# Acclaim for *I'll Be There to* Tell the Story

"With raw honesty and most riveting and courageous story-telling, Maria describes the powerful healing between herself and her mother, after her mother had passed. If you read one book all year, let it be this one."
— Mary Soliel, Author of *I Can See Clearly Now: How Synchronicity Illuminates Our Lives*

"Poetry can simplify, demystify, and transform the most complicated relationships... Maria Weber and her late mother embark upon a spiritual journey ... that leads, ultimately, to a deeper understanding of their eternal connection, to healing, and to peace."
— Lynda La Rocca, Author of *The Stillness Between*

". . . It is a tribute to Maria's writing that Louise springs forth from the pages as a fascinating and wholly alive person, whether or not she was a helpful mother to a young girl."
— Annie Dawid, Author of *And Darkness Was Under His Feet: Stories Of A Family*

"*I'll Be There to Tell the Story* is a compelling account of one woman's supernatural journey. While Weber takes us to unexpected metaphysical places, the story remains grounded in that very human experience: a daughter's complicated relationship to her mother. Weber's particular talent is this combination of detailed storytelling and uncovering the possibility that there may be more to our realities than meets the eyes."
— Amy Frykholm, Author of *Julian of Norwich: A Contemplative Biography*

"Maria, like Rumi who longed for a higher power to create through him, has allowed the intelligence of her deceased mother to create through her. Her book is a treasure trove of information on automatic drawing, and it includes a workbook with exercises for those who want to try their hand at it. She has gone where few dare to go."

— Elaine Soto, Ph.D., Psychologist and Artist

# I'll Be There

## To Write The Story

*My mother Louise and I at home in 1956.*

# I'll Be There To Write The Story

## A Mother-Daughter Journey Beyond Death

# Maria Weber

Piñon Valley Press
Buena Vista, Colorado

The story of the Fairy Queen Thimble Bee in Chapter 1 was first published under the title, "Queen of the Woods," in *New Millennium Writings*, 2003-2004, Don Williams, editor, pages 32-38, Knoxville, Tennessee. While it is not identical to the version published in *New Millennium Writings*, the spirit of the story remains the same.

The instructions and advice in this book are not intended as a substitute for legal advice, psychological counseling, or medical advice. The author and publisher disclaim any responsibility or liability resulting from actions advocated or discussed in this book. Those desiring or needing legal advice, medical advice, and/or counseling are encouraged to seek the services of competent professionals in those areas of expertise.

Because of the dynamic nature of the Internet, any Web addresses contained in this book may have changed since publication and may no longer be available.

Published by

Piñon Valley Press
P.O. Box 4801
Buena Vista, Colorado 81211
www.pinonvalleypress

I'll Be There to Write the Story
A Mother-Daughter Journey Beyond Death

Printed in the United States of America

First Edition

Library of Congress Control Number: 2010900628
ISBN: 978-0-9826301-0-5

Book/Cover design by Nick Zelinger, NZ Graphics
Edited by Melanie Mulhall, Dragonheart
Logo by Kaye Miller
Interior art by Maria Weber
Black & white photographs by William E. Weber
Photograph of the author by James Bassett
Fairy drawing by Stacey Joslin
Printed by Lightning Source

This book is dedicated
to the members of my Monday writing group
The Writer's BLOC,
who have brought me inspiration
through their creativity, humor, and friendship.

*Bury me with a pencil in my hand,*
*For I would wake up—writing.*
*When Gabriel's trumpet blows and his brass bands*
*Begin trumpeting, I'll be there*
*In a front-row stand to write the story.*

Louise E. Weber,
From her poem "A Writer's Last Words," June 23, 1966

# Contents

# Workbook

## Exercises, Tips, and Resources

# Author's Notes

*I'll Be There To Write The Story* is memoir, and the story is true. To honor their privacy, some names of individuals and a few identifying details have been changed.

This book is published in black and white. To view color images of the art, please refer to the website www.pinonvalleypress.com.

# Preface

When my mother, Louise Ernst Weber, was seventy-eight and lived five minutes away from me in a retirement community, she became obsessed with the notion of publishing her best poems in a volume that she had already titled, *This Lively Dust*. I was employed and couldn't devote much time to her project, but I set up a card table and typewriter for her to make edits and prioritize her poems. With over 600 poems to analyze and cull, she quickly became overwhelmed, and her dream sputtered out.

After my mother died at eighty-five, I read all of her poetry. Her writing became a window through which I could view and review our mother-daughter relationship. We were inextricably intertwined, sometimes loving and sometimes guarded. But we never dug back into our past, attempting to heal old wounds. By reading and organizing my mother's poetry after her death, I came to a place of peace with her. In writing this book, I transformed our relationship into a spiritual friendship that exists across dimensions. *I'll Be There to Write the Story* is the result of my own journey, one that started with poetry and took off in new directions. It's not the book of poetry my mother first imagined, but the book that wanted to be written.

After I had finished writing most of the book, I thought some readers might want to venture out on a journey of their own. I created a workbook that parallels my story, chapter by chapter. If you are a reader who likes to participate, I invite you to read a memoir chapter and then turn to the workbook. There you will find complementary exercises. While my story is about healing the relationship with my mother after her death, your journey may take you in a different direction. Select the exercises that speak to you.

By writing about my experiences, I know I will offend some. I can't help that. After sixty years, I choose to follow my intuition and listen to what my gut tells me rather than adhering to any doctrine or creed. My curiosity is too strong to be hemmed in by what can't be. I want to know what might be. While I write about experiences that may sound strange to some readers, in the workbook, I provide lists of books and resources that I found helpful in understanding my journey. I encourage readers to go to the workbook for more information.

After reading, typing and organizing my mother's life work into notebooks, and gathering up all the published material, I shipped several boxes to her hometown library in 1999. Now her collection can be shared with others at a central location in Kingsport, Tennessee.

# Acknowledgments

Writing this book has been a ten-year journey. My heart is filled with gratitude toward all the people who helped me along the way. When I arrived in the Arkansas Valley knowing no one, I found my niche with the local writing group. Barbara Mertus Munyon became my first writing friend and helped me edit my first prize winning story. Nancy Rossen encouraged my poetry. She also introduced me to editor Camilla Beck of Fosilpres, who first tamed the unwieldy manuscript. Jude Silva helped me understand that automatic drawing was an acceptable artistic practice.

With my weekly writing group, the Writer's BLOC, and my monthly Shavano Poets group, I kept my writing muscles toned. Cousins Sandra Doren and Elizabeth Stepp added indispensable family insights. Stacey Joslin, Sheryl Watson, and Heiderose Spang-Martindell helped me put the story back on track after a derailment. Well into the project, I met author and mentor Susan J.Tweit who helped me believe this book could happen. Cary Unkelbach, Sue Greiner and Debby Cason formed my supportive critique group who wouldn't let me give up. I am grateful to the women who read my manuscript: Libby Hale, Mary Soliel, Lynda LaRocca, Marcy Adams, Sandra Doren, Maryann Shephard, Amy Frykholm, and Elaine Soto and to those who provided substantive comments and final editing: Annie Dawid and Melanie Mulhall.

Two dear friends played a role in the story and have since graduated to the Other Side: Sue Elliott and Lanie Mischke. I still miss you.

I am grateful for my patient and understanding husband, Jim Bassett, who time and again rescued me from hardware and software conundrums and put up with me during the pregnant years of being "with book" instead of "with pottery."

All poems by Louise Weber are used with permission of the Archives Collection of the Kingsport Public Library, Kingsport, Tennessee. Martha Egan, the library archivist, accepted my mother's poetry collection in 2000. Brianne Johnson, another archivist, helped me track down numerous citations within the collection in 2008 after it was housed in Kingsport. Both assisted me with the generosity of their time and expertise.

# Chapter 1

## Loose Ends

My mother was dying, and I was not ready. I sat in her room in the Denver nursing home as the April sun's slanting rays picked out the philodendron plant and the stuffed teddy bears that friends had brought for St. Patrick's Day. A large black-and-white photo of our Tennessee woods that my father had developed in the kitchen sink years ago, before Kodak developed color film, hung on the wall next to Mom's bed. I had tacked it there to provide a window into our common past. A beige curtain that divided the space between my mother and her roommate, Mrs. Jordan, was pushed back against the south wall, making the room feel almost spacious. Mrs. Jordan was parked in the hall in her wheelchair.

My mind compressed itself into some tiny chamber inside itself where minutes felt like hours. My eyes clung to Mom's thin form under the cotton blanket. I watched her chest rise and fall, rise and fall, wondering how much time was left.

My friend Lanie walked in. I greeted her with a hug. She had come on her lunch break to visit my mother for the last time. Lanie sat down by the bed and held my mother's hand for a minute or two. Death didn't seem to faze her: she had put her cat to sleep at home, administering the injection herself.

She leaned close to my mother's ear. "Louise," she said, "This is Lanie. I'm here to say good-bye." She spoke with the nasal East Tennessee twang I always liked, since I'd grown up there myself. Mom did not move or open her eyes. "I'm glad I had a chance to know you. You've been a friend and I've appreciated you ever since we met. I'm here to thank you for being my friend." She sat next to my mother for a few minutes, squeezed her hand, then let go.

Dry-eyed, Lanie looked at me, took a deep breath and stood up. "Thanks for letting me come. Your mom is a special person."

Two days earlier, Mom had been sitting in her wheelchair on Mrs. Jordan's side of the room sipping water, nibbling on a California roll, and asking me how I was. Today she dozed, but it was not the peaceful slumber of one taking a catnap, planning to be up and about again after forty restful winks. She no longer wanted to eat or drink.

That evening, a nurse said she was in a coma. I hoped she would awaken as she had before. I didn't want to admit she was dying, although I knew in my gut she was. I certainly didn't want to tell her good-bye. I couldn't. I couldn't for fear I would fall apart. Even with my mother in a nonresponsive state, I couldn't say, "Mom, I'm so glad you were my mother. I love you, Mom." It was too late to be that candid. Besides, it wasn't the way we did things.

———

A question burned inside me that afternoon, but it was much too late to ask it as well. As silly as this may sound, I longed to know about Queen Thimble Bee and whether Mom had written the fairy letters. That unanswered question went way back to my childhood, and it began with Phyllis and the fairy experiments.

Phyllis lived up the street from our home in the Tennessee hills and was two years older than me. Even though other nine-year-olds lived in the neighborhood, I preferred Phyllis because she found endless ways to entertain me. She taught me how to make a grapevine swing and led me through the dark ravine below her house in search of praying mantises. We tended to injured grasshoppers in our bug hospital—after scorching their behinds with a match.

Phyllis and I were bonded—something like sisters, but without the fighting—and we decided to seal the pact. With her dad's razor blade, we each cut a tiny square on the side of our knee and mingled our blood, which, she said, made us blood sisters. Lucky for us, we didn't become infected.

Phyllis insisted fairies were real. We practiced trying to shrink down to fairy size one afternoon because, more than anything else, we wanted to transform ourselves into fairies. Concentrating with all our might, we sat against the shady brick wall of her house with legs outstretched, breathed ourselves into hyperventilation, and commanded ourselves to shrink. When we opened our eyes, we felt dizzy and were convinced that our bodies had shortened, just a little.

I told my mother about the fairy experiments.

I turned ten in October of 1954. Three months later, on Christmas morning, I awoke to find four shiny pink tinsel trees rooted in Styrofoam on my bedside table. A large letter made of aluminum foil and inscribed in swirly script was taped to my bedroom windowpane. It read:

Dear M,

I am a fairy who lives in your woods.

The forest of pink trees is my gift to you.

Remember the Child. It is his birthday.

I look in on you when you are sleeping.

Love, Queen Thimble Bee.

I called my mother to come and see what had appeared in my room. She hugged me and hovered over my shoulder as I removed the foil letter, one corner at a time. We reread it together. Truly, a miracle had happened, she agreed. My whole body glowed with euphoria. I had been personally contacted by a tiny being who lived in our woods. I have no memory of what my father thought about this, but my mother smiled broadly as I experienced the first thrill of magic. Before the day was over, I had called Phyllis and written a thank you note to the fairy. I placed it on my windowsill, and then I waited.

I awoke every morning in eager expectancy and checked the windowsill to see if my note had been answered. Mom asked me if I had heard anything. Weeks passed, and I felt glum. A new letter eventually arrived in the same swirly script as before, but his time it was written on white paper in blue ink.

Dear M,

Thank you for your little message, my Child Friend. Not many Fairy creatures from the Invisible World have Human Friends. Most people think we only live in Fairy Books!

Writing to you takes more time than you would think. I have to first change myself into solid elements—for I am light as thistle down. I love you, dear M.

F. Q.

When each Saturday night rolled around, the magic created by F.Q. Thimble Bee's letters evaporated. In its place, a discordant scene unfolded. Mom would come into my room and say, "Lay out your clothes for tomorrow."

I would whine, "Can't we stay home?"

Her back would stiffen. "No, we're all going to church tomorrow. We are a family and this family goes to church."

"But I don't want to go. Why can't I stay here while you and Pop go?"

My mother never asked me why I didn't want to attend church or what I was afraid of. Had she done that, she might have discovered a shy girl who was fearful of other children, especially older boys who teased her during the weekday school bus ride across town. The bratty boys attended our church, and I dreaded encountering them in the subterranean Sunday School halls.

*A typical unhappy Sunday morning*

The scene repeated itself each week. On the rare Sunday when my parents stayed home, I exulted in the joy of a Sunday without dressing up. I despised wearing dresses and patent leather shoes, white gloves, and hats—all the trappings of someone I wasn't.

I was a tomboy, a tree climbing wood nymph. Cutting paths through our three acres of woods and watching pollywogs grow legs in our backyard pond were my favorite pastimes. On other days, I would find a sturdy grapevine and make a swing over one of our four sinkholes. Our property was filled with oak, beech, hickory, walnut, and ash trees. Grapevines hung from the canopy. Mayapples and jacks-in-the-pulpit sprouted from the understory in the spring. Backlit redbud leaves were my stained glass windows; wind blowing through elms, my organ pipes; and cricket song, my choir. Church, with its sanctuary of starched and primped glazed-eyed sheep, held no relevance for me whatsoever.

The following summer, Phyllis and her family moved to a new subdivision in the county. I never saw or heard from her again.

I kept writing to the fairy, who wrote back from time to time. When she did, I would show the letter to my mother. In fact, together we designed our own "fairy paper" using vegetable oil and food coloring on parchment. I placed the paper creations on top of our upright piano for Queen Thimble Bee and waited for her to find them.

*Dear M,*

*This time I found the paper! How nice the Pond looks! When the moon is full,*

*it makes a silver, shimmering lake and
reflects my "Wand Light." Mrs. W.
thinks I fly in the evening with the
fireflies—She is right! But always higher
than a certain pair of reaching fingers!!!
Have you heard my summer orchestra?
The cricket fiddlers play for you each night.*

*Love, F.Q.*

With each letter, my love for Queen Thimble Bee grew. The letters always appeared during the week, never on Sunday mornings, which was a good thing, because Sunday was my least favorite day of the week. My stomach curdled each Saturday night. I hoped I'd be sick in the morning. I became filled with dread over the prospect of confronting my mother again. Church wasn't so much the issue and neither were the bratty boys. It was the need to exert my will, express my side of the story, and be recognized as a real person in the family. I craved some shred of independence. Sunday morning wasn't the only place and time when it became obvious to me that I was still a child with no rights. I also fought with Mom over dance and piano lessons. But Sunday was the worst. I dawdled in the bathroom. I tried to make us late. I pouted and hung my head.

Mom would say, "Why aren't you ready yet? We're leaving in ten minutes. Come eat your breakfast."

"I don't want any breakfast. I can't find my gloves, my shoes are green, and they stink." In our dank Tennessee woods, shoes mildewed in the closet.

"Well, clean them or wear a different pair."

I knew that she wouldn't resort to spanking on a Sunday morning, but on other days of the week, she and my father often did that to deliver the clearest message in the shortest amount of time. Spare the rod and spoil the child was an adage to which both of them subscribed. My father tormented me with his books, *The Care of Children from One to Five*, and *The Child from Five to Ten*. As a World War II Navy man, he believed in raising a child by the book. It wasn't beyond him to read passages aloud to me to make his points.

None of my excuses or delay tactics worked. Mom stood firm and I caved in every time. I never won a battle with her. My inner fire fizzled and my self-esteem plummeted. It became difficult for me to speak and I was even afraid to answer the telephone.

Mom had grown up in a family of six with three siblings. She stood out from the rest with her blonde hair, blue eyes, and her precocious chatter. As my mother, she talked at me constantly, which left me with little to say. I learned not to express myself so much with my voice , but inwardly. Among the roots of an ancient beech tree, I played with dolls, creating their lives and conversations in my mind.

I assumed she thought that by sending me off to church— as her parents had packed her off to tent meetings—I would become a happy, well-adjusted and religious person. But her strategy only made me more determined to resist. She assumed that I was like her, a social creature who enjoyed weekly contact with friends. I wasn't. Each day of elementary school created stress from having to interact with so many people. As an only child, I needed weekends to regroup, to reconnect with my trees, the pond, sinkholes and the music of crickets. I would return from church feeling depressed and depleted. The weekly clashes with my mother wore me down and helped build the wall between us that existed until she died.

Meanwhile, letters from Queen Thimble Bee continued to arrive on my windowsill, and every time one appeared, I shared it with Mom. Those loving letters saved my soul. They wedged their way like kudsu vines through the crusty wall I'd erected to keep my mother out.

Dear M,

Fairies live mostly on nectar from flowers—that is why we go south with the birds—I had to come back for some "Fairy Business" which I can't explain—a sparrow brought me on his back—I return now until springtime—Thank you for the green honey! Unicorns are Fairy Creatures—We ride them sometimes—I have strange powers—I can grow big and grow strong when I have to—that is how I can write with your mother's pen (Mrs. W.) I am as tall as your four fingers are wide—My hair is golden—I sleep in a leaf on

the tallest tree for I am a Woods Fairy—
I can also make myself very small!
My woods work now is helping with the
seed scattering. Christmas in Cuba then
off to Brazil for the winter. Thank you
my dear M for everything.

Queen Thimble Bee

By the time I was twelve, I was emerging from my shell. I had matriculated from the hated elementary school, where nasty boys on the school bus had taunted me, and entered junior high. My life was a swirl of homework, sleepovers with girlfriends, and boy watching. I was wearing my first almost-flat bra, which meant I was grown up and visible. Larry swished my ponytail. I was in love. Isaac pursued me.

"Dear diary. Well, it looks like I'm done for. Isaac insists on liking me and it's hard to hold back. Oh me, what can I do? I don't know whether to like him or not."

Letters from Queen Thimble Bee tapered off, but I still believed in her and wanted her to write. I was different from my peers in that my budding spirituality was anchored in something tangible: paper and ink. I believed in fairies and the unseen world because I was experiencing a clear and present relationship. I trusted that the letters came from a fairy, a belief that superseded anything I had heard in our church, which, in my youthful opinion, was only hearsay from the distant past. I knew who loved me best.

At twelve, I was eager to draw, paint, and make figures with clay. I credit Mom for letting me glue pieces of stained glass onto our dining room window in a permanent sunburst. She filled one end of our dining room table with a changing display of polished rocks, abalone shells, fresh cut daffodils, dried grass, and Ansel Adams photos. I allowed her into the artist part of myself, as well as the part that revered nature. She was someone I could have loved then, if only she had not been my mother.

Dearest M,

I could not go without telling you good-bye.

I was so surprised to find your lovely letter for I thought you had wrapped me up as one of your pleasant childhood dreams—a secret fancy to remember—now that you have become a Young Woman! It is a rare thing for one of "Us" to ever openly communicate with a "mortal," and rarer still for a Fairy to find a child who believes in our existence as long as you have (At least in This Country of America).

My work in the woods is over now.

The seeds have fallen and the trees are painted

*and the birds are going South. Where did you find the corn-like jewel stones? Scatter it for the birds who stay with you in My Woods. I borrow my gifts from those who will never miss them ... A little here, a little there. My friend Swallow waits to carry me to Brazil. One last Xmas visit, but invisible, I will be with you always.*

*Q. T. B.*

I was thirteen when Queen Thimble Bee visited for the last time. Maybe the fairy knew it was time to stop the letters because I was too old for such things. The letters had appeared on my windowsill for three years.

"December 25, 1957. Dear Diary, It's Christmas! Got two blouses, makeup kit, red pocketbook, and stuffed animals and a note from Santa Claus. Thimble Bee gave me an angel from Brazil."

When the letters and mementos stopped, I felt sad. But Queen Thimble Bee said she would be with me always, and I believed her. Whenever I was depressed, I took out the letters and reread them.

I still have all twenty-six letters from Queen Thimble Bee. They're preserved in a blue talcum powder box as my most cherished childhood treasure.

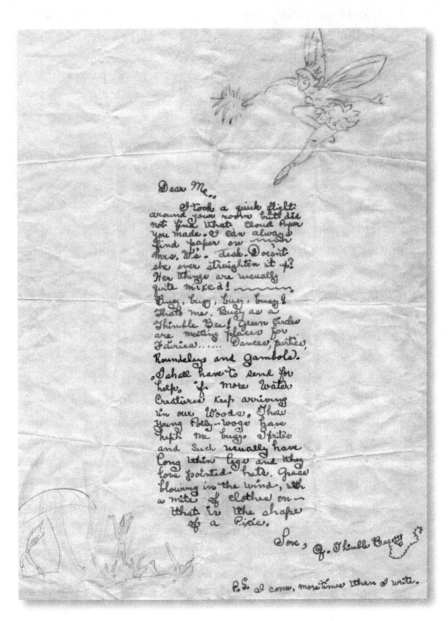

*A letter from Queen Thimble Bee*

Up until I was thirty-five, I believed that the fairy wrote them. Then I allowed myself to doubt. By then, my own spirituality was securely rooted. It seemed possible that maybe, just maybe, my mother had written those letters. Still, I wanted to believe that she had help from the fairy world. Plenty of opportunities arose for me to ask her, but I didn't.

When my mother entered the nursing home, her mind was a blur, but she could still remember past events. A week before she died, I considered asking if she had written the letters, but I hesitated. I didn't want to hear the truth. I wanted some element of magic to remain with me always. I wanted to believe that a filmy fairy queen had changed herself into solid matter and had written those letters. At the very least, I wanted to believe that my mother had written them under the spell of a fairy queen who loved me.

The week before Mom died, I couldn't tell her I loved her. I had never said those words to her. I envied women who could do that, but sometimes it seemed artificial and overdone. The right time for expressing gratitude and affection would have been when my mother was still of sound mind. What held me back was that I would have had to abandon my resentment and forgive her, and to do that, I reasoned, would have taken a lot of explaining. First, I would have had to tell her about my old childhood anger that still hunkered down at the bottom of my heart—the anger that had hatched during our fights about church and escalated during high school. I'd have had to confess that. Then she would have become flustered and soggy or stoic and rigid. I would have felt remorseful for hurting her and would have told her it didn't matter anymore when, in fact, it did matter. I would have felt like a torturer for even bringing it up to an eighty-five-year-old woman. Or I might have lied to make her feel better. I needed her to understand why I'd sealed off my love. It never occurred to me that I just needed to forgive the poor woman.

Heaven forbid, she might have unloaded on me, too. She might have nursed a laundry list of old wounds that I had caused. I don't know if I could have withstood such honesty. I wasn't willing to leap into this quagmire without perceiving the outcome ahead of time. We had never worked any of this out in the early years. We had each kept mum. We had never aired our grievances in an old-fashioned, down and dirty, gut spilling way. Never. In fact, my mother had taught me by example that emotional scenes were to be avoided at all costs. So here she was on her deathbed, and I still carried old grudges from half a century earlier. There were no more chances to say what hadn't been said or ask what hadn't been asked, or so it seemed.

The early relationship with my mother set up two contrasting themes that would shadow me all of my life—regret and wonder. The dark and light swirled together like chocolate and vanilla from my tenth year until she died, and beyond.

# Chapter 2

## The Dream, The Vision, and the Bird Call

The summer of my thirteenth year I boarded a train bound for Philadelphia to visit my cousin DeDe for six weeks. Two weeks after my arrival, Mom called to give me the terrible news that my next-door neighbor and playmate, Linda Brown, had died of a brain tumor.

*Linda and Maria, the summer that Linda died.*

I remember seeing a pink welt on the side of Linda's knee about the size of a quarter. When I first asked her about it we were nine. It was a tumor, she announced, and a second one lurked on the top of her head. She let me feel it under her thick mop of red hair. Her pediatrician had said that she might die from it when she grew older. But at nine, "tumor" was only a word, and "might die" elevated her status in the eyes of her friends for about twenty-four hours. After that, the tumors might as well have been mosquito bites for all the attention we paid them. Normalcy resumed for Linda, along with the neighborhood softball team and the evening games of kick the can.

I didn't return to Kingsport for the funeral because I'd just settled in at DeDe's, but a dark cloud descended that tainted the rest of my summer. Mom said some unusual things had happened that would make me feel better, and she would tell me when I returned home. Life in our woods was never the same with Linda gone. Her parents conceived another daughter, but that baby was stillborn. Burdened with sadness, the parents and their two young sons moved out of our town and into a neighboring county.

The details of that tragedy eventually faded from memory until after Mom died and I paged through her old, black, three-ring notebooks. There I rediscovered the tale she had typed for me forty years prior. What happens after we die? On the day after Linda's funeral, my mother wrote this story for me.

*I have been alone all day. The house is so still. First, there were two strange things—the vision and the bird call—and now three— a dream. Anyone can dream and the bird call might have been a coincidence, but Mr. Brown is not a man to have visions. I have been thinking about these things all day, alone here in the house, where*

*I pass the time waiting for Maria to come back from her long visit with her cousin in the north. I must remember everything so I can tell her. She will want to know, for all she knows now is that Linda is dead and buried. Her best friend.*

*It's over now and all finished. Yesterday I saw them put her in the ground. The thirteen-year-old red-haired sprite with the pixy face is gone from the earth. Or is she? I wish I knew more about these things. My theology has holes. Even the odd brands have holes. I haven't found one that covers everything. The minister, a true follower of Calvin, preached a lovely sermon—just right I suppose for the occasion, for everyone seemed pleased. But he had her straight up in heaven, running about, and that's not what I dreamed last night. Oh, she was well in the dream, just as he said, but she wasn't in heaven. She was here.*

*I dreamed Mrs. Brown, her mother, and I were sitting under the trees in the side yard. Maria was on the grass nearby. We were all quiet and sad, remembering Linda. For the first time we really knew what had happened. The loss was too great to be borne. No one said a word. Mrs. Brown rocked, far beyond tears. I grieved for her, trying to think how it would be not to have my Maria, and mourned for my child because she could not cry. Her life-long friend carried away and buried, and she, come home now to nothing.*

*Then, it happened! In the midst of this dream sorrow, far deeper than waking sorrow, Linda appeared in the woods, far off in the trees where they had always played together. She was dressed in green. Her red hair dazzled in the sun. Specks of light sparkled and darted from her toes and fingers and I could see she had no weight. She was dancing toward us through the trees in a wild sort of joy, arms up, whirling and skipping. Maria saw her and flashed a look at me to see if I saw what she saw. I nodded and then we both realized Mrs. Brown could not see—she continued rocking, eyes closed, deep in grief and memories. Linda floated, soared, and whirled straight to us, pointed to her mother, smiled a mischievous smile, floated right on to her mother's lap. There, Linda (elf, sprite, fairy, spirit-child—what you will) tweaked her mother's nose, ruffled her hair, patted her cheek and loved her in a thousand ways, all joy, thistledown and light. Quick as a bird she was on the grass, silenced us again with a gesture and then danced a dream dance far beyond my telling. We both knew we were part of a great secret and promised with our eyes not to tell. With a final pirouette, she was gone, and I awoke.*

*All day alone in the house I've been wondering—what was the secret we were to keep? Surely not that she was well and more alive than she had ever been. Could it be, that she was—is—close by?*

*And what did Mr. Brown's vision mean? He, who never had a vision in his life, came to a thin place in his hour of agony and saw, through time and space, as he said, an Amazing Beauty. When at last he knew the child would die, he stumbled from the hospital room and walked to the end of the corridor. There, standing alone, saying, "No, and No and No," he saw a Glorious Rose, a Marvelous Rose, a Perfect Rose, full-blown, and he was filled with joy. This he told me afterwards.*

*And now I must write the third thing, while I remember so I can tell Maria. But first I must explain about the secret bobwhite bird call which was the "are you home" sign, used by the five children (now four) who live here in these woods. Three houses join the land, each one shut out in summer by dense woods, so that Tom and Paul and Linda Brown, across the lane, Linda Mellons up the hill, and Maria in the middle, learned long ago to stand at dusk and whistle "Bob White . . . Bob White!" If an answer came from another house it meant, "Yes, I'm home, come over, come down, come up!" No voices ever called in these woods; a low, quiet whistle took care of everything. "Bob White!" We heard it for years. The three girls were the same age and played through mud pies, dolls, and later, secret dens in the woods, first tolerating the younger brothers as lackeys, later using them as scouts and pathfinders.*

*With little warning, it all ended. Maria waved off on a train one bright Sunday for summer vacation. A week later, the dreadful news of a red-haired child stumbling and falling in the yard. Then the X rays, surgery, the nightmare words—Brain Tumor; the watch—the helpless long watch, and finally, a churchyard in the country on a late summer afternoon. Everyone Linda loved was there—all except Maria. The church was full of country people for they had taken her to the home burying ground. Cross-Anchor, last stop of the pioneers working their way inland from the British ships so long ago. There are funerals and funerals. A child of promise is the hardest of all. My private grief at that moment was for my own child far away, who was living this hour alone, beyond help. She knew the time of the funeral and somewhere, was keeping watch and growing old. Then is when the third thing happened. The formal service was over. The minister began one last, small tribute at the graveside, saying, "All of Linda's friends are*

*gathered here together . . ." Across the fields, out of the*
*sunset, in the terrible stillness of that moment, came a low,*
*quiet and piercing call: "Bob White—Bob—Bob White!"*
*The four children heard, looked at each other, transfixed*
*in wonder. Maria! Somehow she had come, across time*
*and space. It was she who called with the voice of the quail,*
*in the sad, pale, golden evening light.*

After reading that letter, forty years later, I thought the bird call might have been Linda signaling she was okay.

At thirteen, I didn't comprehend what my mother believed about the afterlife, but it was clear to me she didn't subscribe to a simplistic heaven and hell. Even though she was brought up in a tent meeting, fundamentalist environment, she and her two sisters broke away from that pattern. Her older sister, Mary, didn't attend church at all, but drew inspiration from nature. Her younger sister, Rachel, became a Quaker. Mom educated herself through stacks of books on theology, philosophy, and mysticism but still attended the Methodist church. Everybody I knew attended church. It was the thing to do. Mom acknowledged that the church's teaching offered only a slice of the truth. Meanwhile, I inhaled every mystical scrap she threw my way. Her dream story, Mr. Brown's vision of a rose, and the bobwhite call printed an indelible stamp on my heart.

When Linda and I were playmates, her father was my idea of an ogre. He stood over six feet tall, had jet-black hair, and yelled a lot. If the kids misbehaved, Mrs. Brown would report to him, and he'd punish them with a belt strap when he came home from work.

Not being one of his own didn't exempt me from his wrath. Red faced, he once ordered me off his property. I later figured it all out, but at the time, I was in a state of terror and confusion. As seven-year-olds, Linda and I were playing in her yard on a warm summer morning. Her younger brother Paul cut into our fun as he always did, and the two of them started to squabble. Linda screamed at him to leave us alone. He screamed back that he had as much right to be there as she did. Indoors, Mrs Brown was bathing two-year-old Tommy in the bathtub. She left her little one alone and stormed out of the house to silence the banshees. I stood back while the frustrated mother swatted both kids and told me to go home. Little Tommy in the bathtub turned on the hot water and injured himself.

Mrs. Brown feared her husband's terrifying temper as much as the kids did, so to spare herself and them even more flack, she said it was I who ignited the brawl. Her fib must have worked, because Mr. Brown leveled his ire on me for at least one horrid day. I wasn't accustomed to being yelled at, nor did I perceive what I had done wrong.

Linda, her brothers, and I would watch for his car around 5:30 p.m., and scatter like rabbits the instant his black Buick hit the top of the driveway. But Mom's disclosure of Mr. Brown's agony and vision transformed my image of the man. Instead of an angry screamer who whipped his children weekly on general principle, I viewed him as a broken father who had genuinely loved his daughter beyond words, and my harsh judgment melted away. I accepted that adults could have more than one face.

When Linda died, I was thirteen and Mom was forty-six. Linda's death brought us together during an interlude when I was brewing and stewing into adolescence. Whenever Mom shared her mystical side, as she had with her story of Linda's funeral, I opened up to her. I wanted more of the same. When she forced me to dress up and traipse off to church, I erected my wall and shut her out. When we talked about spirits, visions, and other strange phenomena, we danced forward. Because my father viewed these subjects with skepticism, unexplained mysteries became the single sacred area I expected Mom to share with me alone. It became our common ground.

At the end of her life, I don't know what Mom expected would happen. Communicating with me from the Other Side, though, was not at all out of the realm of possibility.

# Chapter 3

## Bringing Down the House

After parents are gone, traces of who they were assume new meaning. With hindsight, I realized I had done an awful thing following my father's death. When he died and it came time to clean out my childhood home in the summer of 1988, I wasn't interested in my mother's collection of old scrapbooks from high school on. We left them behind with the house for the antiques dealer to auction off at an estate sale. Twice I read the large box of love letters between my parents during World War II. Then I burned them. My father, Bill Weber, was an attorney in our town. When I cleared out his office, I tossed a lifetime of daybooks into the dumpster behind his building. Not my proudest moment. All of this carnage because I had yet to value my mother and father.

When my cousin asked if I wanted the letters I'd written to her over the years, I said no. It was an act of historical suicide. Since I have no children and saw no purpose in preserving my memories or my parents' memories, it seemed only reasonable to clear the decks. I'm not the packrat my mother was. She hoarded correspondence from family and friends. She even kept her mother's letters from the 1930s. Nineteen years after my father's death and ten years after my mother's death, I was finally ready to sink into my parents' lives. I never expected that to happen and the only reason I could conclude for my readiness was that I finally missed them enough to care.

From my familial cleansing frenzy, I salvaged the journal my father started in 1938, during the early days of his law practice, and all of my mother's poetry. Some inner wisdom kicked in to stay my hand and these things were saved. Mom had written voluminously, compulsively. I wondered if she suffered from the writing disease, hypergraphia. She had written letters to me once a week until she was seventy-six and moved within five minutes of my house. I preserved only a handful of those letters.

On the other hand, I could count the total of my father's letters to me on my fingers and toes, each one purposeful, seasoned with wry observations. I prized them because my father and I rarely spoke to one another without my mother present. Our alone time had consisted of his coaching me in math at a card table in the living room and hikes together around the subdivision. We never knew one another in the way my mother and I did. When I called home as an adult, he would answer the phone. "All right?" he would say instead of "Hello," and then talk about thirty seconds, and then ask, "Do you want to speak to your mother?" I'd say, "Sure," and that would be the end of it. So each letter from my father was a nugget for me and me alone. I packed them away in a drawer, reread them, studied his handwriting, and even sniffed them for his scent.

In the early 1940s, my parents tried to conceive a child without success. Mom told me she had miscarried a number of times. She missed periods and then experienced wrenching cramps, after which she knew she'd lost something. They finally succeeded in 1944. My father, the eminent record keeper, wrote these journal entries in the years before my conception.

*41*

*December 7, 1941—No church today for me. Spent all day cleaning up brush piles in yard and raking leaves, burning trash, etc. Louise sick with pain. At 5 o'clock Louise told me of the news that Japan had bombed Pearl Harbor and other U.S. military bases in the Pacific. Everyone was agog with the news. Radio news broadcasts continued throughout the night. Weather cool—heavy frost.*

*December 8, 1941—Roosevelt asked congress to declare war on Japan. Congress did so . . . We saw "Kitty Foyle" at Fox Theater. Will married men be called to war if they have no children and their wives can work? I think they will, but when?*

*April 2, 1942—Dal, our Dalmatian dog has just finished a very full mating season. It lasted one week. There was a black Chow, a black and white Pointer, a German Shepherd, a half-breed Collie, a mongrel Setter, and various others. We are wondering which is the father of the pups to be . . . Will Hitler invade Turkey?. . . Will I lose my law books to W.A. Allen?. . . Will Louise get pregnant?. . . Will Kenneth Ernst be drafted?*

*May 22, 1942—Tonight at 10:30, May 22, 1942, we, Louise and I, drank heavy port wine and listened to music for two hours. Beethoven's Fifth Symphony, Tschaikowsky's Symphony No 4 in F Minor (opus 36), then Tristan und Isolde— Isolde's Liebestad, Part 1 (Isolde's Love—Death) (Act 3) (Wagner), Kirsten Flagslad, Soprano—all on Victor disk records. Try it sometime. It is of life, Life, LIFE!*

Pop was more than a little tipsy when he wrote that entry in a sloppy hand, but music and wine, together or separately, made him very happy.

Many pages in my father's journal were blank. However, he wrote about being commissioned as a Naval Reserve officer on March 29, 1943. He was then sent to Dartmouth for officer's training, and on July 23, 1944, he finally shipped out of Norfolk, Virginia, on a minesweeper headed for the Mediterranean. My mother was a registered nurse. When my father left for overseas, she rented a room in a boarding house in Norfolk and worked in a hospital there. She terminated the Norfolk nursing job at some point because she was pregnant with me. She then moved to Charlottesville, Virginia, to be near her mother-in-law.

On the journal page for October, 1944, my mother wrote in red ink, "Maria born October 21, 1944. Bill off coast of Southern France and Italy and Sicily." Mail traveled slowly, so she never knew exactly where he was.

My parents were born two weeks apart, Pop in December of 1911, Mom in January of 1912. They met at eighteen and married at twenty-four. Classical music, books, and port wine held them together for more than fifty years. They sustained my mother while Pop was on a ship serving as a naval officer, and re-coupled them after his return. My father was fond of history, especially the events leading up to World War II. My mother read at least fifty books a year. Over a nine-year period, she kept a list of books read, which totaled four hundred and twenty-five titles.

On a normal evening at our house in the 1950s, you would find Mom and Pop tucked into matching wingback chairs, noses in books. Mom would have a cigarette going and Pop might be smoking a pipe. I can't tell you how many times they quit tobacco and started up again. I was raised believing air pollution was normal. The ticktock of Grandpa Pitman's clock kept time with Handel's *Messiah* or Vivaldi's *Four Seasons*. I would be stretched out on the couch under a green colonial tole lamp, engrossed in a Hardy Boys mystery. In the winter, my mother would shake incense onto the hot eye of the central coal-fired furnace, smoking up the house like a cathedral. Ours was a peaceful nest, before television, throbbing with concertos and bookish thoughts.

When I was very young, I took to heart my father's adage, "Children should be seen and not heard." My reptilian brain accepted this warning literally, and I became silent witness to my parents' cerebral dinner table discussions.

Mom was a woman of many words who preferred talking to listening. At least it seemed that way to me. Because I was an only child and her head was packed with information aching to be released, my mother expounded on philosophy, life, authors, religion, the natural world, and just about anything else I ever wanted—or didn't want—to know. What I really wanted to know but couldn't voice were questions never addressed: Why do I feel so confined? Unhappy? Angry? Why don't you make me a brother or sister?

I didn't understand the reasons for my discontent then, but I do now. My parents, and especially my mother, taught me facts that supplemented my school books, but they didn't coach me in the art of growing up. I was taught to obey their orders and rules, but not told that my feelings of discontent were normal. Without siblings to compare myself to, I assumed that I needed to be an instant adult, intellectually and emotionally. All I perceived was failure and jealousy toward my mother. I couldn't articulate the questions that bothered me. Nor was I encouraged to ask. Darkness overtook my soul and I could not find anything good within myself, which is another reason I separated myself from my mother's love and built my wall. What I needed were hugs, words of love, and being told that I was really okay, after all. I received praise for good grades, which affirmed my intellect, but did little for my inner being. Not knowing what else to do with this malcontent, I blamed it on my mother.

As a child, I never heard the words "I love you" voiced between my parents or even to me. There seemed nothing odd about it. To do otherwise would have appeared "soft" and the watchword of those times was stoicism—a holdover from the Great Depression. People respected authority; they cloaked their anger, stifled tears, and refrained from public hugs and kisses. To quote my grandmother, "You must contain yourself lest you appear overwrought."

The words "I love you" were printed on Valentines and uttered breathily on the silver screen. With so much left unsaid, unexpressed, and un-vented, including words of affection and frustration, Mom and I were mutually stuck. Our stiff hearts cried for a thaw. Anger and love are closely intertwined. Freedom to be responsibly angry is necessary for love to blossom. Mom and I played the game called "everything's okay" for most of our lives. We didn't express our love for one another and we weren't particularly empathetic.

My parents spoke with eloquence about books and ideas, but not about feelings. For a year or two, my mother had bouts of bursitis—inflamed connective tissue in her shoulder—and she took to her bed. She also went to bed two days a month with painful menstrual cramps. Since I was too young to be enlightened about the joys of menstruation, I figured she was either seeking sympathy or there was something horribly wrong with her, in which case I had no choice but to pretend it wasn't so. I followed my father's example and left her alone. Both of my parents came from stoic German stock. They were raised not to complain. People were expected to overcome adversity, if not with a smile, at least without whimpering about it.

Since we lived in three acres of dense woods, and neighbors were out of view, Mom was my constant companion until I entered first grade. Had there been siblings, life might have felt more balanced. But I was stuck with her in our house, fuming a lot of the time—about what, I had no clue.

When I looked at myself in the mirror, I saw in my face her crooked nose, her tight lips, her square little teeth, and her serious countenance. I wanted no part of her attributes, especially her deadpan face. Instead, I liked my friend Julie's darkly pretty mother who fried okra and called me "Mae-ree." I didn't want to be like my mother, yet I wanted to be exactly like her: cast-iron smart and wordy.

Mom was famous for saying, "Here's some free advice," and then depositing a load of it on the unsuspecting bystander. Her women friends were delighted. Her ungrateful child wasn't. On the other hand, my father's advice was always welcome because he was an artist of the spoken word. He thought about what he was going to say before speaking. When I asked his opinion, I didn't receive a quick off-the-cuff answer, but a methodical explanation spiked with colorful anecdotes. He was a folksy orator, and he remained in that persona most of the time. He was also very funny. He could transform the most mundane trivia into a carefully crafted tale.

Once he told us why he wanted to learn to fly fish. It was during his nineteen-year tenure as City Attorney when he spent a lot of time with various city administrators. One of his cronies was the City Treasurer, and according to my father, this man was a fine fellow, but fishing for him was a sort of disease. There were several men who suffered from that disease and each tried to outdo the others in the amount of time spent fishing and the number and size of fish caught. But in spite of all their fancy gear and getup—reels, rods, flies, plugs, night crawlers, thermal clothing, waders, and all the necessary equipment to keep from freezing to death—they might fish all day and catch nothing. My father called the disease "piscatorial malfunction syndrome." He reminded us that his only experience fishing had been as a lad in Virginia when a group of boys would take a boat out on the James River, fish for a few hours, and come back loaded with fifty pounds of bass in a bushel basket. They used hook, line, and sinker with crab meat for bait, and they fished to put food on the table. He didn't see the point of spending hundreds of dollars on fly fishing paraphernalia just for the bragging rights and no fish. But, he added with a grin, he was going to do it anyway.

Looking straight at my mother, he said, "So today I purchased a supply of artificial bait—plugs, flies, worms, and lead weights. I'm going to use my old rod and reel and learn to catch a fish mountain style."

I inhaled his exuberance. Fly fishing was totally beyond his ken. He never caught a single fish, but before he quit trying, he bought a live, twenty-four-inch catfish from a bait shop down on the lake, brought it home, killed it, and butchered it in the kitchen sink to demonstrate his fishing prowess. When he was finished, the kitchen was a mess; the mangled fish was too tough to cook, and my mother threw out the miserable carcass. From that failed fishing affair, my father created a story to be told, embellished and re-told to his buddies at the lunch counter.

As City Attorney, his good-natured quips often made the local newspaper, but, according to a colleague, he was a dreaded opponent in the courtroom. By the time I was in junior high school, I realized he was a respected community leader. He ran for state senator when I was fourteen, but lost as a Democrat in a predominately Republican district. His high profile career put pressure on all of us. I viewed him as a public figure rather than "just Pop." My mother was relieved when he lost the senate race. She preferred a nonpolitical life.

Church women said, "You know, Bill is a true Virginia gentleman." That meant he was soft-spoken, cultured, and courteous. He opened doors for women and when he walked with us on a city sidewalk, he placed himself next to the traffic, protecting us from splashes. I envisioned him as a man who would throw his coat over a mud puddle to prevent a woman from soiling her shoes.

"Don't lie, steal, or cheat," he told me so many times that it became my mantra. He fondly reminded me that when he was in law school at the University of Virginia, anyone caught cheating, lying, or stealing was kicked out immediately. He even showed me the exact square foot in Cabell Hall where a classmate had left his overcoat for a year. The coat was never filched, and this was during the Great Depression. With those three "don'ts" burned into my brain, I tried my best to adhere to his code of ethics, even turning myself in to the student authorities as a college freshman for arriving back at the dorm after curfew.

For the most part, all seemed well between my parents during the eighteen years I lived under their roof. Still, there were times when Pop and I ganged up on my mother in an unspoken pact of passive aggression, and I remember one of those times vividly. Mom was washing dishes after fixing dinner. She was irritated because neither of us lifted a finger to help. I could tell she was mad because she was slamming pots and pans around the kitchen. She was in martyr mode and didn't ask for help. I could have helped her, but I had yet to learn the fine art of compassion. My father ignored her. All of a sudden she yelled, "Dammit!" and stormed into the living room holding a blood-soaked towel over her hand. The culprit was a submerged knife. She started to cry and my father rose from his chair. They decided she needed stitches and rushed off to the emergency room, leaving me home to wallow in guilt and finish up the kitchen.

When I left home for college, Mom assumed the role of intermediary between Pop and me. In a letter, she wrote, "Your father loves you, even though he doesn't show it. He cried when we left you at the dorm." I remembered that sentence all my life because it was the first time I realized that my father did love me—enough to shed tears. Deep inside, I thought I had been a disappointment.

Long before that, she had explained that my father had grown up without a father, which had made it difficult for him to know how to be a father. When I asked what had happened to his father, she told me he had died when Pop was a little boy.

I married my first husband at twenty-two and moved to Colorado. Pop and I rarely had a chance to talk alone after that. When I was home for a visit, I was also with my mother, and we two females huddled together with coffee and girl talk. Our conversations were rarely superficial. In fact they might have been judged as deep and meaningful by an outsider. We often stayed up till midnight discussing spirituality, psychology, or predictions for the future—subjects we relished and that kept us safely distanced from facing the flaws in our relationship.

The prime time I spent alone with my father was when we walked the circuit around the neighborhood. He enjoyed pointing out new houses and property developments and rehashing the behind-the-scenes political shenanigans that attended them. "That's progress," he would say. He was upbeat as long as "progress" didn't encroach on "Weber's Gulch"—our three acres of trees, house, shack, tool shed, playhouse, sink holes, parking lot and various pets and wild critters that passed through. He enjoyed my company, even though I was mostly silent. I was silent because he was a man, and I was afraid to speak the truth with him. Truth, in my twenties, would have been admitting to an unhappy marriage. Truth would have included my desire to create art. Truth would have exposed my search for meaning and purpose. Small talk was not my forte even with my father, so I failed to cement the warm, intimate, father-daughter relationship that would have allowed us to share our hopes and fears. I always regretted not having that.

By living so tightly together for eighteen years and never speaking openly about our feelings, Mom and I had created a make-believe relationship that didn't include total honesty. I carried a lot of frustration out of our family home. Never the less, our relationship was a happy one in many ways. The fact is that Mom and I were more alike than not. Both of us expressed ourselves as artists, writers, nature lovers, and spiritual seekers. Mom wove together her intellect and traditional religious beliefs with mysticism. I picked up the nontraditional side of her spiritual interests and explored them further. We both questioned "the way things were." We wondered whether plants had emotions, whether rocks could think, if dead people came back to check on the living. She read William Blake, the great English mystic poet and visionary artist. In college I had studied John Donne, one of the British metaphysical poets. Having spent so many years in our woods, listening to the thrum of cicadas and shivering hoots of screech owls, we shared nature, beauty, song, and awe of the physical universe. And we both carried a hidden side of secret hurt.

In 1984, Mom wrote a letter to her nursing class in honor of their fiftieth reunion. Each surviving class member was asked to write a brief life history for a booklet that was distributed to everyone after the reunion.

*How does one summarize a life of seventy-two years in a paragraph? . . . I have just learned I have a "small" aneurysm of the abdominal aorta. What will be will be . . . I smoke and drink one glass of beer before supper. Go to Methodist Church each Sunday and Wednesday night. (Does that balance out?)*

*Last summer we drove 4,000 miles in our VW camper . . . Since Bill had a heart attack three years ago, we take one day at a time . . .*

*There was time out for World War II . . . my lawyer husband became a deck officer on a minesweeper in the Mediterranean and coast of Japan . . . The war smashed the law practice and we returned to Kingsport as poor as when we had begun. We survived.*

*My most memorable and enjoyable experiences were our three river rafting trips on the Green in Utah, the Snake and Salmon in Idaho. These were ten-day trips on white water in small rafts. The last one through Hell's Canyon in Idaho was in my 69th year . . . There is nothing on this earth like a wild river.*

*I still get homesick for the sea—so in October we take off for the Carolina coast. And yes, like everyone else, in between this traveling, we have shopped for food, drudged through dull times, lived through three major surgical operations, and fought and made up. In August 1985, we will celebrate our 50th wedding anniversary, God willing.*

After writing this, my mother enjoyed two more good years with my father. Then his failing health caught up with him. On top of diabetes and a previous heart attack, he was diagnosed with colorectal cancer. While he was in the hospital awaiting surgery, he was stricken with a second heart attack and died several days later at age seventy-six.

Mom held up through the service and the church ladies' visits with their covered dish kindness, but inside, she crumbled. Within days, she collapsed and was hospitalized for two weeks with pneumonia. Three odd things happened during this time period. At my Aunt Mary's house, a mirror fell off the wall and shattered just minutes before I called her with the news of my father's death. She said it was an omen. Great Grandfather Pitman's clock, which had sat on our living room bookshelf for fifty years, stopped running the day after Pop died. And the diamond Pop had given Mom on their fortieth anniversary fell out of her ring in the hospital. Luckily, we found it under her bed before the cleaning crew swept it into the trash. Those three symbols of dissolution and disintegration punctuated the end of my parents' earthly union.

My mother made the decision to leave Kingsport, Tennessee, her home of fifty years, and move out to Colorado to be near me and my husband Jim. Through a stroke of amazing luck, I found her a small apartment in a retirement community within minutes of my house, where she lived for the next seven years. It was a tiny unit that faced a busy street. I held my breath for fear she wouldn't like it after living in the woods all her life, but she was elated. "I love to people-watch," she said.

When Mom lived near us in Denver, our relationship took on a new shine. Since she was no longer peddling advice or lecturing, we talked about everyday events—well, every day. Aside from the fact that she was still sad, she found much to be grateful for in her new digs. One of the bennies of living near me was that we could go on shopping expeditions and the occasional overnight getaway together. Little by little our roles shifted as she needed more help from Jim and me. I became the mother to my mother, and that felt good.

Mom liked her port wine before dinner. She claimed she'd been sipping a single glass before dinner ever since 1940 when her doctor told her it was good medicine for her nerves. Since she couldn't drive to shop for it, Jim and I schlepped it to her in half-gallon jugs that she stored under the kitchen sink. She worried her Baptist neighbors would see us lugging in large jugs of booze, so we delivered it in brown paper grocery bags. Having her wine and being able to offer something to guests made her feel more civilized in this strange new city.

We enjoyed sharing sunsets. Summer evening skies trimmed with pink and gold cumulous clouds were our favorites. Once, when I saw a good August sunset firing up, I asked if she wanted to take a ride. "Sure. I'll be ready in ten minutes," she said. It had reached ninety-eight degrees by noon, and the day was finally cooling off.

I picked her up at 7:00 p.m. We drove to the highest spot in the area—Sundial Park, where Denver's lovely old mansions surround a lush mown field of grass and gardens. It's a favorite meeting place for all ages. A long flagstone terrace heats up during the day. I pulled out our aluminum lawn chairs and we sat in silence. In the cool mile-high air, we watched families cavort with dogs and Frisbees.

The sky displayed its full gaudy palette: gold to peach to lavender and green, and finally, indigo. We weren't ready to leave when Venus and the stars began to twinkle on, but a chill was settling in. We moved inside the car and sat there talking in the dark, musing about how lucky we were to be in this beautiful place. Mom said she was glad she had come to live in Denver. We moved as close as we ever had to speaking the forbidden words of affection.

Around 9:00 p.m., a police car pulled up. A man in blue walked over to the car and knocked on the window. "We're just talking," I said. He could see we weren't having sex, dealing drugs or smoking pot, and turned away. That brought us back to reality. Sundial Park's clientele changed after dusk. It was time to go home.

One autumn afternoon, as I sat in the rocker across from her, we were chatting about life, death, and the world situation. (We talked about death a lot, which was much easier than admitting our love for one another.) I said, "Mom, when you die, please, let me know you've made it to the Other Side. I want a sign. Remember when Pop showed up in the kitchen?"

A plastic bottle of soda water on the counter had made a loud "pop" as we were talking about him. A month later, while Mom was alone in her apartment thinking about him, she heard a rustling noise in her jewelry box as though "someone" was stirring her beads.

Then there was Uncle Morrie. After he died, the family swore his spirit caused the chandelier bulbs to flicker over the Thanksgiving and Christmas tables.

"I'll do my best, but I can't make any promises," she said.

"Just try, and I'll expect to hear from you."

Keeping the conversation light was the only way I could approach her demise.

The day before Valentine's Day, 1996, Mom fell near her apartment building. Paramedics took her by ambulance to the hospital where she remained for two weeks. The medical staff balanced her electrolytes, alleviated her dizziness, and tethered her to an oxygen tank.

When she returned home, still dragging an oxygen hose around her apartment, she was less able to cope.

Following a second and more serious trip to the hospital, her physician sent her to a nursing facility for rehabilitation. By then she was eighty-four years old. After intensive physical therapy, she was able to trundle about with a walker. The nursing home staff deemed her fit to find a suitable assisted living facility. She and I toured one elegant residence after another, but nothing pleased her: too big, too formal, too posh, too intimidating. She wilted under the prospect of another upheaval and wanted to stay put. The nursing home provided her a shared room on a wing across from the central open-air atrium. From the atrium ground grew a tall, specimen blue spruce and a variety of landscaped shrubs. Birds flocked in to nest and eat the seed scattered by nursing home staff. My tree-loving mother felt very much at home. The rent was high, but this was where she wanted to stay.

Several happy months in the nursing home followed. My mother was free of responsibility for the first time in her life. When I visited her, she met me with a smile and a story—about feeding the birds, watching kittens cavort outside her window, sipping wine served at the Fourth of July party, or listening to traveling musicians in the lobby. We liberated her for dinners at our house and a neighborhood restaurant where the waiters treated her like their own mama.

On the last big adventure of her life, we arranged to take Mom with us on a long weekend to visit the new home Jim and I were planning to move into. We had been carting our worldly goods, load by load, in an old Ford 350 truck. Each one-way trip meant a 135 mile drive and took three hours—the first 45 minutes just to elbow our way through Denver traffic.

Mom needed portable oxygen in transit and an oxygen tank at our house. We three set out on our trek over Kenosha Pass and through South Park, a broad valley that was once an inland sea, surrounded by mountains. Half way across South Park, the truck's distributor died of old age, the truck slowed, and Jim pulled over onto the shoulder. I went into panic mode because Mom's portable oxygen was only good for three hours. I envisioned her turning blue and passing out before we made it to our house.

Cell phones were not common. We didn't have one, but some people did, and we lucked out. I flagged down a car whose driver called a police officer, who called a tow truck. Mom declared this was an adventure and she wasn't worried. When the tow driver arrived, he hauled our truck, fully loaded with moving boxes, my mother, and me onto his tow bed. From our second-story perch, we enjoyed a premium view of the Rocky Mountains for the next hour, while Jim sat in the cab with the driver. A big oxygen tank was waiting for us at the house. The Ford ended up at a garage for repair, while I rented a car from a neighboring town. Somehow it all pulled together, and my mother never passed out or turned blue. She relished her last escape from the nursing home.

⁓

Everything changed in September with her first small stroke. To this day, I believe wine deprivation was the contributing factor. Her short-term memory vanished, although her long-term memory remained intact. She was diagnosed with dementia, and the rest of her body became more impaired. She moved off the walker and into a wheelchair. She couldn't remember coming to the nursing home, how long she'd been there, or what event sent her there. But her memories of Pop, her Tennessee home, and her lifelong love of poetry were still alive and well.

I enlisted the help of a professional care manager, Shirley, to advise and lend emotional support to my mother and me. Shirley was a registered nurse and said I could call her anytime, day or night. The nursing care at the home was adequate but shorthanded. The staff couldn't respond quickly enough to Mom's changing situation. I located a good geriatrician who made nursing home calls, but right after her eighty-fifth birthday in January, Mom became lethargic.

"Your mother is suffering from anemia, and the cause in someone her age is difficult to diagnose," she said. "I recommend a blood transfusion."

I took a deep breath before explaining the situation to my mother. "Mom, it will mean a trip by ambulance to a hospital and an overnight stay." My mother refused. She said she wanted to die.

I called Shirley. "Is this the point where we stop all medical assistance? Should Mom be allowed to die now?"

My mother had repeatedly told me not to resuscitate her, not to extend her life, until I was neurotic about following her wishes and second-guessing the situation. Shirley had managed a Denver hospice before entering the care management business for herself. She understood the needs of people in the last stages of life, and she sensed my mother wasn't finished yet.

In a thirty-minute visit, Shirley explained to my mother why she needed a transfusion, how she would get to the hospital, what would be done, and what results she could expect. For some reason, the composition of her blood had deteriorated. This was why she was feeling so poorly. Fresh blood would probably revive her for a substantial length of time. It was a standard medical practice for her condition.

As Shirley talked, I watched my mother's face shift from depression to hope. Shirley was able to explain in medical terms what I was unable to convey. My mother, who had been an RN herself, listened, understood and trusted. She took Shirley's advice. An ambulance was called. Mom was transferred out of her bed, onto a gurney. I rode with her to a large inner city hospital and sat with her throughout the transfusion. The hospital kept her overnight, and I left her there alone with the misgivings of leaving a child. I saw her the following morning back in her nursing home room. At first she appeared to be in a coma, and my heart sank. But by noon, the transfusion caused a dramatic change. Color came back to her cheeks; she was talkative, cheerful, and glad she had taken that courageous step.

Once she felt better, Mom needed something to live for. She was not going to languish in that nursing home bed waiting for the next crisis if I could help it. "What are her interests?" Shirley asked me. I remembered Mom's poetry collection—her old notebooks we'd transported from Tennessee.

"I know just the person who can help," Shirley said. "Mary has been a caregiver on my staff for many months. She is creative and enjoys working with elders. She especially likes poetry."

I told Mom that Mary would drop by to visit and discuss poetry. I said Mary could help put her poetry in order—one of my mother's wishes before she had become too infirm. My motive was to keep Mom's mind and spirit alive in the nursing home. Mary was honestly wild about poetry, and bonded with my mother right away. She must have been divinely sent, for the two of them made a perfect match.

Mary wrote me about the first time she met my mother. "It was snowing quite hard and she was the only one I needed to go out of the house for that day. I debated whether or not to call and ask to reschedule, but something—that quiet something that will urge one on—told me to bundle myself up and go. I walked into her room. She was sleeping. I reached over and touched her and she opened her eyes to see who it was. She recognized me right away and we began a quiet conversation. As we were talking, the sun broke through the clouds and came suddenly and brightly in through the one window, lighting up the whole room. I remember we looked at each other and smiled and said, both of us, almost at the same time, 'This is a good sign.'"

Their friendship flourished. Mary photocopied and read my mother's poetry collection—all six hundred pages—and put it in a binder. She visited twice a week, sat in a chair next to Mom's bed, read aloud, and asked Mom to talk about the thoughts that had brought on the poems. She was a natural healer of souls. My mother blossomed once more.

We had held onto Mom's apartment for almost a year, paying the monthly rent, just in case she might return. But as the winter of 1997 thawed into spring, I spent the month of March clearing out her apartment, a little bit each day, knowing it was time to wind up that chapter in her life. While I had packed up the Tennessee house in the space of a week, with emotions clamped down tight, when I cleared and packed up her Denver apartment, I probably spent far too much time. I read through her correspondence, and cried. I threw away barrels of litter, and cried. I gave household items and bed linens to charity, and cried. And I answered questions from the occasional visitor who wanted to know how Louise was.

This sad releasing and relinquishing reminded me of the last poem Mom wrote and finished in that very apartment, "Clearing Out Family Papers." In that poem, she noted that there is "no need to longer save that hoarded sorrow." My mother inherited the hoarding gene, so for her to "clear decks of salt debris— / Dried tears, faint scum of ancient sighs," must have been torture, just as it was for me to clean out the last eight years of her life. "A basket fills, an empty file slides shut with ease. / To all but light and sun and wind, / I bid good-bye, good-bye, good-bye."

After all nonessentials are cast aside, a person's distilled essence often comes to rest on the walls and limited flat spaces of the last bedroom. In the nursing home, Mom shared a two-bed room with Mrs. Jordan, whose working life was condensed into an inscription on a plaque commemorating years of service in the Denver Public Schools, and beneath it, a picture of her as a younger woman. Most days, a nurse's aide wheeled Mrs. Jordan out into the hall, where she spent hours in front of the nurse's station. Her head drooped and she stared at her motionless hands. I tried to envision Mrs. Jordan in her prime. Her hands would have danced across a blackboard as she held a piece of chalk. They would have pointed at the student in the back row. They would have filled out report cards and evaluations. Her voice would have influenced each student in her class. Mrs. Jordan didn't talk anymore.

The blank wall next to my mother's bed begged for a bulletin board, which I added. There I tacked her final poem, "Clearing Out Family Papers," and a picture of our Tennessee woods. I taped her poster of the Andromeda Galaxy across from the foot of the bed, and on the closet knobs hung two lattice-work paper valentines made by visiting grade school kids. My mother's life in a nutshell: Poet, Tennessee Woods Woman, Star Gazer, and Handiwork Collector.

Mom had fallen several times that last year. But when the nurses called to tell me of a fall on April 5, 1997, I was shocked to see her bruised, swollen face and discolored arm. By that time, she was a shrunken wisp, and yet, out of her bony face gleamed the same bright blue eyes and intense expression that defined the essence of her personality.

When my mother lost her appetite for food and water, the end was near. I brought in a carton of California rolls from the King Soopers deli across the street. This would usually elicit chirps of delight, but she only raised the morsel to her mouth, took a tiny bite and put it down. I was hungry and ate the rolls myself. A few days of eating and drinking poorly set her up for a bladder infection.

The day the head nurse told me about Mom's bladder infection, I wasn't alarmed until she said Mom would die if the infection was not reversed immediately with antibiotics. How would it be administered, I wanted to know. The nurse said they would set up an IV. This entailed more needles, and I remembered my mother's mantra: *Do not resuscitate me!* It was posted all over her apartment for the benefit of the EMTs who might be called in. *Oh God*, I thought, *now it's up to me to decide whether she lives or dies.*

I informed the nurse of Mom's wish to stop all treatment when she might be nearing death. The administrator searched Mom's files and found her Living Will, but no Medical Durable Power of Attorney, which would have defined her wishes specifically. I had never understood that a Living Will was insufficient to cover my mother's end-of-life wishes.

Mom had been a resident of this nursing home for over a year, and everyone knew us. They cleared the way for Mom to get on with her transition without a Medical Durable Power of Attorney. She was in a coma, and the bladder infection was working its way through her weakened body. I asked for hospice to take over.

A hospice nurse came the following day and when that happened, the nursing home staff relinquished responsibility for my mother's nursing care. The hospice nurse explained the dying process and assured me Mom was starting that process. Although fatigued, I became very alert and began a two-day vigil.

Shepherding Mom through this rite of passage was my last act in our earthly relationship. As my mother's caretaker, I felt fiercely protective. I wanted her to have "a good trip," and yet I was apprehensive. I had only been present for one other death— my father's, nine years prior. That had taken place in a hospital intensive care facility surrounded by ICU nurses, my mother, and me. Now it was up to just me. Jim was on a business trip.

My friend Carol came to sit with me the night my mother died (April 15, 1997). As an RN who volunteered for Red Cross, she had seen many souls into and out of this world. She assured me there was nothing she would rather do. Carol had performed several sessions of Therapeutic Touch on my mother, which Mom had loved. Therapeutic Touch is a form of hands-on energy work drawn from ancient healing practices. We sat together by her bedside. I read from *The Book of Common Prayer*, and we took turns reading some of Mom's poetry aloud.

The floor-to-ceiling curtain was pulled around Mrs. Jordan's bed, affording us a sense of privacy. Even though sound carried through the curtain, it created the illusion of a soft barrier at night. Around midnight, Mrs. Jordan began to mutter. The nursing staff considered Mrs. Jordan a blank slate—a passive, silent Alzheimer's patient. Mom had never heard her speak, but told me she talked to Mrs. Jordan as if she understood every word. Carol and I finally untangled the words and realized she was reciting the rosary. On this particular night, Mrs. Jordan muttered over and over, "Hail Mary, full of grace, the Lord is with thee. Holy Mary, Mother of God, pray for us sinners, now, and at the hour of our death."

I had been awake too many hours and was exhausted. Carol told me to take a nap. The nurses found me a vacant bed in a room down the hall. Carol said she would call me when it looked like my mother was getting ready to pass. Around three in the morning, she came to fetch me.

"Your mom's breathing has slowed," she said.

Carol held my mother's hand, stroked it, and talked to her with soothing words. "Everything is just fine, Sweetie. You're doing fine. We love you."

I was frozen in place, watching and wishing I could muster the words I'd never spoken aloud to her, "I love you, Mom." But they wouldn't come. I was so glad that warm, loving, experienced Carol was sitting with me, holding Mom's hand.

When my father died, I had held his hand. It had been as cold as ice. A nurse had said, "He's going. Tell him you love him. He can still hear you." So I did, and it seemed so out of character, so unlike me. Our family just never said those words. We signed our letters, "Love, Mom," "Love, Pop," "Love, Maria," but never said, "I love you." It was like a taboo, as if speaking those words might bring down the house around my ears. Those words might leave me howling in the night, insane, with all the good and evil flying out of me.

At the end, it was clear my mother's form on the bed was just a shell, still mechanically breathing, going through the motions. There was no sign of the life that had been there three days earlier. Some people open their eyes and speak before they cross over. Both Carol and I felt that my mother was out of her body and in the room with us. The form on the bed took a last breath, and that was it.

Carol and I looked at each other. "She did it. She's free," I said.

I walked to the nurse's station and asked for a pair of scissors, returned to the room, and clipped a small lock of her white hair to save, like the hair she clipped from my head for the baby book. I placed it in an envelope, thanked Carol for staying with me, and we walked out together. That was the last time I saw my mother.

I had the house to myself. After the sun was up and I felt human, I called family and friends. When I reached my friend Libby at work to give her the news, it was nearly noon. She left immediately and picked up lunch for both of us, then came to my house.

"Your mom paid me a visit this morning," she said, about to burst with the news. Libby was at her desk around 9:00 a.m. when, in her mind's eye, she became aware of my mother "whooshing around." She knew it was my mother's energy, although she didn't physically see her. In her mind's eye, she saw a white cloud soar around the office and sensed my mother's delight with her newfound freedom. She said my mother was transmitting the thought to her, *See what I can do!* Mom evidently wanted me to know she was very much all right.

Earlier that same morning, Carol had called, equally excited. Her best friend, Sue, who was part of our monthly meditation group, asked Carol to pass along to me what she had experienced. Later, Sue wrote me a card that said, "As I meditated on Monday night, I was sending light to you and I saw a woman in gold light and I understood it was your mother. She looked very happy, young, and was waving and wishing you well. I hope this is some comfort to you."

It was the most profound comfort I could imagine. I was amazed and grateful that my mother had contacted me through two friends, neither of whom knew she was dying Monday night. I hoped she would contact me, but I also realized I wasn't in a sufficiently tranquil state of mind to be receptive.

At the conclusion of my mother's memorial service, Mary handed back Mom's three-inch thick poetry notebook and urged me to continue the work. "This is too good to let drop," she said. "I would encourage you to still think about publishing a small volume with your own comments and some photos. If it's meant to be, publishing won't present a problem. That's just the way the Universe works, you know."

I had little time to grieve my mother's death since Jim and I were busy wrapping up our lives in Denver. We held yard sales and did a twenty-year house cleaning and final tweaking of the old house we were leaving. Then we planned the logistics for moving our pottery business 135 miles to the mountains. Jim was in charge of having our kiln transported and set in place on its new cement pad. We proceeded to move every stick and stone of our belongings, truckload by truckload, to our new home. Once in place, we spent the remainder of that year retooling our pottery business.

We carted Mom's poetry notebooks and her ashes with us. Her ashes would go into the Arkansas River when my cousins, Susie from Arizona and DeDe from Maryland, came to visit. Mom had wanted her ashes placed in the river where, theoretically, they would join my father's ashes in the Atlantic Ocean. We had placed Pop's ashes in a stream on Bay's Mountain, a park near our Tennessee home. I thought that would be the end of her. I expected a short grieving period, and then I'd be over her. Little did I know this was only the beginning of a whole new chapter of Louise Ernst Weber.

# Chapter 4

## The Healing Legacy

When she was in her seventies, I asked my mother to tell me what she had learned from living her long life—as if she could blurt it out in a couple of sentences. With an edge in her voice, she replied, "Read my poetry."

As a child, I hadn't understood metaphor or poetic symbolism. I had told Mom that if she couldn't write it clearly in plain words, then I didn't care to read her poetry. She had looked at me with her piercing blue eyes and had said nothing. My disinterest in her poetry remained a thorn while she was alive.

I learned to appreciate classical poetry as an English major in college, even studying Milton's *Paradise Lost* for an entire semester, but I didn't write poetry unless it was assigned for a class. I sent Mom the one sonnet I wrote for an English class. She submitted it to *The Lyric*, a respected poetry magazine, and they published it. I still have the copy of that long-extinct publication. Later that year, I wrote some very bad poems and submitted them myself, only to receive soul-killing rejection letters. I never told her, nor did I write poetry again for thirty years. Poetry was simply not a topic I wanted to discuss with her or anyone else.

I was more than happy to read her writing after she was gone. When Jim and I were finally settled into our new log home near the Arkansas River, I started reading Mom's poetry. Her poetry became my new career. Mom had titled one ancient black notebook *Finished Poems*; another, *Unfinished Poems*. Over the next two years, I read, typed and sorted all her poetry, including her yellowing originals and her multiple revisions. Many brought back memories, transporting me to distant days, seasons, and events. One such poem was "Interim, for Bonny von der Meer." I remembered the incident that had, no doubt, inspired it.

In the summer of my ninth year, Mom and I were parked near the post office when she opened and read a registered letter from Herman von der Meer. Her face fell, and she started to shake. She reached for Kleenex in her purse.

"Bonny's dead," she sobbed, and leaned her head against the side window. I'd never seen her in such a state.

"What happened, Mama?"

Bonny was my mother's best friend from her nursing school days, and this was horrible news.

"A car accident," she said. My mother slumped in the seat with her hand to her forehead as she read the letter to me. The family was returning from a vacation to the shore. It was dark. Bonny's husband Herman fell asleep at the wheel and drove off the edge of the highway—a low shoulder—and the car rolled over.

My hands grew cold as Mama read.

Bonny was thrown from the car and pinned beneath it. Herman pulled himself out of the wreckage and tried to save her. She was still breathing when he reached her, but he couldn't lift the car off of her. She died before help came.

I felt sick trying to imagine how it would feel to be squashed under a car.

"And the children?" I asked. I remembered Ingrid and Peter, whom I'd met when the family came to visit us the previous summer. They were several years younger than me, very sweet and well behaved.

"They're all right. They were sleeping in the backseat and were somehow unharmed. Herman got them out, thank God."

I didn't know how to comfort my mother. I just sat, stiff and barely breathing, until she could drive home. Since my emotions were tied to hers, as though we were one, my heart sank and I remained depressed for days.

Bonny had been my mother's friend since they were eighteen. They had roomed together during four years of nursing school at Presbyterian Hospital in Philadelphia. After graduation, Bonny returned to her native Holland to marry her sweetheart who was studying psychiatry in Amsterdam.

My mother completed her graduate nurse's training at the University of Virginia, married my father, Bill Weber, in 1935, and then was hired as head operating room nurse at Holston Valley Community Hospital in Kingsport, Tennessee. As World War II darkened Europe, Bonny and Louise wrote letters back and forth. At the beginning of World War II, Bonny reached out to Louise from Amsterdam.

> *Left alone in the worst agony, wanting to turn to someone, I find that you are the person I need now. I need you desperately.*
>
> *At two o'clock in the night, someone rang the bell and delivered a telegram in which Herman was summoned to go into the army-service immediately. Now he's gone. Why aren't you here so that I can talk to you? Where will he be today? Where will they send him? Will I ever see him again? . . .*
>
> *The sky is slowly getting lighter; birds are singing; the trees are getting such nice buds—nature is so calm and*

*beautiful. How is it possible that maybe in a few days this whole world will be one bloody scene? . . . Louise, if he should die, I don't even have his child as a living memory. Nothing but cold, dead pictures. Pray to God he'll take me too.*

Herman's army duties were short-lived. He was allowed to return to his medical studies. Bonny kept house as the war marched closer to their doorstep.

In January, 1941, Bonny wrote again.

*Before this new year started, we had weeks at a time that we woke up every night from this ungodly noise the anti-aircraft cannons make. Then you could very distinctly hear the shards fall all around on the roofs of the houses and the street. But again, one gets used to everything, and as I said before, the thought of what may be coming frightens me more than I like to admit even to myself; but when we first experienced these things, we were scared and got out of our beds, even dressed so that we could get away as quick as possible, if anything would happen. After-wards, we just got awake, said to each other "there it is again," turned around and tried to go to sleep again with the more or less fatalistic thought if they're supposed to get me they will anyway, no matter what we do to prevent it. So why worry. And so we go on, knowing that each bomb may hit us, as well as our neighbors, hoping to get through all this alive; hoping for a better future. We live from day to day and try to make the most of it.*

By the winter of 1941, letters were being opened and read by German censors and then stamped with the German swastika.

Bonny could not write details of what was happening in Holland politically, because the censors would not pass the letters through.

> . . . *Louise, you say that maybe you would be ready to fight if your president were set aside and the government overthrown, but you doubt it, as long as you could live quietly and in peace. Those last words are very important, Louise. Don't underestimate them. And don't think you will live quietly and in peace if that ever would happen. Ask me and I'll tell you all about it . . . some day.*

She ended her letter by saying:

> *My dear Louise, if anything would happen to us, I want you to know I've only had one friend all my life; one who has taken complete possession of all the friendship I ever had to give; one who has proved to me that friendship, as described by poets is possible in this world. Love always, Your Bonny.*

Bonny and Herman survived the war. They adopted two Dutch children and eventually returned to the U.S., where Herman established his psychiatric practice in Pennsylvania.

After Bonny's death, Mom wrote "Interim, for Bonny von der Meer." In it, my mother says she dreams of Bonny, joyful dreams that seem real, from which she doesn't want to awaken. In the end, my mother wonders whether Bonny, on the Other Side, misses her as intensely she misses Bonny.

> . . . In dream we talk with care
> Of things no others share.
> The joy is past belief,
> Night's respite far too brief.

. . . Does she, too, wrapped in light,
Endure this self-same plight;
Stalk love with memory clear,
Meet silence in the ear,
And wait with bated breath
For news of my own death?

Weeks after Bonny's death, Mom came to me excited and relieved. "I must tell you what happened to me today while you were in school . . . I saw a vision of Bonny."

Mom told me she was trying to rest that afternoon. She was lying on the bed with her eyes closed and feeling very sad. Suddenly she saw a light. "The light became a face, and it was Bonny! My dearest Bonny! She looked perfect, young and whole . . . and she was smiling. She told me she was all right."

"Did you hear her voice?" I wanted to know.

"No, she talked to me in my head, through ESP, and said my grief was causing her to be sad. She said I should stop grieving because she is fine. She was so beautiful. I am so happy. I just wanted you to know that I'm finally going to feel better."

Mom's vision sparked my interest in the afterlife. I reasoned if Bonny appeared happy and even spoke to my mother, then contact was possible from another realm. I had no cause to doubt Mom's vision, because I witnessed her overnight shift from sadness to peace.

Bonny's tragic death even benefited me. Mom allowed me into her private life for a short time, which made me feel very grown-up and of use to her as someone she could confide in. This interlude defined common turf where we could be friends instead of Lecturer-Mama and Listener-Maria.

This incident became another milestone. The unseen world, perhaps the most intriguing territory I'd ever encountered, captured my full attention. By sharing extrasensory experiences such as her waking vision of Bonny, and later, her dream about Linda Brown, I learned from my mother that there was more to life than what I experienced with my five senses. These weren't stories in a book. They were my mother's true, firsthand experiences. Mom's poem, "Interim, for Bonny von der Meer," brought back the scene and sensations of my nine-year-old self.

Sitting in our loft, with her poetry spread out around me and a view of the Sawatch and Sangre De Cristo Ranges out our south facing windows, I often felt Mom's presence—the subtle energy field that settled around me when I worked with her writing. I wondered where Mom was and if she had reunited with Bonny in the afterlife.

That was just one question out of many. I wanted to know who my mother was now. I didn't know how to picture her. Linear time had little meaning anymore. Should I think of her as the shriveled wisp in the nursing home, or as the woman I resisted as a teenager? Should I remember her as the middle-aged woman who repeated stories about the war years, or as the seventy-nine-year-old mother with whom I drove up to Sundial Park on summer evenings for sunset viewing? Was she the mother who nagged me to become more sociable, or the woman who wrote poetry at midnight? Which image and which relationship would stick with me now that she was gone? Furthermore, I was confused about our relationship, because I held warm memories from recent years and troublesome memories stemming from my first thirty-five years. In the end, I arrived at a benign image of my mother in her middle years, between forty-five and fifty. I envisioned her with graying hair, as she had appeared when I left for college. Regardless, our relationship remained in flux while I dug into her secret life of words.

During my reading marathon, I dwelled in my mother's mind and glimpsed into her soul. Many poems praised God, while others cried out for a palpable connection with the divine. She described dreams and paranormal experiences. She wrote dozens of antiwar rants and an equal number of poems in honor of creatures and trees. She wrote about the process of writing and the creative spirit. She wrote tributes to her friends and family, living and dead. She struggled with anxiety, depression, doubt and fear. My mother was a woman of intellect and ideas. She could hold her own in discussions on science, philosophy, art, and authors. Her poetry, though, showed me the naked truth about her. I sensed I was on the brink of a new relationship with her, one based in honest sharing between equals. I was ready to exhume our common past for reexamination.

Certain poems moved me to tears, consoled and reassured me that her love persisted. I craved a heart connection with her more than ever and actually felt a warm vibration, a loving glow around me that was indisputably Mom. Some of her poetry was about me, and I cried when I realized the intensity of her love for me. Loving words I couldn't remember her ever saying to me came out in her poetry. "We had almost gotten used to your leaving," she wrote in a poem called "The Visit." After I married my first husband and moved to Colorado, I returned to Tennessee to visit my parents in 1969.

> The way you flop in a chair, and walk, and stand;
> The motion and sound of you . . .
> Found again after two years—these are the things
> We had almost gotten used to not having.

She wrote that she had to grieve my loss a second time after I returned to Colorado. I could have written similar lines about missing her voice on the phone or the sight of her sitting in a wingback chair, legs resting on a footstool and a book in her lap. Much of the time, I was on the edge of tears while absorbed in her poetry, existing in my own skin and hers.

I began to make sense of who she and I really were. I read everything, every draft of every poem. Not only were there poems, but journals and notebooks of her random thoughts. I started to see her as more than just my mother. She was becoming a woman with dimensions I never knew as a child . . . or even as an adult. Here was someone I would have sought out as a friend had we been closer in age. As a friend, I would have supported and encouraged her. I could have shared in her guarded private world. But as her daughter, she didn't allow me into the crevices of her life, and as her daughter, I never asked to go there. The beauty of reading her self-revealing poetry was that I felt she had accepted me as a trusted friend.

In her poem, "Prescription," I learned she had experimented with tranquilizers.

> I'm grateful for these days and waiting, watch
> The magic of the medicine unfold.

I can only guess what was bothering her enough to use them.

> Must every river, then, be traced back to its spring;
> Must every wandering road be trod back to
>   the fetal home,
> The very sod which nursed me into life?
> If this is true, I can't stop at my father's door
> And linger with his sins and mine, considering
> What he has done to me, and I to him.
> A primal father waits for reckoning . . .

She never confided to me anything improper about the relationship with her father. I assumed his parenting was healthy, for when I saw them together, they looked happy and normal. Maybe an abusive stretch erupted in her upbringing that I never heard about, never suspected. Something had caused her to hide who she was from me. Something had caused her to suffer and plead for forgiveness in her religious poems. I wondered, too, if she unwittingly shielded me from my father because of some incident that happened with her own father.

In her poem, "Inertia," she questions her lack of motivation.

> Paralyzed and dumb, I wait
> For that which I'm told
> Will surely come. Meanwhile,
> I'm useless, helpless, cold.

I began to view her as "Louise," rather than "Mom." Mom was the woman who raised me and hid her weaknesses. Louise was the writer who disclosed the wounds of her heart, which made her seem more reachable. I had used tranquilizers a number of times. As for inertia, I battled that myself.

My mother became Louise to me as I read all of her poetry. She was a compassionate listening ear to her friends' woes. She held those burdens close to her chest, but in "Empathy," she unloaded. Poetry was her refuge, her outlet, her therapy. When my father had gone to his office and I to school, Louise had the house to herself until the next phone call disturbed her.

> The morning mail is heavy with travail;
> The phone brings woes, north and south

> My friends meet blow on blow,
> And if I cautiously admit the least entrance
> Of world news, the eastern half alone
> Would lay me low . . .

What did she do to lift her spirits? For if she, too, fell limp as wet plaster, she would be no help to anyone. She said her strength came from the scenes out her windows, her faithful trees, mountains, rocks, and leaves. In other words, she turned to nature to steady her will and open her heart.

My own friends began to suffer blow on blow when I reached my fifth decade. First, the husband of a friend died of brain cancer. Next, one of my best women friends succumbed to the same fate. Like Louise, my heart sank with loss, and I hiked in the hills to restore my balance. I experienced empathy for Louise that I'd not felt before.

In "Stormcloud and a Three-quarter Moon," Louise said she received answers only in flashes, as when moonlight flickers across trees and then retreats behind a cloud.

> . . . I see for an instant, then the mind dims,
> Goes into shadow and uncertainty again.
> BUT, bright as these stark illumined trees,
> And real as this mottled moon, I know I did see—
> Though beyond recapturing—answers,
> Burned for one streaking instant, on
> The dark sky of my wondering.

It was knowing that she did see, if only for a second, that sustained her. My insights came in bursts and then dimmed into mist, as she described. How I missed talking to her about insight and the workings of the mind. Even though thirty-three years separated us, we had had many good talks when she came to live in Denver after my father's death. Poems such as this one reminded me of those conversations in her apartment.

Reading Louise's poetry allowed me to roll back the years and hear her forty- and fifty-year old voice, not her intellectual voice, but her introspective voice. She wrote for herself, as therapy, as I would write in a journal, except she was careful not to name names.

Louise's written words and thoughts became a curious kind of time machine for me. I began to read her writing when I was fifty-four. Where was she at fifty-four? At sixty? At seventy? At eighty? How would my thoughts and feelings compare to hers on comparable birthdays? At age fifty-four, my mother wrote about the empty nest, and she made her first trip out of the country with my father. At fifty-four, I summited my first 14,000-foot mountain peak. At age fifty-seven, Louise witnessed the Apollo 11 astronauts' first moon landing and wrote her poem, "Moon Men." This event changed her world. At age fifty-seven, I witnessed two hijacked planes hitting the World Trade Center. This event changed my world. While the global events we witnessed were very different, our genetic makeup was similar. With her poetry as a compass, I could see where I might be headed.

Buried in Louise's life and newly arrived in my rural community, I needed some fresh air. I joined a local writing club, where I found people who were interested in my "poetry project." I'd been looking for like-minded friends, and I developed several friendships from this group. The writing club customarily presented poetry readings for the community each summer. Since I'd written almost no poetry of my own, I asked if I could read my mother's. I imagined her astonishment as I spoke her words aloud from a podium during two summer performances. Here was the daughter who showed no interest in poetry during her mother's lifetime, now eagerly reciting her lines. I could almost hear her words from beyond the veil, *"I thought I'd never live to see the day. . ."*

I volunteered to read at a local fundraiser, on a school stage and to an audience of over one hundred. The poem I chose initially caused me to cry. It was a children's poem about a house that faded away into the deep, dark woods. In the last stanza, the writer—my mother—also unraveled and disappeared. In my practice sessions, I kept breaking down at the end of the poem where my mother unraveled. So to fortify myself, I commandeered my friend B.J. to hear me recite it over and over again until I could read without choking up. I learned the value of practice, practice, practice.

Shortly after that performance, poetry began to happen for me. I submitted two pieces to the writing club's anthology contest and both were accepted. Not only did Louise's poetry resuscitate my memory and influence my thoughts about her, but it inspired my creative process. I began to discover my own original writing voice. A respected regional journal bought two of my nature poems. Some of my early poems contained a bitter edge. They mellowed over time. I discovered the healing power of poetry.

One day I noted that certain poems I'd written complemented my mother's poems. For example, they might have similar themes—say, the weather, or the sun. I put the two side by side and thought, *Wouldn't it be fun to see where I can take this? Maybe I can write poems that will answer hers and we can talk back and forth in verse.* But my writing juice wasn't in the weather or the sun, it was in the old anger from my teens and twenties. I abandoned writing for fun and followed the urge to contradict my mother, exactly what I was forbidden to do as a youngster.

I read Louise's poem containing some platitude or advice that had rankled my flesh as a sixteen-year-old. Then I wrote about it until I was spent. The anger flowed fresh and hot. I could play off any emotion I was able to dredge up—guilt, self-pity or frustration. This was great stuff. Regurgitating our argument in poetic language allowed me to finally have the last say.

In "Old Wine," Louise wrote about a time when she was beset by memories of "sad, unspeakable, ancient sorrows." She wanted to "exorcise the past" and give a "Christian burial" to those sorrows that had "leached her days for years." When I read this poem, I saw the long face my mother sometimes wore and I remembered thinking, *she's got that martyr look again.*

In response, my poem, "Old Whines," emerged from the angry fifteen-year-old self that still resided within my fifty-six-year-old self, during a time when I viewed my mother as a religious fanatic determined to pound me into a copy of herself. At fifteen, I felt powerless and totally unsympathetic towards the spiritual longings and emotional pain she voiced in her poem. At the time, I had no understanding of the origins of these feelings, but I caught glimpses of them in her tired, drawn face. Furthermore, my mother had brought me up to believe what others thought of me was more important than what I thought of myself, and I vented that anger in "Old Whines."

In my poem, I recalled being told, "Don't whine / Don't curse or raise your voice," and that I must always "Maintain decorum lest the neighbors cast / their overwhelming judgment on this house." This seemed like a phony way to live.

In "Old Wine," Louise professed her religious belief, that, "Kindness is all, and merciful Christ is kind." She said she sought, "Grace, perhaps . . . this easing of old hurt; / The stinging scene recalled in peace." Louise was still tormented by childhood traumas unknown to me, but hinted at in her poem, "Prescription," and other painful events she tried unsuccessfully to repress. She prayed to Christ for mercy, forgiveness, and peace . . . but still she suffered.

I offered no sympathy in my answer to her. "A stoic German household you installed / with Thee and Thou unspoken but implied." Her sanctimonious attitude irritated me, as she pled "for grace and forgiveness in a minor chord." Since she had never shared her anguish with me, I had no way of knowing what, specifically, bothered her, so my heart did not soften.

"Old Wine," continued: "A cup of tears must never spill beyond / Its wide round rim to utter hopelessness."

*Oh, please!* I thought, *You are way too melodramatic. Get a grip.* Extending my mother no latitude, I retorted in my poem, "Your long-suffering expression . . . with lips held in a waxen half-smile— / Madame Tussaud would have been proud."

In her poem, Louise talked about the losses of her life, and because she was growing old, she found "the earlier bitter losses settling / Down and down—to near forgetfulness." She ended her poem by saying, "And if I gently pour my long life's wine / the red comes clear." In other words, she didn't need to drink the dregs of childhood fear because they had settled once more to the bottom of memory.

My fifteen-year-old self continued to goad her, saying, "You refused to spill a drop / of strangled melancholy." And in a final wallop, I called her "my manikin mother" whom I wished would "come unglued," so I could finally hear her admit "in the light of day" that I, Maria, wasn't "the only one irreparably flawed," but that she was likewise flawed. At fifteen, I really didn't like myself very much, acknowledging only what wasn't right with me.

"Old Whines" was my first venting poem—satisfying to write. With my mother recently deceased, I could regress and be as outspoken as I liked without fear of her slapping my face for cursing. "A slap across my face for muttering, 'Damn,' / . . . shut off my water / behavior unbecoming a daughter," I wrote in the first stanza of "Old Whines."

Although she and I reached common ground as adults when we could talk for hours about nearly everything, such was not the case when my personality and psyche were being formed. Back then, I applied pressure and looked for fissures in her persona whenever she presented herself as all-knowing or flawless. I was such a brat!

In spite of reading everything she wrote, I was never able to figure out precisely what it was that caused her so much pain and guilt that she needed to ask for divine forgiveness over and over in her poems. That mystery remained fodder for conjecture.

———

As I wrote various call-and-response poems, I shed a lot of tears for Louise. Her poems were the very breath of her, the very voice of her, and it seemed she was almost alive again. When I read her poems, I felt the subtle essence of her energy. I sensed forgiveness from her. I sensed her encouraging me to release the pent-up venom out of my system, and this brought me closer to her. It's difficult to explain how I "sensed" her, because it was a combination of "knowing" she was there, coupled with a loving feeling in my heart, and remembering how her energy felt to me when she was alive. I was in tune with her from reading her poetry and writing back to her. I thought of her constantly, and this, I believe, drew her to me.

---

One of my pet peeves as a child was my mother's opinion that anger should be stuffed. Louise maintained that negative thoughts should be contained and never expressed. This was the 1950s, before the Human Potential Movement, before conflict resolution, or win-win psychology. She didn't know how to talk about anger and neither of my parents wanted to hear any "guff." Instead, they required obedience, manners, and a pleasant disposition.

Being an "only" child, added pressure to the pot for me and created its share of internal conflict. As an only, I was forced to shoulder the full measure of my parents' expectations. They expected no back-talk, no expressed anger, and no criticism of them. I tried hard to be the perfect daughter they wanted. Punishment was the alternative, and I didn't fancy that. Had there been other siblings, we'd have plotted an insurrection.

"Anniversary Reflections" was Louise's advice about how to create a harmonious marriage. When I read it as a twice-wed woman with twenty-seven years of marriage under my belt, Louise's wisdom didn't seem far off the mark. She observed that verbal abuse kills love as surely as physical abuse.

I looked at Louise's poem through the lens of my parents' marriage. They rarely argued in front of me. Only two or three times in eighteen years did I hear them raise their voices, so I grew up thinking married people were never supposed to get mad at one another. Louise advised that to achieve a loving, successful marriage, partners should refrain from unpleasantness. When angry, they should zip their lips.

In "Anniversary Reflections," Louise wrote, ". . . they said love is forever, constant, unwavering! . . . One thing is for sure: love, too, has its seasons." She remarked that "spring flames to summer, smolders and wanes," but then the chill of cold weather descends without any warning or reason. When a relationship falters, Louise said, "wait out the weather." And furthermore, "to bend and not break is Eve's part"—the woman's responsibility. Later she said,

> Remember the softness of feathers.
> Hoard fluff; fill all the spaces with foam;
> . . . surround your love with puff.

My response poem, "Reflections," had roots in my 1970s awareness that women did not have to be silent or the only ones in a partnership to yield. Women no longer waited out the weather—they confronted and cleared the air. In my late twenties, I was married to my first husband. That was during the Women's Liberation Movement of the 1970s, when women attempted to establish their equality in the workplace and bedroom.

In my poem, I recalled a moment from the 1950s when my mother raised her voice and perhaps should have done more. I took her to task in my poem. That incident from my childhood was not typical. We were normally quite civilized.

"Remember the time Pop brought home the air gun?" I asked Louise in my poem. "It was after supper and he was laughing and playing / Vivaldi on the Hi Fi . . . He wanted to practice a pot shot at my behind."

In my poem, I imagined that Louise had held her tongue and let me talk.

"How much will it hurt?" I asked Pop.

"Not much," he said. "It's only a cork." He showed me an innocent looking ball the size of a dime.

Pop lined me up in front of the bookcase and took aim at my backside from ten feet away. "You watched from inside the kitchen door, blue eyes smoking," I reminded her. "I willingly played the target / to watch you steam.

I said, "He laughed when I screamed. / He wouldn't stop laughing till you finally yelled, / 'For heaven's sake, Bill, enough is enough!' / Did you unstuff the fluff that night or / Smother your angry thoughts in puff? / As for your advice, I burned my bra and said good-bye to Mr. Ex."

My first marriage lasted thirteen years. It didn't survive the Women's Liberation Movement, which encompassed years of social upheaval on many levels. To leave Mr. Ex, I had to find my voice and a new set of rules, rules that were different than my mother's.

Louise had been the model 1950s wife: She stayed at home with me even though she was a registered nurse; she stuffed her anger when my father brought home more and more stereo equipment while she was not given "play" money to spend; she kept the peace and taught me, by example, not to speak up for myself. Now, I accept that Louise came from a generation in which women were expected to absorb hurt feelings, not make waves, and not contradict men. When I was finally able to crawl inside her skin and realize her views and beliefs were formed from her rigid family upbringing in the early part of the century, I forgave her for teaching me to stuff my emotions.

My rush of pent-up passion poetry lasted for about a year and resulted in a collection of call-and-response poems. I didn't dredge for her proudest and best hour when I was scrounging for poems to blast, but rather poems where I felt something rise in my throat. I was continually surprised when I felt my mother's presence as I wrote. I assumed she could still hear me and knew very well what I was writing about her, but I felt she was encouraging me instead of raising her spirit eyebrow in disapproval.

⁓

The poetry collection, *Tangled Vines*, captures the voices of fifty-four different women talking about the complicated union between mothers and daughters. In her introduction, editor Lyn Lifshin writes that many women grapple with questions of how to create healthy relationships with their mothers without merging with or being absorbed by them. Even when mothers and daughters are separated physically or by death, Lifshin says the bond remains and the issues remain. I found that to be true. Lifshin captured the dynamic between my mother and me: resistance, which stemmed from my need to individuate—not merge with or be absorbed by Louise. I needed to block out the weight of her personality in order to find my own identity.

My early anger and grudges hatched when I needed to discover who I was as a unique human being. Louise and I were so much alike: both of us were artists and writers; both of us were wild about nature; both were spiritual seekers. I viewed my mother as the person I wanted to emulate when I was young, but assumed I'd never come close. To bolster my teenage ego, I belittled her whenever possible. Case in point: I challenged her poetry, saying it was too obscure. Couldn't she just write something in plain English that people (like me) could understand?

Answering my criticism, Louise penned her poem, "Why Don't You Say Things Plain," to explain why she wrote in symbolic language:

> And when you ask me why I must try
> To put my thoughts down in poems,
> Why I don't say things plain, I can only
> Answer: for the same reason I buy
> Colored threads and paper designs to
> Embroider prosaic items such as dish towels,
>     pillow slips and pockets,
> All quite useful unadorned. Something urges
>     us on to beauty . . ."

When I rediscovered this poem, it became my touchstone. I had begun writing my own poetry and I needed all the help I could conjure. I wrote my poem, "Trying To Be A Poet," not in anger, but in supplication.

"You read me your poems from time to time" and "I resisted your riddles, rhythm and rhyme." Instead, I became "collector of details, conveyor of clarity, chronicler of rules / like my father, the lawyer."

I had worked in the business world for thirty years, and most of that time I wrote technical manuals, newsletters, instructions, forms and procedures.

Louise said poetry was like "layers of tones, / Chords; meanings in meanings, teased out by / Suggestion—sharps, flats, striking sparks."

I replied, "I've finally become, like you, an unraveler of puzzles, explorer of mysteries . . . seeker of symbols, questioner of coincidences . . . And now, with your legacy of six hundred poems

in front of me, I need your help! Please send your word weaver /
Lend me your muse."

Louise didn't promise to send her muse back in 1964 when
she wrote her poem, but her last piece of advice reached my now
receptive ears:

Take the petals of roses and the
Pain of your thumb pierced by thorn: think on
That a long time. That's how poems are born.

I thought about those rose petals and the thorn pierced
thumb for at least seven years, and she was right. My poetry
often, but not always, arrived in a flash of inspiration after I had
pondered a notion until it distilled into metaphor or paradox.
At age twenty, Louise's poem drove me crazy, but at age fifty-six,
it made sense. Maybe Louise was becoming my muse after all.
One thing was clear: I wasn't angry at her any more. I finally
opened, finally wanted to listen. From her place beyond the veil,
I almost heard Louise say, "*There's hope for you after all!*"

Louise was a good storyteller. Not all of her poetry was obscure.
Lots of it created word pictures so precise that I could see
through her eyes and hear through her ears. She grew up on a
farm in Lemasters, Pennsylvania, where her mother—Granny
Ernst to me—cooked three meals a day for a family of six plus
three hired hands. They lived in an 1800s stone house within
view of a low mountain range. Soft hearted, animal lover Granny
Ernst would hide in the house and cover her ears during hog
butchering.

At twelve, Louise, her two sisters, one brother, and her parents
walked to a neighbor's house to catch the first ever radio

broadcast. In her poem, "How Things Are," she wrote about hearing that signal crackling from the box: "KDKA, KDKA Pittsburgh," and commented that her parents were silent. Louise lived through an era of great leaps in technology, beginning with the first telephone and the first automobile and, later, The Bomb and astronauts on the moon.

It wasn't until I read accounts of her childhood traumas that I really began to love and understand her. In "The Well of Un-remembering," Louise relived the harsh memories of her own early years that had been fraught with fearful events. At three, she heard the screams of her older sister having a rib removed and a rubber tube implanted in her chest on the Morris table in the living room. At six, she and her family almost died in the 1918 influenza epidemic. At seven, she watched her World War I, shell-shocked uncle being hauled away in a straitjacket, insane. At nine, she survived appendicitis and peritonitis in a distant hospital. As a teenager, she moved to the city because her father had lost the farm in the Great Depression. And yet her mother, Granny Ernst, had survived and had imbued her children with a love of nature that my mother passed down to me.

A love of nature was Granny Ernst's legacy to all of her children and grandchildren. Without Louise's poetry to remind me, I might have forgotten many delights: catching fireflies, creating a backyard pond, rock-hounding for ammonites in the Tennessee hills, weekend getaways to mountain hamlets, the chorus of insect and frog songs on summer nights in our woods, a vase of fresh-cut iris unfurling at midnight, and on and on. Were it not for Louise's legacy of poetry, I might have forever lost this collection of memory gems.

After two years, I had read everything, dredged up ancient emotions, written plenty of poetry to Louise, and purged myself of judgments about her. It was my way of grieving and letting her go. But I was also a compulsive organizer. I had it in my mind to do something significant with my mother's poetry collection. Putting it in storage under my house was not useful.

I had typed into my computer every single poem, from the shortest four-line snippet to the longest ten-page prose poem. I made one set of copies and organized them chronologically. When I read everything in date order, I discovered how stressed Louise had been during her forties, while I was an oblivious teenager. The year Linda Brown died was a gravely painful time for Louise. Her mother had died of cancer that spring, after a long illness. In August, Louise's beloved Aunt Lillie had died. Around this time, her friend Janet committed suicide. Too much death and loss!

The memories I carried from that period were all about me and my adolescent snits. Although I had lost my buddy, Linda, and our woods just weren't the same, two new boys had moved into the neighborhood. Suddenly my attention shifted to Butch, the skinny softball ace with green eyes. The fall after Linda died, I started eighth grade with a whole new set of concerns. My mother was still sad, but she didn't cry on anyone's shoulder. She kept her grief to herself and wrote "No Time for Mourning." She'd had "too much of bright and cheerful death"—funerals that shun tears with words of "Weep not; she would not have it so!" Louise said that the day of her mourning was overdue, and when it came, she intended "to mourn her fill." Much later she would "live again, answer ringing bells and even sing."

From my adult perspective, I empathized with her. No wonder she had seemed closed, stoic, and demanding to a contrary, self-absorbed, adolescent daughter. I thought about how

I would react under those conditions and felt nothing but compassion toward her. Reading her poetry in sequence, from 1920 to 1984, allowed me to forgive everything.

I sensed her relief, too. As I have mentioned, her essence stayed with me through this process. When I came to peace with her, she came to peace with me. Although she was not in body and I could not see her spirit in the room, I often felt her, and picked up mental messages. I would hear her words in my inner ear, but more often, I would just receive a flash of understanding that she was transmitting. I knew she was happy that I was past all the old grudges.

---

I was an organizing maniac. I cataloged all of Louise's poetry and placed it into six two-inch ring binders. I made a list of her published poems and boxed up the journals and magazines in which they had appeared. Louise had entered and won a few writing contests. She also had submitted poems on the subjects of spirituality, religion, nature, family and antiwar protest to publications. A number of these reached traditional publishing channels, including one that *Arizona Highways* published across a two-page art spread in their 1977 Christmas issue.

I contacted her hometown library in Tennessee, where a vibrant archivist welcomed the entire collection. On my mother's birthday, January 11, 1999, I shipped the binders to the library. Four contained her originals, arranged alphabetically. An organized person in all areas of her life, Louise had saved and dated even her earliest drafts of many poems. For future researchers, I saw value in following how a writer progressed from pencil scratchings on the backs of envelopes, through marked-up revisions, to the final typed copy. In the fifth and sixth binders, I placed the entire poetry collection that I had entered into my computer, grouped by theme. I wrote introductions to each section and explained what I thought was happening in my mother's life at the time of her writing. That done, I patted myself on the back and felt closure. Louise's life's work had found a new home, and I was free. My grieving period was over . . . or so I thought.

Even after I had shipped off the poetry to Tennessee, Louise's words were still inside of me. I found myself talking to her as if she were here, especially when I hiked. The early morning was my favorite time to walk. I'd say, "Mom are you there?" I'd wait a few seconds and then begin to talk. Sometimes I could sense her subtle presence. Other times I'd just have to trust. I could not prove that she showed up for me, but I believed she did. I heard answers in my head that sounded like her voice—no long conversations at first, but a few words. If I asked her something that required a longer answer, a flash of understanding might enter my mind several minutes or hours later.

Because I still remembered every poem in her collection and since I was in touch with her thoughts and feelings, she seemed especially real to me. The wall I built to keep her out had crumbled. I was finally able to say, "I love you, I forgive you, I understand why you treated me the way you did." Those sentiments trickled into my heart over the weeks and months. I also needed her forgiveness, for I carried a lot of guilt. That happened too, as my tension relaxed. I came to a place of gratitude, where I could feel thankful for everything she was.

I learned it is never too late to say the things that could not be said in life, to speak or write those things. It is never too late to forgive or be forgiven. It is never too late to say, "Here's what really bothered me about our relationship," or to say, "I love you; I understand you now; I'm sorry I didn't understand you then." I believe the ones who are in nonphysical form can hear us from the Other Side. It helps to talk to them as though they are sitting across the table listening.

The practice of writing poetry to and about my mother was the tool I used to heal my relationship with her. Four years had elapsed since her death. After that length of time, I didn't have the urge to write poetry to her anymore. However, I soon discovered our work together wasn't finished. It was Louise who made the next move, using art as the medium to reach me.

# Chapter 5

## *The Art of Communication*

I sat on the floor next to my computer and told myself I needed a break from wrapping gifts. It was early December. A fire in the woodstove warmed our log home. Outdoors, our Colorado sky shimmered a frosty blue. I stared out the picture window toward Mt. Princeton to clear my mind. I wanted to draw. I had retreated to the carpet, my favorite place to do my art.

*Let's see if I can still do this.* With a Bic pen in my hand, I gazed at a page of used computer paper, clean side up. The last time had been three years earlier. I rested my hand on the paper and waited. In a second or two, the muscles clamped down and my hand was madly looping, scribbling, blackening in areas on the page, leaving other areas white. Energy flowed through my arm as this continued, and it was focused in my right hand, which was out of control, or being controlled by a force that I allowed to seize me. I could have stopped it at any moment by raising my hand from the page, but I didn't wish to.

If this had been happening to me for the first time, it would have alarmed me. But I had done it many times before. The motion was familiar, yet unfamiliar. Never had the energy moved my hand so quickly. I was feeling a rush of love in my heart and excitement in my solar plexus as the scribbling continued for two minutes. A picture took form, a doodled sketch in black ink, six inches high by eight inches wide. Nothing fancy. It was a body, torso, head, shoulders, arms and hands. There were eyes, eyebrows, nose and smiling mouth. And then the motion stopped. I stared at the sketch in front of me. Who was it? I had no idea. Was it my muse cheering me on?

I first felt that kind of movement when my mother bought me a Ouija (pronounced weeja) Board. The two of us sat together a few times and played the word game. We'd ask a question and the pointer (or planchet) would move under our fingers, both of us touching the heart shaped planchet. It would spell out answers—silly answers that we didn't believe. When I asked whom I would marry, it said, "Gene Foster," but that didn't come true. The Ouija Board game was the most fun I'd ever had, and I pestered my mother to play it over and over until she finally said, "No more." We discovered either of us could cause the planchet to move without the other one. Any slick surface would do. The Ouija Board wasn't necessary to create the movement. In fact, my hand would move with an oil pastel just as easily as it would move a Ouija Board planchet, which is how I learned to draw automatically.

I was fifty-seven when I drew that picture with the Bic pen. My mother had been dead four years and in the interim, I had read all the writing she left behind—a binder of six hundred poems, plus notebooks of short fiction and journals. I had even been writing poetry in response to hers. Sometimes I felt like the daughter, and I thought of her as "Mom," but more often, I viewed her as a poet, woman and spirit in her own right, and thought of her as "Louise." She was still on my mind every day. I kept the page with the drawing where I could look at it. Two days later, it hit me. It was my mother. Her face—the shape of her face, the crinkly smiling eyes. I looked at the arms spread wide, greeting me with beckoning fingers. She was reaching out to hug me. Right after she died, I wanted a sign that she was okay, but I hadn't asked recently. And yet, here she was. I wiped my eyes and stared at the picture. *Thanks, Mom,* I whispered.

*Through automatic drawing, Louise greets Maria with a hug.*

When I was a teenager, Mom shared with me that she had attempted automatic writing using the typewriter. With fingers poised on the keys, she waited. Eventually her hands took over and her fingers typed wildly by themselves. The result was gibberish and the experience, alarming, so she didn't type automatically again. I tried this too, but with no luck. My fingers stagnated on the keys where I placed them, with nary a twitch. Some well-known writers have successfully typed entire books automatically. Jane Roberts, writer of *The Seth Material* and *Seth Speaks,* typed a manuscript automatically that she believed was authored by William James, although the content did not resemble James's writing or teaching, according to researcher Arthur Hastings in his book, *With the Tongues of Men and Angels: A Study of Channeling.*

Susy Smith, wrote *The Afterlife Codes: Searching for Evidence of the Survival of the Soul.* Her first experience with automatic typing happened as she was composing a letter to a friend. Her fingers rested lightly on the typewriter keys as she was thinking about what to say and questioning whether she would say it right. The next thing she knew, her fingers started typing of their own volition. They typed words that were totally different from what she wanted to say, and to her shocked surprise, the words spelled out a communication from her dead mother. Susy's experience of typing automatically happened after months of writing automatically with a pencil.

Although automatic typing didn't work out for my mother, she was successful in her efforts to draw automatically. From the time I was small, I remember my mother taking art lessons. She was a founding member of the Kingsport Art Guild, and she sold her work at guild fund-raisers. As a teenager, she wanted to become an interior decorator. She loved wallpaper and fabric designs. She bought original oil paintings from accomplished regional artists and hung them on the walls of our home alongside her own oils and pastels. Because the hand of an artist sometimes takes off on its own, it's no wonder she discovered how to do automatic drawing.

I remember that we discussed automatic writing and drawing when I was home on college break. I wanted her to use the Ouija Board with me.

"No, Maria," she said, "I won't use it with you anymore. I was wrong to give it to you in the first place." She said she had learned that low-level souls like to play the Ouija Board. That is why the answers were never true. She told me to throw the board away.

That's how one of our long-into-the-night discussions started about all things weird, such as UFOs, coincidence, and ESP. Louise bought *Fate Magazine* at the newsstand whenever our family of three went to the movies. She couldn't talk to my father about any of these things, but she was eager to tell me what she knew. I learned about her automatic drawing and typing experiments during those midnight talks.

After Louise died, I combed through her personal effects and discovered dozens of automatic drawings she had created in her fifties and sixties. On several occasions she jotted, "Who writes?" Answers in a meticulous scrawl, as if done left-handed, varied from "Louise," to "Zos," to "Your Muse." She drew her self-portrait, the family dog, a law conference speaker. She drew the faces of people she knew who were living overseas. And when I say, "she drew," these were executed in a single line, spontaneously, without conscious direction. She dated most of these drawings, as she dated most of her writings.

In the folder of her automatic drawings, I found a series of abstract concepts, each labeled and dated. The designs she produced were Dark and Light, Death and Dying, Birth and Becoming, Deep Inward Peace, Fury and Anger, Blessedness and Love, Light of Light, Crashing Noise, Deep Silence Like a Pool, and Power of a Surging Wave. In an envelope, I found a solitary drawing of a human heart. Each drawing appeared as a quick, continuous line sketch.

Louise sketched her final automatic drawing the morning I went in for surgery. She was eighty-three years old and I was fifty. I had tried every way I could think of to shrink the fibroid tumors—herbs, healing audiotapes, meditation, and visualization. Nothing had worked. I read that myomectomy to remove only the fibroids was a surgical answer for women who were still of childbearing age, but that it was riskier. I decided to go ahead with the hysterectomy and eliminate the problem once and for all. While under anesthesia, I imagined that I would enter the void—the place of the Great Mystery in Native American belief—the creative source. I might even die. The *Medicine Cards* said that the totem animal Raven gives us the courage to enter the void and possibly experience a change in consciousness.

I believed the Raven symbol would lead me safely through my journey into the void, so I asked Mom and my friends, Libby and Lanie, to invoke the protection of Raven for me. While I was in surgery, Libby sat with Jim at the hospital and held a raven carving that I'd given her. Mom stayed home and waited for news. A raven landed on the ground at Mom's front door that morning. She made an automatic drawing of the bird and gave me the drawing after I had my surgery.

*A Raven, Louise's last automatic drawing.*

In my thirties, I had discovered that my entire body would move automatically if I allowed it to do so. The first time this happened, I was seeing a spiritual counselor who led me through some warm up exercises. I was standing with my eyes closed, following his instructions, when my arms began to move without my willing them. Before we were finished, my arms had performed quite a dance. I was astonished by this and never forgot it. What force guides the body to write, draw, or move automatically? I wanted to find out the cause behind this peculiar spontaneous phenomenon.

My search into the roots of automatic drawing felt important. I wanted to know how and why it worked, and who besides me and my mother did it. The more I learned, the more I relaxed about it. In the beginning, the only term I knew for it was "automatic drawing." As I searched, I found references to psychic art, channeled art, raw art, spontaneous art, soul drawing, expressive art, and intuitive art. All seemed to describe the same drawing technique, depending on the field discussed. Disciplines that referenced automatic movement included psychology, religion, spirituality, fine art, art therapy, psychic phenomena, and channeling.

First, I followed the path that my mother had explored: the writings of Dr. Carl Gustav Jung. During Louise's nurse's training in the 1920s, she had practiced psychiatric nursing. As a result, she was forever interested in the human psyche—psychology, psychic phenomenon, and religious experience. For six months, I read books by Jung, just enough to be dangerous. I learned that he did automatic drawing himself and taught his psychiatric patients to draw automatically. In following that course of treatment, his patients produced amazing symbols that Jung helped them interpret. He called some of these "authentic unifying symbols." Jung believed that the source of these drawings was a part of the mind that he called the unconscious. Jung thought that if we were in touch with our unconscious, we would also be in contact with our creative source.

The day that I rediscovered a packet of my mother's automatic drawings, I found that she had jotted a note at the bottom of one, saying, "An authentic unifying symbol," with a reference to one of Jung's essays. I tracked down the essay, read it, and concluded that her readings in Jung had inspired her to draw some "unifying symbols" of her own.

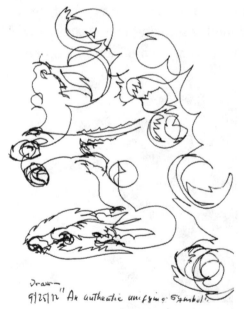

*Louise's automatic drawing of a unifying symbol.*

I don't know whether Louise's foray into Jung was inspiration for her automatic drawing or whether that had happened independently. She was an avid doodler when she talked on the telephone, and doodling often leads to automatic movement of the hand. If I begin to doodle, my hand takes over. The main symbol my doodling hand wants to create is a five-pointed star. My mother doodled connecting boxes.

The same afternoon that I drew the picture of Louise hugging me, I pulled out my oil pastels and asked which color my hand wanted to draw with. I let my fingers move loosely over the box. My hand drifted of its own accord and came to rest on the color brown. The results from that drawing were unsettling—a hand reaching up from a skull. I didn't know how to interpret this, for the hand symbol might symbolize the pottery and writing that I create. However, I deciphered the skull and hand combination as a message from my mother to mean, "Hello from the grave. This is your dead mother speaking, and I want to draw!" I decided to follow my intuition and do more automatic drawing.

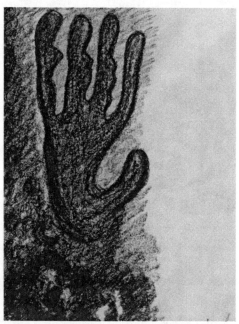

*Maria draws automatically. She believes Louise is showing her that she wants to use Maria's hand to draw.*

Although I received next to no formal training, I have enjoyed drawing for most of my life. When I was around twelve, Louise and I collaborated on a little booklet of poetry and art. The poems we chose possessed clear imagery. They were poems that I liked and they conjured interesting scenes. I illustrated them as any child would, with amateurish colored pencil drawings. We punched three holes down the left side and fastened the eight-page booklet together with brads. That was the only time I ever illustrated Louise's poetry until after her death.

The idea popped into my head to see if "the drawing force" could illustrate one of Louise's poems. I chose "Housekeeping Lesson for a Young Daughter," which reminds the child "when you wax wood," to "never forget the tree / Which living stood." Louise reminds the child that the wood in her house comes from a living tree with feelings, so the tree has made a great sacrifice for the homeowner. Louise says, "If no one remembers the 'once-green bough' or the 'forest in which it dwelled,'" then "Floor, sash, sill are served ill."

As I drew, a freshly cut log with its fiery red life essence bleeding out appeared on my drawing pad. My hand created this picture in an energetic whirlwind of color. Some force wanted to make this image. Since I held the oil pastels, I took credit for being the artist. But I didn't know whether the designer was my subconscious, my mother, angels, demons, or some other phantom artist. I was more than a little bit worried.

*Maria's illustration of "Housekeeping Lessons for a Young Daughter."*

I decided to take my pictures to Sheryl Watson and see what she could tell me about them. Sheryl was a professional intuitive, clairvoyant, and medium I had met the previous year at a metaphysical fair in Crestone, Colorado. A pretty woman with short, curly blonde hair and blue eyes, she was reading palms that day. I talked to her about my mother's poetry and the possibility of my publishing a book with both of our writings. By then I had accumulated a collection of call-and-response poems as well as poems I'd written that complemented Louise's. Additionally, I was now beginning to illustrate Louise's poems using automatic drawing. Sheryl affirmed that the work was to be a joint effort between my mother and me, and Louise wanted me to do it.

I drove two hours to Sheryl's house outside of Denver to show her the automatic drawings. She took me upstairs to her ceremonial room, where sweet incense was burning.

"Sheryl, what about these pictures? Are they just coming out of my subconscious or are they coming from my mom?" I wanted to know how I could be certain that their source was of the light and not the dark. "Take that dark picture of the hand and skull, for instance."

"Well of course they're coming from your subconscious," she said. She explained that my subconscious is where the information is stored. When those in the spirit realm wish to send information and concepts, they place them in the subconscious. When I draw, I bring those concepts out of my subconscious. My subconscious contains symbols that I recognize. When a soul from the spirit realm wants to communicate, it uses my own symbology to convey the message.

"But how do I know this is a good communication and not a low-level one?" I asked her.

Sheryl said that my mother was working in the angelic realm on the Other Side. My artwork was being guided by Spirit, and I wasn't to be concerned about the source. I should just do it.

"Let it flow through you," she said. "Just show up and enjoy it. Know it's Spirit working through your mom and you. It's really a trip to be over there and try to come back into density. Your mother is saying, 'I did the best I could!' It is really hard for her to transmit these pictures to you."

According to Sheryl, not only was Louise telling me she was alive and well on the Other Side, she was also saying she wanted to collaborate on this writing and illustrating project. I valued Sheryl's opinion and breathed a sigh of relief. Since she was a professional medium, I figured Sheryl knew plenty I didn't.

Apparently, I had received two kinds of automatic drawings: literal and symbolic. The picture of "The Hug" was literal, and it seemed my mother had literally used her energy to guide my hand. However, the picture of the shadowy hand and skull was symbolic. Mom's message was placed into my subconscious mind in symbolic form. I just wanted to know the mechanism that caused my hand to move.

Sheryl said Spirit was working with me, and I wasn't to be concerned about the source. Nevertheless, I wanted to learn what others had to say about the source of automatic drawings. That's when I discovered Susy Smith.

Susy Smith, author of thirty books on the paranormal, wrote of her experiences with automatic writing, both by hand and typewriter. Early on, she successfully contacted her dead mother this way, but also was disturbed by intruding energies and non-physical meddlers that would worm their way into her mind and take over the communication. It took Susy quite a while to learn how to get rid of them. She advised people who communicate in this way to use protection, such as envisioning themselves cloaked in white light or mentally encasing themselves in an impervious tube of plexiglass that acts as a barrier to souls who have crossed over but have remained at a low level of evolution and pretend they are spirit guides.

I asked Sheryl about my own protection. I didn't want intruders taking over my drawings. Up to that point, I hadn't envisioned a protective shield or even asked for divine protection. I simply sat down and said to my mother, "Okay, Mom, let's draw." I asked Sheryl if I should worry about an entity inserting its influence.

Sheryl said, "You can call in the protection of Archangel Michael with his sword upraised before you start writing or drawing. Michael and his legions of Light above and below are great protection."

Her advice was corroborated in Doreen Virtue's book, *Archangels and Ascended Masters*. Virtue characterizes Archangel Michael as a leader among archangels whose chief function is to eliminate fear from the earth and its inhabitants. His sword cuts the cords of fear and protects those who call upon him.

While I wanted to believe that I was drawing pictures that were sent by mother, I also wanted to be convinced that the source was, indeed, otherworldly. I continued to read for more information.

I discovered a gem of a book that began to shed more light: *With the Tongues of Men and Angels*, by Arthur Hastings. Hastings had dissected the writings of C.G. Jung, and said that Jung had investigated many mediumship cases that in today's jargon, we would call "channeling." These included metaphysical teachings, messages from the deceased, and visions. Jung was open to the possibility of discarnate spirits, although he thought it was likely that the entities could be constructed by the unconscious mind. He believed that the unconscious could create "autonomous complexes"—parts of our psyche that act contrary to what we consciously wish—which could behave like spirits.

I learned that there are other strange ways in which autonomous entities can seem real to people. For example, a wise figure named Philemon showed up in Jung's mind and talked with him, giving Jung insights when he began his own inner work. Napoleon Hill, who wrote *Think and Grow Rich*, created his own council of advisors in his mind, which included, among others, Emerson, Darwin, Lincoln and Carnegie. These imagined characters became real to him, and carried on conversations with him. Authors of novels and short stories often create characters who take on lives of their own during the writing. They can appear unexpectedly in the author's mind, and dialogue with the author or one another, sometimes giving perspectives that differ from the author's.

Besides Jung, other well-known and lesser-known individuals in the field of psychology have written anecdotal accounts in the area of channeling, automatism, and a plethora of other Exceptional Human Experiences. My eyes opened to a new world of interesting phenomena when I read in this area, but I failed to find definite answers to either side of the argument. Do all exceptional experiences take place within the mind or do some originate from the material world or the nonphysical world?

Given Sheryl's advice to keep writing and drawing, that's what I did. I went back to Louise's poetry and kept creating more pictures. I didn't worry about where they came from, but simply enjoyed the process.

# Chapter 6

## *Uncharted Territory*

Talking to trees and rocks? Who would do such a thing? I'm admitting it right now. I've talked to trees since I was young, growing up without brothers or sisters in a Tennessee forest. Trees feel like friendly beings. They're good listeners, and hugging one can do almost as much good as hugging a fellow human. Ponderosa bark smells like vanilla—definitely my favorite in the huggable tree category. As for rocks, while I've always liked them and collected small ones, I can't say that my urge to get personal with a rock happened until recently.

When we moved from Denver to our town in central Colorado, we bought land that was covered with boulders. I delighted in the fortress-like feeling the rocks gave us, forming a visual and sound barrier between our homesite and the county road. Instead of a perfectly flat two-acre lot peppered with piñon trees, our lot came rockscaped. Our acreage had been overlooked by other buyers. From the road, it resembled an unfriendly jumble. Some of the rocks were as big as a pickup truck. One towering monolith was shaped like the Matterhorn.

I envisioned our chunk of land as a rock garden with potential paths and secret nooks. Boulders created a protective environment for trees, yucca, rabbitbrush, fringed sage, wild current, gooseberry, mountain mahogany, snakeweed, and dozens of other high desert plants and shrubs. They provided cover for rabbits, chipmunks, and ground squirrels. They even served as a snow fence during winter blizzards. I had never lived among this many rocks in my life. I singled out my favorites and the ones that formed a hideout were high on the list. The ones that I could scramble on top of and lie down on brought me the most pleasure.

Today, when I walk on our property alone, I mutter out loud. I talk to our three ponderosa trees, encouraging them to hang in there during drought. I've even carried buckets of water to them. I talk to my ancient piñons that are as tall as the house, and I pat my rocks on their tops. When pine beetles struck our oldest, tallest piñon, I learned how to make a deal with the bugs so that they wouldn't spread further. I've made friends with the land, our trees, and the rocks.

Machaelle Small Wright is considered a spiritual pioneer who actually sees and hears the invisible forces of nature. In her first book, *Behaving As If the God in All Life Mattered*, she describes awakening to her extrasensory abilities and how Nature guided her to develop the Perelandra nature research gardens, where she is carrying out and documenting her life work. She describes communicating with varieties of matter—rocks, flagpoles, computers, cars, as well as with members of the plant kingdom. She writes, from personal experience, that every material thing is conscious and can be communicated with— which means things don't just listen, they talk back. According to Wright, all matter is aware and responds to our thoughts. This, too, is the belief of many indigenous peoples.

Unlike Wright, I don't hear back from Nature when I talk to it, at least not with the certainty she does. But that doesn't stop me from trying to hear and imagining that I do hear. I'll share a little story about the day I might have succeeded.

I was eager to hike one April morning. I had just returned from a trip to the East Coast to visit my cousin, DeDe. Back in Maryland, spring had already arrived, whereas in our valley, there were no signs of new life. I set out walking across the railroad bridge over the Arkansas River, through the campground, down the road, and up the jeep track. It was a route I had taken a hundred times. My turnaround spot is forty minutes out. I hike up a steep hill that eventually crests a low mountain of the Mosquito Range at about 10,000 feet. I quit at about 9,000 feet. Dryland shrubs, piñon trees, and granite boulders punctuate the slopes along the jeep trail. Ponderosa and aspen nestle into the dry washes. The spine of the Sawatch Range with its world-famous 14,000-foot peaks stretches out, north to south, across the valley.

I always stop in a grassy glade, protected by one chest-high granite boulder and a piñon tree with its eight massive arms that reminds me of an octopus. This place feels like a chapel, my sacred retreat. The rock is my father confessor. On many a day, I have rested my torso against it and asked it to take all the fatigue, grief, or frustration from me and do with it whatever rocks do. When I lean over the rock, I assume it absorbs the crud and channels it into the earth. The tree, a captive audience, has no choice but to listen. It's the rock that I always dump on.

That morning I was lighthearted, hiking fast and breathing hard. The rhythms of hiking and breathing put me into an altered state, feeling detached and floaty. As I hiked, I talked to Louise, saying, "Okay, Mom, we've got to get back to the book today. I'm going to be writing again and drawing. Are you ready?"

I sensed that she was glad I was eager to begin again after my vacation.

By the time I reached the grassy glade, I was winded. Leaning across the top of the rock, I said, "Good morning, Rock; good morning, Tree."

Sharing my trip to the East Coast felt right. I figured the piñon would have no concept of eastern trees—the pears, crab apples and magnolias—and might be intrigued. How to describe crab apple flowers to a short-needled piñon tree? I took it slowly, as if talking to someone from another planet. Pinecones might serve as an analogy for flowers—wooden flowers.

Addressing the piñon tree, I said, "Crab apple flowers look something like your pinecones, with extremely thin bracts. Imagine flowers that are shaped like piñon cones, but are made out of very thin bracts. Then imagine that the flowers are white or pink. Imagine that the trees are spindly, like the little branches that grow out of your trunk. Imagine that the tree has leaves like the current bush growing at the base of your trunk."

I closed my eyes and waited for an answer. Was the tree listening? Did it catch on to what I was saying? In my mind, I heard, "Yes," and in my mind's eye, I saw the tree wave its octopus arms.

"The trees back east were covered with hundreds and hundreds of flowers," I added. "Do you follow this?"

Again, I heard, "Yes."

I also sensed that the tree was interested. I didn't know if the interest was related to the information I was conveying or if it was just happy to be recognized as a fellow conscious being.

Turning my attention to the rock, I said, "The rocks back in Maryland and Virginia weren't exposed as they are here. They were covered up with vegetation. It's different back there. The west is a much better place to be a rock. That's my opinion."

I wanted to explain the eastern seacoast and the concept of

ocean. I started with rain, then rivulets, then rivers, then lakes. Each time I explained a concept, I asked the tree if it understood and waited for an answer. I asked the rock if it understood and waited for an answer. If I perceived a "no" from one of them, I assumed it had no frame of reference and tried to explain in terms more germane to the rock or tree's life.

The piñon didn't understand "lake," but it understood "river." The Arkansas River runs in the valley at the foot of the trail. The rock understood "lake," perhaps because it had been around so long and had seen glacial lakes. But the rock didn't understand "ocean," perhaps because of its igneous, rather than sedimentary, origin.

Once they understood "lake," I explained that oceans are vastly larger, salty, and have great fish swimming in them. They both knew what fish were.

At one point I stopped and asked if I was insulting their intelligence. I heard an amused "No." They seemed glad for the diversion.

I asked if they were picking up mental pictures from me. I heard, "Yes." So I proceeded to tell them about the Chesapeake Bay Bridge. They said they could see it from my mental image but didn't understand what it was used for.

I explained to the rock that the bridge was made of elements from the earth and was used by people like me to cross the water. The rock followed that.

It takes much longer to tell about this odd conversation than it did to experience it.

Before I left, I told the tree that I wished I could see the Piñon Deva, or tree spirit, who resided within its trunk. Some people can see the tree spirits. A friend of mine came upon one while hiking. She was alone in a meditative mood, and the face of the tree spirit suddenly appeared in the trunk of a large

ponderosa. I wanted very much to experience that, but nothing happened.

I felt euphoric about that conversation with my rock and
tree as I walked toward home down the rutted jeep road. I also
started thinking about Louise and the poem I wanted her to
help me illustrate.

When I was home, seated on the floor with my pad and
pastels, I asked Louise to help me illustrate her short poem,
"Nature's Logo."

> Power curled
> In the coiled spring
> Unfurls a flower
> And spins worlds.

What occurred was a complete surprise. The first color out of
the box was brown. The first gesture on the page appeared like
a question mark. After a few minutes, I could see that the picture
was becoming something quite peculiar, especially when an eye
appeared. Because I could feel Louise's energy when she used my
hand to draw, and even receive some of her thoughts in my head,
I understood that this was a picture of the piñon tree spirit up on
the hillside. Louise was drawing my heart's desire.

As I drew, I understood from her that the tree spirit was
shimmery and the colors around the face were of light. The
image was the face of the tree spirit, a funny looking creature.
Its nose was shaped like a pinecone bract. The semicircular "hat"
or "hair" followed the pattern of the pinecone rosette. She swore
that this was a fairly good representation of how she had seen
it that morning. The spirit of the piñon tree was androgenous—
neither male nor female.

*Automatic drawing of a piñon tree spirit.*

I needed to be in a happy, relaxed state when I connected with Louise's poetry and drew automatically. Sometimes I used headphones and listened to classical music. I sensed that she enjoyed illustrating her poetry, especially the ones about trees.

Louise loved the natural world more than anything, writing at least one hundred poems about nature. She took me on a propeller airplane from Kingsport to Knoxville for my twelfth birthday, just so we could experience flying through cumulous clouds. She hiked Mt. LeConte in the Great Smoky Mountains and many of the trails in the Appalachians. She and my father took me camping every chance we got. She saved wounded birds, and made friends with butterflies. She was exceptionally fond of trees, all kinds of trees, and she handed down that tree-bond to me.

When I moved to Colorado, living in a semi-arid land for the first time, my spirit wilted for lack of green lush. I wrote to my mother that I was homesick for trees. Our state's dry plains and exposed hillsides possess their own beauty, but I was used to a green cocoon of oak, chestnut, black walnut, beech and elm. As the years passed, I came to appreciate what the west offered: postcard blue skies, soul feeding expansiveness, invigorating air, raw geology, he-man-sized canyons, and even trees, where each tree mattered. But for the first few years, I needed trips back to Tennessee to restore my equilibrium.

As I read through Louise's nature poetry, nostalgia grabbed me. Her stories transported me back to the green thickets of my childhood where we understood the meaning of dank. Humidity wasn't a number—it was visible. Some mornings mist hung in our woods until noon. Trees transpired a sticky liquid that fell like little raindrops in the evening. The goo was difficult to remove from car windshields. On a perfectly still summer evening back in 1957, our woods pulsed with life. You could almost hear the trees breathe. The Cherokee called trees the "standing people." Although Louise didn't use that term, she connected with tree consciousness.

In her poem, "The Sky is Falling," Louise bemoaned the loss of a redbud under the weight of spring snow. To her, each tree was an individual personality. I was home with her during that April snowstorm. Our trees had already leafed out. We opened the door and heard the pistol cracks of breaking limbs that felt like shots through our hearts.

"Another one has died this instant," Louise said.

She became frantic, racing around with a broom, beating

the hemlocks beside the house. Then it happened. The perfect redbud tree came crashing down "splintered and severed to the heart." We both recalled when that wild tree had sprouted up beside the birdbath, just a sapling.

"Fifteen summers of green gone with a tearing rend," she lamented. "The scream of split wood fills my ears."

That redbud with its "glorious cloud / Of purplish pink" was framed by our front door. Now it lay "Broken and open, the heart of this tree, beyond repair." We watched helplessly as the sky continued to fall "in shreds and patches / Feather shaped, white as wool, heavy as lead."

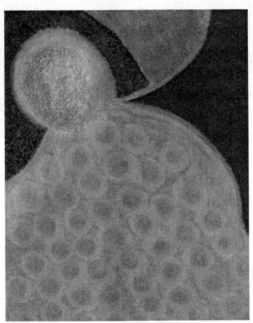

*Maria's illustration of Louise's poem, "The Sky Is Falling."*

My drawing showed the loss of that tree-being. The redbud produces tiny pink bud-like blossoms in the spring and heart shaped leaves that turn gold in the fall. This automatic drawing captured the leaves in pink rather than gold. My drawing hand depicted "the final ring of the ax" as a solid red wedge at the neck of the tree, whose spirit appeared as a woman wearing a cloak of pink leaves.

⁓

One April afternoon I sat on the floor with pastels and paper. "Mom," I said, "do you want to draw your poem, "Second Childhood?" Using muscle testing, I got a strong "yes" from her. Muscle testing, also called bio-kinesiology or applied kinesiology, is used by many chiropractors to determine whether a part of the body's electrical system is weak or strong. When I say, "I got a strong yes," that means my electrical system tested strong when I asked the question. In the years since her death, I became aware of her energetic essence—when it was present and when it was absent. Sensing her near me, I could connect my consciousness with hers and get "yes" and "no" answers from her.

"Second Childhood" was never published, and it was one of my favorites. When I said, "Mom, do you want this poem in the book?" she answered with, "Yes." In the poem, Louise described her memories when she was "barely ten plus two," and lived on a farm in Pennsylvania. She was so moved by a winter sky that "beauty pierced me through and through." Images that would leave her weak were:

> Strings of wild geese flying high . . .
> White sheep upon a distant hill . . .
> Purple cockles in the wheat,
> Bleeding poppies in the sheaf . . .
> Wind-waves rolling through green grain . . .

Certain sounds, such as "the poignant call of whip-poor-will," and odors, such as "the haunting smell of tasseled corn," left her breathless. To shield herself from "a nameless, wordless pain" she "thickened skin / Stopped ears—dulled sight." That worked for decades. But one night she forgot her armor while peering through her binoculars at the "pin-point moons of Jupiter. . . Beauty pierced me through and through," once again, "tonight, aged five times ten, plus two."

A subtle current energized my hands as I began to draw. Having no idea where this drawing would lead until it was finished, I was surprised by the completed piece. I reread "Second Childhood" and then looked for the images. Often I ignored the emerging images until after a drawing was complete. Sometimes an illustration would present a mystery that needed unraveling, but this one was easy. I found the whip-poor-will, the fields, and the wind-waves right away.

*Maria's automatic drawing of Louise's poem "Second Childhood."*

I drew pictures with an 11 x 14 inch sketchpad and a set of oil pastel crayons. I experimented by drawing with my left hand as well as my dominant right hand, and the results were different. My right hand charged along, while the left hand crept, as though it needed coaxing.

When alive, Louise was a far better artist than me. She had taken art classes for years. She hung her own oil paintings on our walls and sold her pictures at art guild fundraisers. She encouraged me to draw as a child, and so, when the urge came upon me to illustrate one of her poems, I always called upon her spirit to help me.

When I worked with my mother's poetry, before I began a picture, I would set the intention for Louise to illustrate her own poem, then I would choose the poem of hers that I wanted to illustrate. I would read the poem aloud a couple of times and keep the poem in mind as I drew, but didn't reread it until I was finished. I would sit on the floor with the pad to the right side of me. This position allowed my hand and arm to swing freely. To stay focused on the task, I watched what I was drawing, but tried to stay separate from it. In other words, I didn't mentally focus on specific words and I didn't try to guide my hand.

The movement usually started up slowly, gaining momentum after a minute. Each picture took approximately an hour to complete. Most drawings unfolded in sections. I might begin with a shape resembling a fat question mark, and then I would retrace the perimeter fifteen or twenty times until that shape was firmly outlined. My hand would gather speed to complete each section, and when finished with a particular color, my hand would stop moving. Then I (consciously) reached to the box of oil pastels and asked for the next color. My index finger would move back and forth across the crayons of its own volition, stopping on top of the next chosen color.

After selecting that color, I would move my hand back to the page, where it sketched in another block of design and color. Before I was done, I might have selected two or three layers of color to cover a single area. This technique always surprised me. I tried not to guess what the picture meant or how it would look before it was done. It was best if I remained detached. Sometimes that was difficult!

When I drew automatically, I did not attempt to "draw what I saw," for I saw nothing except the page. Some force—be it Louise or otherwise, in collusion with my subconscious mind—worked with me within my capacity to manipulate the medium. It guided me step-by-step in selecting and layering the colors. I didn't design these things; they revealed themselves over the course of a sitting. When a picture was finished, my hand stopped moving.

Is automatic drawing an activity too bizarre and uncomfortable to share? I thought so at first. I kept reading and searching for answers about others who did automatic art. In his book, *With the Tongues of Men and Angels: A Study of Channeling*, Arthur Hastings described automatic art that was apparently channeled. There were some contemporary artists who seemingly downloaded new work from old masters. Brazilian medium, Luiz Gasparetto, for example, drew rapidly, creating some pictures in three to five minutes, sometimes in a darkened room or with the paper upside down. The resulting art has been critiqued and acclaimed to be in the styles of the original artists.

I shouted "Eureka!" when I found an article in *Artnews* magazine, about the "American Action Painters," a term coined by artist Harold Rosenberg (1906-1978) for a style of painting that started with the surrealists and was later called abstract expressionism. Here at last was what I was looking for—legitimate artists using automatic movement to produce their works of art.

"Action painting" did not define a school, but rather the creative act itself. The works "emerged spontaneously, unpremeditated from the artist." Painter became actor, allowing the psychic state to take over. As I perused their works, I could see reflections of my own spontaneous style. Aside from Rosenberg, some of the other named action painters were Arshile Gorky, Willem de Kooning, Mark Rothko, and Jackson Pollock.

Jackson Pollack is well known for his free-flowing paintings. As a child in the 1950s, I remembered seeing his abstract art and thinking it bizarre. It didn't look like "art" to me, but play. *I can do that!*, I thought. Didn't we all, back then? He would lay out a huge canvas on the floor, take a bucket of paint and a brush, and drizzle one color after another onto it. It looked like fun. Then I read Pollack's own words, in which he said that he starts painting without paying conscious attention to what he is doing. He doesn't worry about making changes or even destroying an image because "the painting has a life of its own. I try to let it come through."

When I read, "the painting has a life of its own," and "I try to let it come through," I knew exactly what he meant. Pollack was painting out of his body's own subconscious movement.

I discovered a wonderful book on Carl Jung, *Jung: A Journey of Transformation*, which was illustrated in part by Freydoon Rassouli, a contemporary Iranian artist living in California. On the page, Rassouli's sensual forms appeared to move like water and fire. He labeled his unique style Fusionart. In his artist statement, he said that to initiate a painting, he climbed a mountain peak at sunrise. He would sit and observe plants opening their leaves. He would commune with nature until he felt a serene unity with the divine. As soon as he experienced creative energy from the OneSource, he rushed to his studio, where he dipped his brush into paint, and "let it move freely on canvas."

Once more, I had found an artist whose creative hand was moving on its own, from his soul. Many of Rassouli's exquisite pieces flowed in a circular motion from a central core, a process that felt similar to the way my drawings evolved.

When I sat down to illustrate Louise's poem, "Fifth and Main," my right hand was guided in a different way. The circular motion was absent.

Louise wrote "Fifth and Main" when she was eighteen, the earliest poem I located. She was captivated by a solitary tree:

> Bare black elm
> Towering high,
> Etched against
> A winter sky.

Its branches reached upward toward heaven as if to "Mirror man's supplication." She was entranced by its beauty, enhanced by a flaming sunset behind it.

> Yet hurrying feet
> Pass it by,
> Eyes on earth
> Instead of sky.

How many times have we witnessed a spectacular rainbow, sunset, or even a rare bird and been amazed at others who seem blind to that special moment?

*Maria's automatic drawing of Louise's poem "Fifth and Main."*

Pictures that came through sometimes taught me new techniques for working in the medium of oil pastel and, therefore, something new about the process of spontaneous art. This picture drew itself with clear, crisp lines, whether under Louise's instigation or some other force. While drawing the tree was quick and easy, filling in the background took forever, as the force moving my hand insisted on layer upon layer of color to achieve the luminous painted effect. I didn't expect an extended session, but layering the background over and over with different shades of lavender and peach took two hours. In the end, the sunset's glow pressed my little Pentel oil pastels to their limit, showing me what they were capable of.

The stylistic diversity surprised me. I felt that Louise was working with me on "Fifth and Main," and I was intrigued with the abrupt stylistic change from abstract to literal. Later, I received more abstract images with subtler symbols. "Second Child-hood" was an example of a picture that contained multiple symbols. As that picture came to life, I had no inkling where it was going, although it seemed that there was a plan from the very beginning. Even though Sheryl had assured me I was channeling my mother's artwork, I still had doubts.

~~~~~~

I questioned that Louise was the source of my drawings until the day after Jim and I had to have our most-loved kitty put to sleep. Fritz, a longhaired gray tabby with green eyes, had been the runt of the litter when Mom bought him for me as a birth-day present the September after she moved to Denver. Since Louise had left her cat behind in Tennessee, she cuddled and cooed over Fritz every time she came to our house.

At the age of two years, Fritz was hit by a car in our neigh-borhood, but he recovered. Each year thereafter, his medical file grew fatter because he suffered from innumerable disorders. We took Fritz with us when moved to the mountains after Louise died in 1997. He was nine. Finally, when he reached fourteen, Fritz's little body was as thin as a rag. The malignant tumor on his front paw would have meant amputation, and I simply didn't want to put him through any more medical torture. I made the date with our vet to come to the house at 7:30 p.m. and euthanize him. I was a wreck on the day of his appointed demise.

My intuitive friend B.J. called on her cell phone around noon. She was driving to Taos and my mother had just contacted her from the Other Side. "I love it when these things happen to me," she said. "Your mother said to tell you that she will be with you starting at 3:00 this afternoon. She will be with you when you have Fritz put to sleep, and will stay with you until 3:00 p.m. tomorrow. And she said to tell you that she's going to do something special for you, but I don't know what that is. It will be a surprise."

I felt Louise's presence throughout the evening. Fritz died gently. Jim and I sat still in an altered state for the longest time. The energy in the room was so supportive and loving that we felt like something extraordinary had happened. The following morning, we wrapped Fritz in blue tweed wool and buried him in a deep hole among the rocks. The ground was still soft enough that January to allow grave digging.

Remembering what B.J. had said, I spoke aloud to my mother at around 1:00 p.m. "What's the surprise you promised? You said you were going to be around until 3:00. Should I take a walk?"

I thought I might hear something from her in my head if I walked. But instead, I had an urge to draw. I pulled out my pad and colors. For the next hour, I sat on the floor and let my hand loosely move where it was directed. Louise picked the colors by moving my hand over the box until it stopped over an oil pastel. What emerged was a picture of my cat, not a dark silver-gray tabby, but a cat drawn in lavender and pink. I kept asking Louise questions while I drew and received answers in my mind. She said that this was the way Fritz looked now. He was with her. She was drawing him "from life." She noted that the colors on the page didn't do him justice. As a spirit cat, his coat was made of glowing lavender and silver light. His eyes were gleaming emerald green. By 3:00 p.m., the picture was finished. After that experience, I had no doubt my mother had used my hand to draw the portrait of Fritz, and some of the previous pictures as well.

*Fritz as drawn by Louise using Maria's hand.*

I was watching *The Today Show* on television one morning, when Katie Couric interviewed Dr. Jane Greer about her new book. I almost dropped my coffee mug! Here was a professional woman talking about receiving messages from her mother after death. I immediately ordered and read her book, *The Afterlife Connection*. Dr. Jane Greer was a psychotherapist practicing in New York City. After her mother died, Dr. Greer received so many clear signs of her mother's survival after death that she began counseling her clients about communicating with their departed loved ones. Many of her experiences sounded familiar. The most striking parallel was that, like me, Dr. Greer had asked her mother, while alive, to try to reach her after death. Perhaps that simple and profound request set the stage for contact.

"What might be" is the imperative behind all great explorations. When Edgar Mitchell became an astronaut and went to the moon on Apollo 14, he was a scientist—and he made history while achieving a technical triumph. But when he was headed home, he experienced an epiphany that changed his life. He saw Earth floating in the vastness of space and was overcome with a feeling of awe. After his safe return home, he founded an organization called The Institute of Noetic Sciences (IONS), whose purpose is "to explore the inner world of human experience with the same rigor and critical thinking that made it possible for Apollo 14 to journey to the moon and back." The word "noetic" was derived from the Greek, "nous," which means something close to "intuitive ways of knowing." IONS is committed to expanding knowledge about the nature and potential of the mind and spirit, and it applies that knowledge toward advancing health and well-being for humankind on our planet.

I like what Henry Rolfs, Director of IONS in 1990, had to say about the question that bedeviled me: Am I really communicating with my "dead" mother? When asked whether it was possible to speak with beings from beyond our dimension (channeling), Rolfs responded that there is no irrefutable proof that the phenomenon exists, nor will channeling ever be an accepted reality for the general public. However, he asserted, those who have communicated with beings from other dimensions do not doubt the validity of the experience. For them, channeling is real. During his research, Rolfs even discovered "hard-nosed critics and cynics" who had changed their minds after coming face to face with the unexplainable.

The question of whether my dead mother was communicating with me was answered first in the form of synchronicity, as when I walked into the kitchen on an October afternoon and looked at the digital oven clock. I had just mentally asked Louise if she was still interested in the book, since I had not touched the manuscript in a week. The clock read 11:11. Louise's birth date was 1-11-12 (four ones followed by a two). The display changed to 11:12, and I knew this was her way of saying, "Yes, we are still in this together."

I was gaining confidence in our communication skills between dimensions. I could reach my mother through muscle testing for "yes" and "no" answers, and she could reach me through synchronicity. I could hear her voice in my mind when I called upon her. We collaborated on the pictures I drew, and I sometimes felt her presence around me. She knew that she could guide my drawing hand if she wanted to. These were the ways we communicated.

I was comfortable with automatic drawing, and I wanted to continue illustrating her poems, especially her metaphysical ones. But she had other ideas for the book, which I was about to discover in a shocking turn of events.

# Chapter 7

## The Blast

I had no way of knowing how my writing project would evolve when I began the book. My plan was to showcase Louise's excellent poetry, providing my narrative and automatic drawings to accompany it. But books have a mind of their own—particularly when they are being guided by someone on the Other Side. The book also became an account of my journey toward healing my relationship with Louise. Even then, I was just at the beginning. The book's ultimate purpose had not yet been revealed.

On April 8, 2004, I sat down to draw a picture for a new chapter. I had an outline and a tentative title: "Seasons of the Heart." I intended to use several of my mother's poems about people near and dear to her. But Louise led me on a detour. I placed her poem, "The Leaving," on the floor beside me. It chronicled my parents' return, at age sixty-six, to the Maryland shore where they had courted as teenagers. In the poem, Louise assumed this moonlit stroll, with fingers locked together, would be the last walk they'd ever take on this stretch of beach. I read the poem a couple of times to seal the words in my mind, and then I reached for my first pastel.

Although I resisted guessing what an automatic drawing would look like while it was unfolding, I became accustomed to pictures developing with a mood or spiritual climate that matched the tone and essence of the poems. "The Leaving" evoked a poignant, quiet, reminiscent scene that did not match the picture unfolding before my eyes.

I was guided to select a cobalt blue pastel, and I initiated a curved, broken line. My hand carved across the page with the force of a knife digging into wood; there was no hesitation, no doubt. As soon as blue was finished, my hand picked out gray-green and drew an intersecting ribbon across the bottom of the page and another gray-green wavy ribbon across the top. Next, my hand selected a deep red pastel and quickly drew a wavy, ear-shaped line. I didn't stop to analyze anything. This happened much faster than what I was used to. As the picture came through, I knew it represented something entirely different from a placid walk on the beach.

I picked an orange pastel next, and my hand hit the paper repeatedly. It felt like a bronco rider. The pastel in my fingers slammed onto the page in miniature explosions. What was going on? Then an ominous red eye drew itself, and finally, an enigmatic blue-green half-moon. This picture was completed in all of ten minutes, though I was usually drawing for an hour for one of Louise's guided pictures. When I was done, I felt ill. I sat in a stunned cold sweat. I needed answers. Normally I didn't quiz Louise about a picture, but this was different.

*The alarming automatic drawing.*

With a shiver running down my spine, I connected with Louise. "Mom," I said, "are you there?"

This time I could hear her say, "Yes," in my head. I didn't need to muscle test.

"I'm totally bewildered with this image. Help! Mom, is the picture meant to represent the past, present or future?"

"In the future," I heard in my mind.

I pushed the bewildering artwork aside and pulled out my spiral notebook, prepared to take notes.

"Mom, what does the picture mean?" I put my pen on the notebook page and my hand drew a mushroom cloud next to a stick man with a spear. I asked in disbelief, "Are you showing me nuclear war?"

"Yes."

"Does it happen in the United States, as well as in other parts of the world?"

"Yes."

I took a deep breath and pressed on.

"Does the stick man with a spear mean that civilization survives, but returns to a Stone Age existence?"

"No. It means that mankind reverts to a barbaric way of handling world tensions."

These were not her precise words. Rather, a download of information that I put my own words to. I waited for sixty seconds before asking another question. I wanted to know what other parts of the picture meant.

"What can you tell me about the red eye?

"The eye means evil," she replied. "Evil will bring this about." Again the answer came in my mind as a download.

I paused again. This wasn't getting any better.

"What does the wavy green ribbon represent?"

"The bomb in your picture will fall near mountains—the green ribbon," she said.

"How about the red line?"

Was I making this up?

"That ear-shaped line means that you will hear the blast. It will be so loud that you'll be able to hear it, Maria, even if you can't see it."

I was taking notes—my questions followed by her answers.

"What about this blue-green half moon?" I asked.

"It represents the mushroom cloud. The blue-green color is a reaction in the atmosphere caused by the detonation."

I was still sitting on the floor with my notepad, writing questions and taking down answers. Her answers arrived as packets of information in my mind. I didn't hear specific sentences, but concepts that I put into my own words. I gathered that, in Louise's view, the planet would not be physically destroyed, but would be ruined for civilization as we know it by radiation and nuclear winter. Sturdy, self-sufficient people would endure by using primitive survival skills.

Detached from my emotions and not quite sure what else to ask, I said, "Mom, is this disaster inevitable?"

"No," she answered. "It's not inevitable. Mankind can change and change his future. Nothing is fixed. Changing thoughts from hate to love, from doubt to trust, from fear to compassion will help create a new future. Mentally picturing a different world is important. People must change their minds to change their future."

She said she was fearful for me as her daughter. She didn't want me to have to experience this, just as she didn't want to experience it when she was here.

I got up from the floor where I had been taking notes and left everything on the carpet. I had to leave the house and go for a hike. Louise had just given me a headache and shattered my concept of what this book was about. I felt that the book was out of my hands. Louise had come forward with a new agenda—a warning to citizens of Earth of our planet's possible destruction by nuclear war. I was shocked that she would turn a compelling story of mother-daughter reconciliation into such an ominous prediction. Furthermore, I felt sorry that she wasn't at peace in her heaven. I wondered if we still agonized over the fate of our loved ones and our lovely planet once we were freed from mortal existence.

Apparently, Louise wanted to convey the message that there is still a threat of nuclear war if humanity doesn't change. I felt compelled to follow where she led, so I pulled out the folder containing all her antiwar poetry from the 1960s and 1970s and asked her preference. I wanted to know which poems she felt had relevance for today. While she had written antiwar poetry during other decades, her fear of nuclear holocaust had peaked during the Cold War and spilled over to the Vietnam War period.

When I asked the question, "Which poems do you wish to illustrate?" and muscle tested each poem in the antiwar folder, "Grass Cover Us All" was the first poem she selected. The accompanying picture drew itself in only three-quarters of an hour. Like the nuclear war picture, this one flowed from my hands with an urgency I wasn't used to. As far as I knew (at least in my conscious mind), the intense fear of nuclear war wasn't my issue; it was Louise's.

Louise wrote "Grass Cover Us All" in 1965, after she "stepped through time in a nightmare dream." In the dream, she thought that "hell's holocaust was stalled, / But pride and greed have won." She lifted a fallen tombstone, and on it were inscribed these words in an unknown language, "Ye would not love." Her dream mind translated the words, and below them was etched the outline of a dove.

*Automatic drawing of Louise's poem "Grass Cover Us All."*

For Louise, who was raised under the cloud of World War I and experienced World War II through my father's eyes, peace never took root in her heart. The shadow of planetary destruction hung over her like a wraith for most of her life. I personally remembered the nuclear missile silos planted in a hillside across the fields from my uncle's home in Pennsylvania during the 1950s and 1960s. Silos like those were a presence across our country, positioned strategically and filled with live Nike anti-ballistic missiles. The Soviet Union was armed to the hilt as well. Friends of my parents had built bomb shelters in their basements, and people seriously thought they might have to use them.

In 1962, President Kennedy risked nuclear war and bullied the Soviet Union to remove its missiles from Cuba. That Bay of

Pigs crisis took place during my first month of college in Virginia, an incredibly tense week. I remember going to a college orientation picnic. People weren't talking to one another. Laughter was absent. I won't mention what I thought might happen or what I planned to do if it did happen. Life resumed for me as a college freshman after that crisis, but not without a sense of impending doom. I started smoking cigarettes during that first semester.

Normalcy evaporated for my mother. She watched the television news every night and developed a stomach ulcer. In the 1960s, our news media showed all the gory details of the Vietnam War at supper time. My parents' black and white television sat next to the dining room table. Pop tuned in every evening and my mother worried constantly. As one of many poets and people of conscience who wrote against the Vietnam War, Louise did her share. Her 1965 poem, "Grass Cover Us All," summed up her fears of nuclear annihilation. She talked to the grass:

> Promise me you will hide one seed from the blast.
> Find a cleft so deep, so small
> That fingering death will shun your sunless hall
> . . . let centuries pass;
> Bloom at the last, grow tall.

She asked the grass to cover our bones and the dead seared earth, and "in thy mercy, cover us, cover us all." That poem expressed her sentiment: humankind in its barbaric mode really wasn't worth saving. God's experiment had obviously failed. Humanity hadn't learned, so it was best to just wipe the slate clean and start over—except for the one seed. There was the possibility for redemption as long as one seed was saved.

`As I contemplated her poem, I found it chilling to think about how nations around the world today are creating "doomsday seed banks" to ensure food supplies in the event of environmental or nuclear disaster.

Three days after I drew the bomb picture, I decided to change the theme of this chapter. Since Louise had brought up the topic of war and destruction, I figured that was the direction she wanted this writing to go. I abandoned my outline and my plan for illustrating more poems and turned the book over to her.

Louise wrote some of her harshest antiwar poetry in the decade between 1965 and 1975. Even in the 1980s, she was still writing against war. As an elder in the 1990s, she watched sanitized snippets of the Gulf War on television without putting pen to paper, and she died during a time of relative peace before September 11, 2001. Her friend Joan wrote to me that it was a good thing Louise wasn't here to witness the Iraq War. Little did we know. Apparently, the state of the world was still on Louise's mind, even after her transition to another dimension.

When Louise was living in her Denver apartment, she told my friend Malika that she was a pacifist. It was the first time I ever heard her say that aloud and I was surprised by her intensity. The Gulf War was heating up with Operation Desert Storm, and I believe it reignited every antiwar fiber in my mother's eighty-year-old body. Considering that patriotic fever was rampant, it was a pretty gutsy admission. This was the same woman who wanted to hide the fact she drank a glass of wine every night for fear the Presbyterians and Baptists in her retirement community would disapprove.

In her 1965 poem, "Men Whose Business Is War," she scorns men who "champ like chained beasts / Through the dull intervals of peace." She said those men would do anything to stir up a war, and recalled one who was quoted in the press as saying, "What we need is to get a small war going" in order to pump up the flagging economy.

⁓

After three years of drawing pictures and writing text, I found it hard to believe that the book had assumed a life of its own. I hit the wall. When Louise dropped her own "bomb" on me, I thought I was coming to the end of my first draft. My intention to heal our relationship through writing and pictures had worked. My anger had evaporated. I had studied Louise's poetry, felt her loving presence around me, and had promised that I would publish her poetry. She could see that I was serious about it and had been kind enough to let me get through my healing process before blasting me with this new agenda. Now I was stunned, stopped, and stymied. Not only was I mad at her for doing this to me—I was also scared out of my skull.

I became conflicted in how I perceived my dead mother. Ever since 1997, the year she died, I had assumed she was moving through whatever steps one takes on the Other Side to become an enlightened soul. I believed that she could do this and simultaneously visit me to work on our mother-daughter issues. Without knowing what really happens over there, I imagined she was attending soul advancement classes on the Other Side. Because she was a multidimensional being, I imagined she could take time out to answer my questions and involve herself in the book's progress. I also sensed that our time together was drawing to a close, because I would soon wrap up this book and release her.

But suddenly a new vision of my mother had asserted itself. The young, outspoken side of her personality was back. In fact, it was quite a shock that a personality beyond her earthbound poetry voice had presented itself. On some level, I knew I must find the person she had become. This was not the same mother I remembered in her declining years. Who was she now? Where was she? What was she really thinking? I no longer even trusted my own communications with her. What if I had been wrong about the nuclear war prediction? Why did she want me to see the bomb picture? This was more than I had bargained for and I had only a vague idea about where to begin. Answering questions such as these felt like an insurmountable task.

She had waited seven years to send me this picture—seven years on the Other Side and she was still connected to the fate of our planet. Did she still love Earth so much that she couldn't bear the thought of its destruction? Was she sending out her warning and cry for peace through this book? Hijacking the book was out of character, but on the other hand, she and I didn't communicate all that well across dimensions. She probably needed a baseball bat to make her point. If scaring the bejeebers out of me was what she intended, then she had succeeded. I was not happy. This was a showstopper.

As a child, Louise "drank war with her milk," and later in life, "ate war's moldy residue," including irradiated meat. In her poem, "Enough is Enough," she asked, "Do you wonder my bones are brittle, my heart bleached?" Why should this distress continue to pursue Louise on the Other Side? There was much I wanted to know about her new life.

If prophecy had been one of Louise's gifts in her earthly life, it had been about predicting war. She had once confided that she had known World War II would happen and that our country would be sucked in long before the war began. No one had believed her then. She had felt like Jeremiah in the Bible. He had tried to convince the people of Judah that their kingdom would fall, but no one would listen.

Returning to the antiwar folder, we selected another poem from the stack. In "Jeremiad," Louise entreated readers to pay attention to the nuclear threat. "Weary of sighs and dreary prophecies, my pen / Scratches a sad song on its own accord." She warned that we could blow ourselves up. "Jeremiad" was based on a dream in which she saw "drowned sailors of pre-historic wars." The sailors "heave from their watery beds" and call out, "We cannot sleep." The final words of the drowned sailors were, "Tell them—tell them—/ this time, the whole earth shall die." Louise's greatest earthly fear had erupted through her dreams and, poetically, into her typewriter.

In the realms of myth and ancient history lie stories about civilizations destroyed by nuclear war. According to Zecharia Sitchin, author of *The Wars of Gods and Men*, humankind has built and destroyed many advanced civilizations on this planet for eons. The fear and reality of total destruction is embedded in our collective unconscious. Because it has happened before, we believe it could happen again.

I could not follow where Louise was leading me. I wanted to stick my head under the covers or take a long vacation to a sandy beach with palm trees. I needed a change of scene.

# Chapter 8

## Side Trips to Non-ordinary Reality

For months after Louise had guided me to draw the nuclear war picture, I was stuck and could not move forward with the book. Even my friend Camilla was stumped. "You can't end the book like that," she said. "It's just such a downer."

I wasn't getting any more hot leads from Louise either. Try as I might, insights weren't coming. I felt that the book was out of my hands. Louise had come forward with her own agenda, one that I wasn't too surprised about since her fear of world destruction had been present to varying degrees ever since the 1950s.

I had no idea what dead people thought about or worried over in their new digs. I figured whatever it was, it probably had more to do with spiritual growth than the boring mess down here on Mother Earth. I felt sorry that she couldn't be at peace with our planet's outcome, for better or worse, from her new-found perch above it all. I desperately wanted more answers from Louise. Now was the time I absolutely had to sharpen my communication skills in order to reach her.

It so happened that in February of 2004, I signed up for a beginning course in shamanism through the Foundation for Shamanic Studies, founded by Michael Harner. It would take place in early May. The class included teachings on shamanic journeying, which can allow the journeyer to pose questions and receive answers directly from the spirit realm. I thought I might acquire some further insights from Louise if I took this workshop. I was hoping for instant gratification and clear insights.

To compound my confusion, I was also suffering a dark time in my soul. I had recently broken off a friendship with a close female friend. This was my second friendship split within five years, and it hurt more than the divorce of my first husband twenty years prior. I had been emotionally preparing for thirteen years before I split with my husband. The most difficult part had been admitting to him that the union had not worked for me.

My friend Zoe and I had volunteered within the same small organization and become friends after attending a spiritual workshop. Within a year, I felt I had known her forever. We talked on the phone daily and met after business hours and on weekends. We fixed dinners together with our husbands and even camped and hiked as a foursome.

In the organization, I worked on special projects while she managed accounting. The year I accepted a leadership position, trouble started. I was unsure of myself and leaned on Zoe to back up my decisions in board meetings. She didn't enjoy my dependence and it seemed to me that she scheduled herself to be out of town during many meetings. Meanwhile, our personal friendship had developed into a rich and rewarding relationship—one of acceptance and support, in which neither of us criticized the other. Since we were friends outside of work, I was afraid to jeopardize our personal lives by confronting her with my job-related complaints.

During the fourth year of our friendship, I was leading a doubly deceitful life—a dishonest work relationship in which I didn't voice my displeasure with her lack of support and a dishonest personal friendship in which I pretended nothing was wrong. It was a recipe for disaster. Pretending negative feelings didn't exist and stuffing them if they arose was a trait I'd learned from my mother and it was coming back to bite me.

Zoe had her own reasons for being peeved with me. She sensed my stuffed anger but didn't confront me directly. Try as I might to wear a happy face, I grew grumpy and depressed. We became snippy with one another—a little criticism here; a little sarcasm there. Underneath the veiled conflict, we still loved one another. That's what I clung to. Nevertheless, the friendship was unraveling.

One day we leveled with one another. She risked saying she knew I was angry with her, and I risked admitting that was true. She said that she had known this for several weeks. Thinking that our honesty had cleared the air, I was relieved. As we hugged good-bye for the day, I sensed that our friendship hung in the balance. Shortly thereafter, she quit the organization, sold her house and relocated to another part of the state. Her life moved in a different direction. I, too, quit and tried to put my emotions back together. Although I was happily married, the loss of her friendship unstrung me. Self-recrimination that I had never experienced with the dissolution of my first marriage came to bed with me each night.

As a chronic people pleaser who hated conflict, I assumed expressing anger spelled doom to a relationship, especially between female friends. This perception played itself out exactly as I had imagined it would. Zoe wouldn't take my phone calls. We weren't talking, and I tried my best to stuff this black blot back into the recesses of my consciousness. Afraid of what I would find, I searched my soul for answers, hoping insight would appear in neon lights, unmistakable and clear. I found only emptiness. Had I been too insensitive and abrupt toward Zoe? Too critical toward everybody?

Self-criticism was a stellar talent of mine and I fell into a pit of self-flagellation. Extending myself no mercy, I examined all the rooms of my personality including the basement, attic and storage shed. As an only child, I had believed I must be perfect to please my parents. Therefore, in my relationships with other people, I also had to be charming, giving, a good listener, cheerful, responsive to everyone's requests, and so on. I was afraid of anger—mine and others'. I could have won the Jungian award for self-analysis, but could not find peace. In 2004, I carried on, faking happiness and balance when, in fact, I was miserable.

⁓

The shamanism workshop was on my calendar for May. Four months earlier, in January, I had been bitten by the shamanic journeying bug. I had attended a midwinter weekend poetry festival in the town down the valley from me. One of the two-hour workshops was labeled "Poetry and the Shamanic Journey." While I had lain on the hard floor with twenty others in the basement of a bank, eyes covered with a bandana, an image had appeared in my mind's eye. In it, I was suspended above desert sand dunes under a black, star-studded sky. Below me sat an old Indian, wrapped in a blanket, in front of a small fire. I came close and sat in front of the man. Neither of us said a word, but when I looked into his face, it changed into a frightening toothsome mouth. I almost shook myself out of the journey, but instead, gathered up my courage and took the hand he offered. At the touch, I felt a wolf's paw. When I touched my own hand, it had changed into a mountain lion's paw. A black jaguar materialized beside me. Then the black jaguar and I set off roaming together as big cats.

I moved with power and grace in my mountain lion body. Together we bounded up a fourteen-thousand-foot mountain, the very mountain I viewed daily from my south-facing windows. The jaguar perched on the summit, black as midnight, staring down at me with emerald eyes. I didn't challenge the cat for that position, but turned and hurried down the mountain. When the drumming brought me back into the room, I realized that the black jaguar symbolized Zoe; she owned a jaguar pin that she frequently wore. In my vision, the jaguar was queen of the mountain and I wasn't prepared to share that pinnacle with her. The journey had shown me a piece of my unconscious mind: I was envious of her position on a summit I couldn't reach. My envy stemmed from a lack of self-confidence. I had put that fresh insight aside for the time being.

With a mixture of anticipation and trepidation, I set out on a May morning to attend my first real shamanism workshop near Estes Park, Colorado. Since I lived about 150 miles from the workshop site, I needed to leave home early in the morning. I planned to visit a friend on the way and arrive with time to spare before dinner. It was a difficult trip. A spring snowstorm had descended on the Front Range. I drove most of the day in snow. Dusk was settling in as I drove up the canyon to the Presbyterian camp. Wet snow stuck to the aspens and spruce with the low sun dusting all with evening gold. Upon arrival, I lugged my bags to the bunkhouse and collapsed.

Julia, our teacher, walked over to me before dinner and introduced herself, explaining that she recognized me from having seen me while journeying in preparation for the workshop. Perhaps she intuited my feelings of self-doubt, because she said her foreknowledge of my attendance validated that I was supposed to come. I did appreciate her validating my decision because this was a baby step toward trusting my inner guidance. I thanked her for the information and told her that nothing could have kept me away. I had been doing an excellent job of tearing myself down. Now I needed to learn how to trust and appreciate myself.

"What can I write about next?" was the specific question that I was hoping would be answered during the workshop. I needed some direction, some clue. After Louise's message about the possibility of nuclear war, I was stumped. How could I go on with the book? Where could I go when the pictures and text pointed to the end of the world? According to my original outline (before the bomb picture), I was going to wrap up the book with automatic drawings of Louise's metaphysical poems. I had planned to ask her to draw me pictures of what she saw on the Other Side. But now I knew that plan had to be scrapped. Louise was in charge and I was listening for direction with all six senses.

At the beginning of the workshop, Julia emphasized that these workshops were not for the purpose of teaching us how to be shamans. True shamans studied for many years, experienced life-or-death initiations, and could work miracles. They never said, "I'm a shaman," for that would be bragging. Besides, real shamans were chosen by the spirit world and were recognized as such by other true shamans for the results they achieved. The reason we practiced the shamanic journey, she said, was for personal growth and healing, which could be realized through communication with the spirit realm and the use of divination. Through doing this, one could find the answers to personal questions. But often the answers would arrive in symbols or metaphors and it was up to the journeyer to decipher those things. The riddles might be solved later rather than sooner. Although religious symbolism might come up, shamanism was not a religious belief system, she said, but a spiritual practice that could deepen one's understanding of self and the world, and ultimately, could be used for healing self and others. I was ready to heal my broken relationship and receive messages from my mother. This teaching was for me.

Shamanism came with its own jargon. Common to most shamanic traditions was the real estate: the Lower World, the Middle World, and the Upper World, which were collectively known as non-ordinary reality. To a first time journeyer, these places seemed to exist only in the mind's eye, similar to a waking dreamscape, but some shamans insist that the three worlds actually do exist as invisible realities and that we do travel to them. Each world had its special landscape and its own method of entry. The Lower World had nothing to do with hell. It was a place of deserts, jungles, forests, and rivers, which we would enter through a hole in the ground. The Upper World was an ethereal place of many levels that we would enter by climbing a ladder or climbing a tree, and possibly flying through clouds. The Middle World was a spiritual dimension of our physical world, where shamans traditionally went to find lost objects or do long distance healing work. However it was also a place where spirits of dead people, who didn't know they were dead, still existed. We wouldn't go to the Middle World in this beginning class, Julia said, but would travel mostly in the Lower World.

For our first assignment, we would find our power animal in the Lower World. Twenty of us stretched out in a circle on mats with blankets for warmth and bandanas to cover our eyes. Being blindfolded closed out our immediate surroundings,

147

allowing the inner vision to come forward. Julia drummed for us during the entire time. The drumbeat carried us into an altered state where we could see, or otherwise experience, non-ordinary reality.

I could "see," much like viewing a daydream, but I didn't hear words. Some people experienced journeying through the other senses, which included just "knowing." My power animal appeared at the end of a long tunnel, standing with his back to me: a golden eagle, unrealistically large—taller than me. I took him with me on all subsequent journeys during the workshop. Power animals can lead journeyers to answers and protect them in fearful situations.

For our second exercise, Julia told us to find our teacher, the one who dwells in non-ordinary reality. To do this, we would go to the Upper World and we would take our power animal with us. To reach the Upper World, I mentally exited through the chimney of my house and flew straight up into the sky. The scenes that followed were like a waking dream.

I landed in a small Bureau of Land Management park called Penitente Canyon in the San Luis Valley, near Del Norte, Colorado, about seventy-five miles south of where I live. I had walked through the park, three times, which, incidentally, was home to rattlesnakes and rock climbers. In the 1800s, this canyon was used by the Penitentes—a Catholic brotherhood known for their self-flagellation rituals. They were secretive about their ceremonies, which included mock crucifixions around Easter. The brotherhood still exists today, although they emphasize doing good deeds in poor rural communities of the southwest, rather than the more bizarre practices. Much later, it occurred to me why I had started my journey in Penitente Canyon. I had been flagellating myself over the breakup with

Zoe, and I needed to be made aware that this was what I was doing to myself.

During my shamanic journey in Penitente Canyon, I came upon a circle of white robed figures. I removed the hood from each face in turn and asked if he was my teacher. No one spoke, but one figure was filled with light when I removed the hood from his head. As soon as I asked if he was my teacher, the scene changed and I saw an empty Egyptian sarcophagus painted with blue and gold. Next I saw scenes from ancient Egypt, as if I were on a flyover of temples. Outstretched wings painted on a wall appeared briefly, and my thought was, *my teacher must be Isis.* Next appeared the head of an Egyptian god, the ibis headed one. I didn't recall who it was, but knew I'd seen him illustrated in books about Egypt. It seemed that ancient Egypt was important to me.

Our third exercise was a rock divination. Divination was defined as getting answers from an object. We had all been asked to bring a baseball-sized rock with us to the workshop. My rock had a matrix of blue-gray limestone with red chert embedded in patterns all over the outside. We worked with partners in this divination. First I asked a question that I wanted answered from images on the rock. I examined two sides of my rock and told my partner what I was seeing. She wrote down what I said. The idea was that I would then interpret the pictures as they related to the question. I was hoping to receive an answer about where to go next with the book, but the images I saw on my rock seemed to indicate some kind of disaster by flooding in an ancient part of the world. Taken as an answer to my question, "What should I write about next?" it seemed to me that I should write more about death and destruction. That was out of the question. I was no seer. I was no prophet, and I couldn't interpret images on a rock with any certainty. One chapter on death and destruction was enough.

By the end of the first day, I had learned a lot from the exercises, but I had more questions than I had answers. I realized that I would need to practice a lot of journeying after I returned home.

On the second day, we practiced more advanced techniques. But by the end of the workshop, I had not found an answer to my question. I had, however, honed my journeying tools, which in turn, allowed me to trust my creative imagination.

Upon returning home, when I hiked my trails alone, I went into the altered state I had become familiar with during journey practice. I didn't need a drum. The rhythm of my footsteps on the trail transported me. This state felt quite natural, for it was a reverie where conscious thoughts dropped away, and I tuned in to my surroundings and emotions. Without the mind chatter in the way, without analyzing things, I felt close to the land, the sky, and the trees. There were times when I felt I became the land or the sky or the trees. Those experiences were so poignant that I was usually moved to tears of gratitude or tears of joy. There were times on the trail when I sobbed for no reason. I no longer felt weird talking to the rock and tree I visited on my hikes, and I habitually greeted the sun as a grandiose sentient being. Shamanic teachings validated for me that all so-called inanimate objects were conscious and that we could talk with, or merge with, anything.

That same year, I signed up for an October weekend shamanism workshop in the foothills south of Boulder, Colorado, still hoping that I could reach my mother through this avenue. I wanted so badly to reach her myself, to talk with her during a shamanic journey. Fittingly, the workshop I'd signed up for was titled Shamanism, Dying, and Beyond. Part of the reason I was attracted to it was the timing. It is said that the veil is thin at the end of October. Many cultures honor their ancestors around the first of November and it is thought that those who have crossed over can come close. I hoped I would learn something definite about my mother and her new place of residence.

Zoe called me the night before I left for the workshop, on the date of a solar eclipse, saying that she was finally able to talk to me again. Our hour-long chat shook me up because I was getting used to her silence. I might not have been ready to hear from her, but it had happened; the door opened a crack. An earthquake rumbled through my psyche. Something shifted.

The workshop flyer said this event was for the purpose of personal growth and awareness and also for those who wished to help the terminally ill or souls who had already passed on. I arrived with an open mind.

To introduce ourselves, our facilitator (Julia from the previous workshop) asked us to talk briefly about why we had come. My mother had passed on over seven years ago, I told the group, and I wanted to know more about her existence on the Other Side. It wasn't until after all the others had spoken, that a secondary reason dawned on me: I needed rejuvenation.

Events of the past two years had done me in. Not only had the broken friendship depressed me, but I was burned out, overcommitted, and out of balance in other areas of my life. My salvation was hiking, the one activity I allowed myself that didn't require an iota of responsibility. I tried everything I could think of to exorcise the roiling emotions—self-help CDs and tapes, classical music, writing, drawing, massage, bodywork, energy work, shamanic journeying, and my own forms of prayer and meditation—with only temporary relief. What I didn't do was go to a psychotherapist, take drugs, or belabor it with friends. Simply put, I dealt with my burnout alone. The only thing that could resuscitate my spirit was healing the relationship with my ex-friend.

I would continue to wilt until I understood how I needed to change—and did it—and healed the rift between my friend and me. The rift and its healing seemed karmic to both of us. And until I began to heal the rift, my writing would remain stuck and my mother wouldn't talk to me. These were intuitive knowings. I could not explain why the two were linked, except that I needed to be in a clearer place spiritually to continue on my journey.

The workshop contained many exercises, none of which allowed me to contact my mother. I kept hoping they would and I was feeling sad about not achieving what I thought I'd come for. However, two healing incidents happened that seemingly had nothing to do with the workshop.

I was up early on the second day of the workshop. The previous day, I'd hiked during our lunch break with a woman from our group, and I wanted to return and repeat that hike alone. The inner call to hike was very strong. Our workshop location was at the foot of the upthrust where the Great Plains meets the Front Range of the Rocky Mountains. In Boulder, this area is known as the Flatirons. Red sandstone slabs rear up, row on row and layer on layer, like the flat sides of a hundred laundry irons. It was an area I'd never hiked, although I'd driven past it countless times.

A cold front was moving in. While the previous day had been warm and clear, this particular morning was chilly and overcast with a breeze blowing. A dozen cars were parked in the lot when I pulled in. The trail zigzagged gently up through prairie grass and sandstone boulders, with an occasional cotton-wood tree by a creek. I planned to hike in for half an hour and then back out for the same amount of time to arrive at the workshop opening ceremony by 8:00 a.m. Happy to be stretching my legs and pumping uphill, I got into a rhythm. I was familiar with the trail from the previous day and looking forward to a new section. On a small scale, I thought the landscape as profound as the Grand Tetons in Wyoming. I felt confronted with nature's incredible geology. In the back of my mind was a question: Did this happen all at once, in one day, or was it a slow evolu-tion? I just couldn't escape the sensation of enormous earth forces that were asleep for the moment but could reawaken anywhere, anytime.

I hiked and sang, hiked and breathed in rhythm with my feet. And not wanting to waste a chance to question my spirits (in the spirit of shamanism), I began to ask, "What can I do to heal the pain of this broken friendship?" I didn't want to reopen a relationship that seemed dead to me. But as Zoe had said, "Spiritually, we cannot allow this division to remain unhealed." My ego feared going there again. So this was my mantra as I hiked. I tried to get into a walking shamanic journey. I called in my power animal. The rhythm of my footsteps became the beat-ing drum. I encouraged my consciousness to travel beyond my physical body into the place where visions happen. But it wasn't working. I continued to ask what to do with my friend, the sadness, the fear, and the resistance.

All of a sudden, *ka-boom*! My eyes fixed on the path under my feet. There, in the dried mud from August's abundant rain, was a footprint of a mountain lion, six or seven inches across, and next to it, a smaller version of the same animal. I knew what a mountain lion print looked like, but I had never seen one in all my years in the outdoors. Bobcat prints, yes; bear prints and poop, yes; and abundant coyote hairballs. Not that I wanted to see one in my neighborhood, where I walked three times a week. This was a magnificent find. I had covered this exact ground the previous afternoon with my companion, never spotting the tracks. We had been gabbing, not watching our feet. Evidently, a lioness and her cub had crossed the trail on their way to the creek that ran about twelve feet to my right, down in a little gulch. The tracks were probably two months old and deeply embedded, crisp and clear, in what had once been mud. They were like fossil prints of dinosaurs that had roamed this land and become encapsulated in the sandstone of the Flatirons.

My mind took a turn, rerunning a slew of news stories of mountain lion sightings in the foothills around Boulder—solitary runners followed, chased, and sometimes mauled or killed by the beasts. People's pets had been dinner and the big cats had been known to sun themselves on family decks. New neighborhoods were encroaching on their territory. Suddenly I felt eyes staring at me from every outcrop. *Don't be stupid*, I thought to myself. *Time to turn around*. Looking over my shoulder every thirty seconds, I hustled down the hill to the parking lot.

Our workshop resumed at 8:00 a.m. with a long candlelight meditation to honor our ancestors. It was Halloween morning. I thought about my parents on the Other Side. During the lunch break, I took a stretch outdoors. Weather was moving in. Emil, a man also attending the workshop, was enjoying a cigarette. Emil was a handsome young man, tall, with a South American accent, recently married to an exotic looking woman who wore carnelian velveteen robes in the workshop. He stood up and approached.

We had been sitting across from one another for a day and a half, but had not spoken. Emil said he had a strong feeling that he needed to talk to me, as though there were something I needed to tell him. I didn't know what I possibly could tell him that he needed to hear. We commented on the beauty of our surroundings. I mentioned the cat tracks I'd found and said I would look up the meaning of the mountain lion in my book, *Animal-Speak,* when I returned home. I thought there might be an answer for me in the spiritual meaning of that totem animal.

Emil said he wanted to tell me that he'd seen a tall Native American man standing behind me during the workshop. He'd seen him a couple of times the previous day as well. I didn't know what to make of that. I thanked him for sharing his gift of second sight. I didn't sense the presence of this being, but I would try to find out more.

Within a month, I had figured out who the Native American spirit fellow was. First, I discovered his name as I was walking across the railroad bridge over the Arkansas River. I asked, "Who are you? What is your name? What is your purpose in my life?" I vowed to trust whatever I heard, and the name Shining Star popped into my head. That sounded hokey. I muscle tested and also heard, "Yes. That is the name." I asked if he was one of my spirit guides and I got, "Yes." I asked if he would be here for the duration, and again, "Yes." Three nights later, as I read through some material on the Smithsonian's National Museum of the American Indian in Washington D.C., I spotted the name Panapuchiv (Shining Star, in English), a quiet man, recently deceased, and revered by the Southern Ute Indian people, who had led their tribe for thirty years. I asked my new spirit guide if he was *that* one. I got, "No." Nevertheless, I didn't discredit the name Shining Star that I had received while hiking. Seeing that name in print was a synchronicity I could not ignore. This was confirmation that I had heard correctly. I sensed some gentle masculine laughter in my head chiding, "This doubting one needs double and triple reassurances that she is not making up a tall tale!"

A day after the workshop, I investigated symbolism for the mountain lion. According to *Animal-Speak*, the mountain lion totem meant coming into your own power. The answer to my query ("What must I do to heal the pain of this broken friend-ship—how must I change?") arrived in the unexpected form of a mountain lion track, a mother with her cub. The book also noted that mountain lion meant *power with gentleness*. This was a double message for me: that I was coming into my power, and in so doing, would be able to handle the relationship on a new level, and; that I did, indeed, need to be gentle with myself and all that I touched.

One day, Zoe called again. This time I could talk to her with-out my heart falling to my feet. We agreed to meet for lunch. Enough time had passed that the painful reasons for our split had faded. Eventually, the relationship with Zoe healed, thanks to both of us making the effort. I was learning to love myself, nurture myself, forgive myself, and stop beating myself up for not being perfect. It was a dark period for Zoe and me. We each had our lessons, and when they were learned, we were able to laugh together again.

The symbol of mother and child lion tracks—the cub was surely a daughter—possessed additional significance. Footprints symbolized forward movement, putting one foot in front of the other. The lion tracks were a sign that I was emerging from the stuck place with Louise and the book.

Although I didn't reach Louise during the workshops offered through the Foundation for Shamanic Studies, I continued to practice journeying on my own. In one of those journeys, Louise showed up in an Egyptian setting. The images were clear, but I didn't hear messages or words while journeying, so I wasn't able to ask her anything specific.

In desperation, I asked Louise for a sign to continue. I asked her to give me a sign as big as a house that the depressing chapter about the bomb was necessary and essential for the book. That sign came on Easter Sunday.

# Chapter 9

## Eden's Tree

Jim called to me, "Look out the window. Quick!"

It was Easter Sunday and I had gone downstairs to heat up a pot of soup. There, sitting on a rock, not twenty feet away, was the largest raven I'd ever seen, about two feet tall, with a massive bill. Immediately I knew: *It's a sign from my mother.*

If my mother had wanted to grab my attention in the form of an animal, she would have sent a raven. Louise would have remembered my connection to the raven totem that I had called on for protection during my surgery in 1994. She had drawn me a picture of a raven on the day of the surgery. When I saw the huge raven practically on our doorstep, I knew it was a sign, and that Louise was telling me to keep moving on the book, and to include the strong warning message. In the years since that day, no raven has landed close to our house.

Louise showed up again on Mother's Day. Evidently, she was growing impatient and doing her best to give me some direction. Jim had painted the upstairs bathroom and bedroom. I was putting the bedroom back together. Pictures were stacked against a wall. I picked up the framed photo of my Grandmother Weber that had been in my possession for thirty years or longer. Louise had framed it, and we had all agreed that it captured my paternal grandmother's impish personality. I turned it over to check the wire and noticed that the brown paper backing was torn. As I turned it face up, something fell to the floor. I retrieved it and couldn't believe my eyes—a black-and-white snapshot of my mother in her late thirties, sitting on a chair in the house where I was raised, looking straight into the camera as if to say, "Yes, it's me. I'm still here. Lay aside your doubts and let's get on with it!"

*Photo of Louise that fell from the back of a framed picture.*

I had no idea how that photo had landed in the back of the framed picture, or who would have put it there. But there she was, staring at me. I wanted to think of her as young now, not middle-aged with gray hair or depleted as she was before she died. She was young and expressive with clear blue eyes.

*Where do I go from here, Mom?* I asked silently as I stared at the photograph.

An answer to that question began to take form in a most unexpected way. During my annual physical exam, I gave my physician's assistant a laundry list of complaints. Among them was stiffness and pain in my lower back. "Is it okay if I use one Ibuprofen a day?" I asked. She said yes, but added that some physical therapy might also help. She asked if I'd ever had a tailbone injury.

"Funny you should ask," I said. I told her that my father had invited me to play tennis at the municipal courts when I was fifteen. During a game, I ran backwards to pick up a high ball, jumped, and reached for it. When I whacked the ball, the force tipped my body backwards. I fell, as if in slow motion, to the concrete, landing on my tailbone and left arm. There would be no more tennis for me that summer. I sat on a pillow for a month, and my tailbone was crooked from that point on.

My physician's assistant said that an early tailbone injury could cause structural problems later in life. She knew from personal experience, for she had hurt hers at age four. She recommended a physical therapist who specialized in spinal problems. He came to our town once a week, and she thought I'd like him.

Bob's business card read Physical Therapist. I soon learned that he did more than stretch body parts and assign home exercises. I explained about my crooked tailbone, spinal curvature, and low back pain. What he saw was a woman with depression, a lethargic physique, low core energy, and foggy brain function. He put his hands on my head to assess my energy and emotional balance. I asked him if he was doing cranial sacral work and he said yes. Later I learned that intuition guided his physical therapy, and that it generally began with how he read the client's brain.

On that first visit, I told Bob I wanted to finish a short story, but all creative juice had stopped. He worked on my rib cage, sacrum, skull and facial bones. When I walked out of his office,

I could breathe with what seemed like a whole new lung capacity and my pelvis felt like it had been lubed. After that session, my mood changed from bleak to optimistic and I was able to write again.

I told him about my book at our next appointment. As he loosened and balanced my body, my mental processes and emotions continued to revive. It had taken me a long time to slide into that depleted state, so the recovery wasn't overnight. But in time, my body, mind and spirit came back to life. This work was the missing piece that would allow me to carry on with the book. I envisioned how I could move the story forward: I would seek answers from professional channelers, people who could contact nonphysical beings on the Other Side.

When Louise commandeered the book, I had conceded that she was my writing partner on the Other Side and had much to tell me. But we seemed to lack the telecommunications equipment that would allow me to receive her messages with clarity. No longer was I the daughter trying to heal our old relationship conflict from the past—that phase was finished—but I had a new job as co-author, and I was waiting for the next download of information from the Beyond. I wanted to call her up on the phone for a long chat, and that was obviously impossible. I wanted to become an overnight psychic medium, but that wasn't going to happen either. I decided to enlist the talents of three professional intuitives: Sheryl Watson, Stacey Joslin, and Heiderose Spang-Martindell.

I can't convince anyone that channelers speak truth and only truth. There are charlatans out there who will tell you what they think you want to hear. I want to emphasize that I trusted the three women I picked to channel for me.

Sheryl has been a professional medium and clairvoyant channel for many years. I already knew her from our get-to-gethers about my automatic drawings. She teaches workshops from her home and seminars at metaphysical bookstores. As a medium, she possesses the ability to communicate with those who have passed on. As a clairvoyant channel, she can speak with spirit guides and other nonphysical beings.

One of the beings Sheryl communicates with is the Archangel Metatron. I had never heard of Metatron before seeing the movie, *Dogma*, where he was characterized in a leading role. Metatron lived on earth as a human before being elevated to an Archangel, so he has a special affinity for helping humans. In one of my sessions with Sheryl, it was Metatron who chose to give me information about my mother.

I met Stacey at a metaphysical fair in a nearby town, where she was creating exquisite pencil drawings of people's spirit guides. I asked her if she could see the Native American who Emil said was standing behind me. She said she could, and drew me a quick sketch. As she drew, Stacey said he was from a past life. Stacey and Sheryl have both seen him and agreed on his appearance. He wears a feather in his hair and carries a bow. Later I contacted Stacey for a reading about my mother, since she can see and talk with beings in other dimensions. In the ensuing years, we've become friends, and I have taken her classes in expanding multidimensional awareness.

I made my first appointment with Heiderose on the recom-mendation of friends who had experienced readings with her. She is a dark haired, soft-spoken woman with an infectious sense of humor. In a lilting German accent, she explained that her most intense desire was eternal truth, not just beliefs. She was living in Colorado Springs when I set up the appointment.

She told me she wouldn't be channeling my mother, but an evolved being who knew my mother. She described herself as a messenger of hope and prophecy who channels the angelic realm and ascended masters. I wanted to be certain that whoever came through in the channeling would be able to answer questions about my mother, and she assured me that would be the case. She has since moved from Colorado to Arizona, where some of her recent work has included assisting the dying in their transitions.

The day of our appointment, Heiderose didn't know which ascended master or member of the angelic realm would come through for me until the channeling started. Before she began, she told me she would channel in an altered state, merging energies with whoever had chosen to speak with me. It was Tsen Tsing, an Ancient Chinese Master, who greeted me in a booming male voice.

"This is Tsen Tsing. We are of the Council of Light. We are with you many times, so we do know you and we peek in on you at times! How are you feeling today?"

I was taken aback to hear Heiderose's gentle feminine voice change to a man's voice with a completely different accent and cadence.

I made separate appointments with Stacey, Sheryl, and Heiderose. I typed up a list of questions for each channeler, and some of the questions were identical. In repeating the questions to the different channelers, I wanted to determine if the women's insights from the spiritual world concurred. They did agree, in general, and yet each delivered information that I felt was influenced by the particular woman's background.

After interviewing the three women, I transcribed the recordings. Then I looked for ways to weave the information together. I sometimes grouped two or three intuitive voices, plus my mother's voice, into a dialog, as though we were all sitting together in one room. At other times, I used the interview transcription from only one woman.

During one visit, my mother had told Sheryl that people must change their minds to create a different ending for our planet. I wanted to hear more about that idea. I wanted to know how we humans can improve our chance for peace. I started my interviews with that question.

⌒◦

I began with Stacey since she could see and hear Louise and I was able to talk directly to Louise through her. We sat in her living room, and I asked my first question, directly to my mother.

"Mom, what did you mean by, 'Mankind had better change its mind?' Do the mental pictures we carry with us actually create the world and its future?"

Stacey closed her eyes as she heard my mother reply. She said that Louise was concerned about the human race. From Louise's perspective, we were misusing our potential by not soaring, but attacking one other. Louise thought people were a disappointing lot, but that they could still change. If people changed their mental images about what the world can look like, they could change the outcome of the planet.

Stacey added, "She's quite passionate about that. I can feel that in my body. Even though your mother is on the Other Side, she's really concerned about what is happening here. But at the same time, she's not holding humans in judgment."

This sounded like my mother, and I finally felt as though I were having the telephone conversation I so badly wanted.

I asked, "Why should you care, Mom, now that you don't live here anymore?"

Stacey closed her eyes, and then told me Louise said she still wanted to be a part of this Earth because she feared for its future. The Earth was in transition, and she still cared deeply about it.

Tsen Tsing agreed that Louise was anxious to reincarnate on the planet and be effective here again as a part of the whole scenario, but Spirit was holding her back.

Tears welled up in my eyes, because this sounded so much like my mother. Mom wouldn't choose to be done with the Earth and never come back. She would want to help in any way she could.

Thinking about my mother's frightening picture of nuclear destruction, I asked Tsen Tsing to describe what was in store for Earth. In his emphatic masculine voice, he told me that Earth was in a period of time called The Quickening. He said it was a shift in consciousness that went hand in hand with disasters such as floods, fires, earthquakes, and so on. (The "and so on" bothered me.) A lot of people would experience fear and depression, so it was crucial to remember this was a positive transition for the planet. There was nothing wrong with the world or with us, according to Tsen Tsing.

I cornered him on the subject of "the bomb" picture and grilled him about the source of the drawings. What he had to say was interesting. According to Tsen Tsing, the pictures that came through my hands as automatic drawings arrived from several sources. The picture that I called, "The Hug," was one hundred percent from my mother. She had reached out to me and used my hand to draw. The picture of my cat Fritz, drawn the day after he died, was a combination of my consciousness and hers.

"Just know that some of your creations in this book really come from you two putting your work together. It isn't just all from her. You're co-writing it indeed," he said.

When I specifically asked about the bomb picture, he dodged the question and asked me what I thought. I told him exactly what I had heard the day I drew it, and that it frightened me. He said I needed to trust what I received from intuition and sit with it until clarity arrived.

It was June of 2004. I was still under a cloud of inertia. Where does one go with a story that ends with nuclear destruction? To jar myself loose, I made another appointment with Sheryl. Her skills intrigued me, but I didn't want to depend on her to interpret my life. I knew it could become a temptation to ask for advice instead of trusting inner guidance. However, the wall I had hit was still standing firmly in front of me, and I needed help.

This would be my third session with Sheryl in almost two years. We planned to meet again at her house. I loaned her the manuscript so she could glean a sense of the book up to this point. I told her I was at a place where I had to know more than I could intuit myself. Still not trusting myself, I needed verification that the picture was Louise's creation and not something I had made up.

I met with Sheryl on June 8, the day when Venus transited the Sun. The morning news remarked that it was a rare astronomical event. Sheryl had spent a couple of days with the manuscript. During our visit in her meditation room, Sheryl channeled Archangel Metatron. He explained why Louise had sent me the picture of nuclear war. My mother stood behind me throughout most of the channeling. She wasn't visible to me, but she was to Sheryl. The participants in the channeling were Sheryl, Louise, Metatron and me.

Metatron said that my mother was accompanied by a temporary guide he called "the Way-Shower"—one who shows the way. He described the Way-Shower as a tall, dark being of power and positive character who walked with Louise. It was his job to assist Louise after she crossed over at the moment of death and to help her with her life review.

For starters, I asked Metatron to answer a question. I wanted to know whether it was Louise's plan to predict nuclear war through the book.

Metatron didn't answer that question directly, as I was hoping he would, but he explained why Louise had sent me the picture. He said that when people die, they usually arrive on the Other Side with psychological filters of fear, which are like colored eyeglasses. At first, everything they see and experience on the Other Side is fear-based, just as it was on Earth. Also, when they arrive, some souls are shown movies of the mind that seem real, but are not. Those movies are projected on the Field-of-Possibilities Screen. The Way-Shower took Louise to the Field-of-Possibilities Screen and prompted her to use it. I'd never heard anything like this before in my life. A movie-screen on the Other Side? I wanted to believe, but it was a stretch.

Metatron said that since Louise presumed that war and destruction were real, she had to view a playing out of all her fears—the very outcome she didn't want. She wished she had not seen these events on the screen. She was afraid World War III might happen and she would have to be the one to foretell it, just as she foretold World War II and other wars when she was on Earth. I remembered how Louise feared that World War III would start during the Bay of Pigs crisis and during the six-day Israeli War. She was constantly fearful of another world war. Full-scale nuclear war never broke out, so she wasn't always right.

Sheryl stopped a moment, and then said that Louise was standing behind her left shoulder, and she wanted to say something. I looked in that direction, but saw nothing. Sheryl listened, and then spoke.

"Your mother is saying that she's doing the best she can to understand what she sees from her new dimension of reality. She says the movie of nuclear war scared her, and she didn't want her beautiful planet Earth to be lost in that way."

I sympathized with my mother's fearfulness and felt sorry that she still suffered from it. And yet, I was glad that Louise was present with us in the room. I wished I had the ability to hear her as Sheryl could. I strained to remember everything. I was thankful that we were taping this session.

Metatron continued through Sheryl. He told us that the Way-Shower had shown Louise that the old Earth was disintegrating, shifting. It could happen quickly—boom—or it could shift gently. How it shifted would depend on whether the people on this planet could handle the change. Right now, Spirit was being very gentle. "God has immense time and immense love, and patience," Metatron said.

I asked, "Why, then, is Louise showing me this horror when it may not even come to pass?"

Metatron replied through Sheryl that some who have crossed over wish to relay what they see and experience to people on Earth, and this is the case with Louise. She wants to relay what she sees to me. That made sense to me. My mother had always loaded me up with information, whether I wanted to hear it or not. Knowing her, she would have wanted to tell me about the Possibilities Screen—the technology of heaven, so to speak. She also would have wanted to give me a heads up, as her daughter. Since she was scared by what she saw, and knew I was writing a book, it would have been like her to try and warn readers through the book. She had tried to warn people through her poetry when she was alive, so why not now that she was on the Other Side?

Since I lacked a distinct, articulate transmission from Louise, myself, I was grateful to hear what Metatron had to say. He added that the book must carry a message of action. I gathered that this was Louise's desire as well. People could change the planet's destiny by changing their thoughts. He added that thoughts preceded actions—a universal law. I interpreted this to mean two things. First, to change destiny, we must believe that the planet can be saved, visualize it as healed, visualize a peaceful planet, pray for the planet, and so on. Second, we must do things—take action— to help the planet. There are a thousand things we could do. We must look into ourselves and determine how our talents, occupations, and thoughts could be turned toward good every single day, so that we didn't bruise our mother, the Earth, or bruise our fellow human beings.

Metatron ended on an enigmatically ominous note.

"The Way-Shower showed Louise one possibility for Earth. She did not know what to do with this information other than relay it to you. She wants her beloved Earth to remain. But it will evolve, even if a flash of light means the end—the end of three dimensions—the birth and death wheel. Welcome it."

*Egad, this is scary,* I thought. *There's no way I'm welcoming the end of my planet.* Sheryl turned off the tape recorder and we talked for a while. She behaved more upbeat than I felt. Sheryl's background in metaphysics and channeling various angels and ascended masters had led her to think in positive terms about the future of the human race. She was hopeful that humanity would make the right choices. My view wasn't that rosy.

Glimpsing into my mother's new life cheered me, nevertheless, because it meant she was still learning and growing. I hoped that she would soon move on from her fearfulness. On the other hand, as long as she was connected to the book, she would try to hammer the message for people to envision a new peaceful Earth and not dwell on the negative. Metatron and Louise had both emphasized that outcomes began with thoughts. This idea was not new to me, but I had not made an effort to follow through. Perhaps it was time.

After that channeling with Sheryl, I let the manuscript rest again and awaited inspiration for the next chapter. I took long walks during which I conversed with my mother. I tuned in to her voice directly, as best as I could, and tried to improve my intuition. Sometimes the voices flowed back and forth, but usually the conversations were patchy. I continued to read books about life on the Other Side and then I picked up where I had left off with Heiderose and the Ancient Chinese Master Tsen Tsing.

I asked Tsen Tsing why he thought Louise had sent me the bomb picture. I told him I thought it was because she wanted me to include her antiwar poetry in the book and, of course, to goad people to change their thinking.

"What was your inner guidance?" he asked. I hated it when he did that.

"My inner guidance? That Louise wants to warn the world and shake people up so they'll get motivated to help the planet."

"Peace," said the inscrutable one. "Love and peace."

He didn't elaborate further on that point. He didn't need to. I knew, on a higher level that Louise's intention was to move peace along, not to create more fear.

As for my inner guidance, Tsen Tsing said I should keep working on that. Not what I wanted to hear. But a real master knows the heart of the student and I must have been an easy read. Thank goodness he was also filled with love and compassion.

"One of the things you're practicing is trusting yourself and getting confirmation." He explained that I received an initial perception, and then I questioned it, analyzed it. He said not to stop there, but to stay open until I'm in a very clear place. It could take a couple of weeks to be clear, he advised. The key was to continue *asking for clarity*—to hold that intention and allow Spirit to work on it. In Tsen Tsing's dimension, time had no meaning. A couple of his weeks could translate into a couple of years for me.

Tsen Tsing said he would check in with me from time to time.

A new year dawned—2005. My friend Libby and her husband from Grand Junction drove over to spend the weekend and celebrate the holiday. Libby and I sat at the dining room table on New Year's morning, drank coffee, and silently pulled our angel cards with healing messages. Next we moved to the runes. I asked a question of the runes.

"What is my outlook for 2005?"

I dug my hand into the bag and pulled one rune with a character inscribed on its face shaped like the letter "R." Its name was Raido and it meant, "Journey." The reading for this rune concerned communication and the ultimate reunion that comes at the end of a journey. It advised that this was the time to focus on "right action," not through relying on personal power, but by asking for help from the Inner Teacher. It recommended being content to wait and said that the urge to "try to make it happen" would eventually disappear. This message echoed Tsen Tsing's advice.

Patience was a virtue I was short on, and yet patience came up repeatedly as a quality I needed to practice. I'd been trying to make the book happen for the past year. There was much I needed to learn about patience and asking for help from the Inner Teacher. I read on. The symbol Raido meant that the journey is toward self-healing, self-change, and union of self with Self. That reading mirrored one of the themes of this book— my spiritual journey.

Winter rolled into spring. In the upper Arkansas Valley, at 8,200 feet, we live in a forest of aging pines the size of fruit trees. I gazed out my second story window onto the tops of our piñons. Patches of snow lingered on the land, almost a foot deep in some places. Mountain peaks refused to release their snowy bonnets, which was unusual for March. A year and a half earlier, we had seen our last snow by November; the spring snows had never materialized. The year before that, dust whipped down the valley whenever the wind kicked up. The year before that, Zapata Falls, on the flanks of Mt. Blanca, had dribbled to a trickle, and fires had raged across the state.

In our alpine valley, instead of spring flowers, we settle for jaw dropping views: Collegiate Peaks to the west, Mosquito Range to the east. The Sangre de Cristo Range slashes across the southern horizon at an angle with its pink tinged crown morning and evening. After five years of drought, the heavy March snows should have cheered me with the promise of July wildflowers and a full-bellied river. But it was another spring-less day, without crocus or tulips, and *I'll Be There to Write the Story* was still going nowhere.

Two days prior, I had felt Louise's presence, her warmth and closeness, for the first time in quite awhile. I believed she had flown in with the bluebirds. That would have been like her, that she would return in the spring. I'd heard a voice in my head, "Finish the book; finish the book."

I was feeling pressure to get on with it, but had no handle to turn on the spigot. In the meantime, I read more books, wrote short unrelated pieces, and compulsively made beaded jewelry, in addition to handling the other quarter of my life that I share with my husband—pottery.

In February, I attended a workshop given by my friend, Amy, on overcoming writer's block. It helped me take a badly needed step: attach rear end to seat of chair. I received some important guidance from another writing friend. In a nutshell, she said, "Shut up and write." Since I wasn't writing any new material, I decided to start reediting the chapters, hoping to jump-start the juice.

I read Janet Catherine Berlo's *Quilting Lessons*—the story of how the author overcame her own writer's block through quilting like a maniac. At forty, an accomplished professor and scholar, she had hit a wall in the middle of her sixth book. She literally couldn't stomach the thought of touching the computer. For some reason, she was consumed with an urge to make quilts, a skill she learned from her older sister. Designing and fabricating helped her regain her balance, along with therapy for her depression. Eloquently, she wrote a series of essays of her own desert experience with the project she desperately needed to finish, while she hid the dearth from her colleagues. She cloistered herself in the third floor of her house, cutting and piecing through the night. Finally the balance she needed came clear to her. She had engaged in too much mental energy and not enough play time. Her inner guidance had said "time out," and she had to go along with the agenda of her unconscious.

I wasn't clear yet about my own time-out. Was I waiting for guidance or simply afraid of finishing? How on earth was I to wrap up this thing? I asked for guidance and a sign, preferably the two-by-four level of guidance, the kind that I couldn't miss.

New insight sprang along with the spring thaw, a rivulet I could follow. Louise had called for action, and here was a poem she had written about taking action. "Eden's Tree" had meant little to me when I came across it several years earlier. One of her last poems, she had written it in 1984, when she was seventy-two. This poem honored antiwar protest marchers.

**Eden's Tree**
Protest Marchers 1984

Over centuries
An abiding NO rises again and again.
This and not these shall not be
Forever borne. A turning tree, blackened by fire
But rooted still in lively dust, remembering spring
Stretches one pleated leaf toward primal sun.
Never a total darkness; never None,

For light, buried deep, remembers Light
And always this race of fumbling men
Retains a remnant soul called forth
To rouse the conscience of the world,
Even this day, hemmed in by serpents' eggs,
Death in a thousand shades laid deep
In the earth and sea, or riding the wind,
Even today, Life's Tree says NO,
Circling again to its own true sun.
I see thin lines of women, children, men,
Walking silently, beaten, pulled down, tramped on
But more come, and more, and more,
Whispering the ever-abiding No to woe,
To war, to arrogant pride, to man-made sun.

It wasn't easy to understand. As I teased it apart, I discovered that Louise had employed a tree in the Garden of Eden as the poem's unifying symbol.

When my cousin DeDe came to visit, she read the poem and gave me a quick lesson in the Book of Genesis. There were two trees in the Garden of Eden: The Tree of Knowledge of Good and Evil and the Tree of Life. Because Eve ate fruit from the Tree of Knowledge and offered a bite to Adam, the first couple saw their nakedness and understood the meaning of evil. God perceived they were no longer innocent, and therefore did not allow them to eat from the Tree of Life, whose fruit would grant immortality. God cast them out of the Garden rather than granting them immortality.

Their lot would be a long journey: learning to love, and thereby transforming evil into good. This is the journey of Everyman—all of us. Once we learn how to love, then, and only then, can we taste the fruit of the Tree of Life and gain immortality. DeDe said it wasn't until she became a Waldorf teacher and taught the Adam and Eve story to first graders that she realized there were two trees in Eden. This was news to me as well.

Louise's religious background was rooted in Christianity. In "Eden's Tree," I believed Louise was looking at the fruits of war—death and destruction—caused by the original sin of mankind. Original sin was symbolized by the Tree of the Knowledge of Good and Evil. I believed she assumed readers understood that there were two trees in Eden, and the Tree of Knowledge was the cause of war and of all mankind's trouble. However, it was the Tree of Life (immortality, which can be granted only by God) that was taking a beating in her poem. On that scraggly tree, only one pitiful green leaf remained.

The Tree of Life, in her poem, had been burned and blackened by war's fire, but it was rooted "in lively dust." It stretched its solitary remaining leaf toward the sun, its source of life. Comparing humankind to the tree with one leaf, she said that there is never total darkness, no matter how far down the wrong paths humans wander. Like the single leaf on the Tree of Life, people will retain a remnant of conscience that can be aroused.

In her poem, Louise asserted that when people finally wake up, they will take a stand against those who would create more and more war. In typical Louise poetic language, she referred to bombs as "serpents' eggs—death in a thousand shades laid deep in the earth and sea, or riding the wind." Both the Tree of Life and people of conscience would say "NO" to the false sun— the blinding light of nuclear blast.

Louise singled out protest marchers as the people who remembered the light, those with insight and conscience. She said that more and more would march for peace in spite of the scorn and abuse. In "Eden's Tree," Louise said marching for peace was one way of taking action. She pled for more than just a change in thought, but a shift from passivity to action, even though taking a stand might be risky.

"Eden's Tree" embodied one of the book's themes: take a stand. I uncovered my pastel oil crayons and, together with Louise, illustrated her poem, "Eden's Tree."

*Maria's automatic drawing of Louise's poem, "Eden's Tree."*
*Protest marchers witness the effects of war on the Tree of Life.*

"Eden's Tree" contains all essential elements of Louise's life's message. We are children of God on a journey to learn to love. Along the way, we go astray, kill, maim and destroy. Some people wake up and see that this path leads nowhere but to continued destruction. They take a stand, refuse to fight, and say, "Enough." They get trampled, but more follow their example until, finally, the voices for peace win out.

Louise's poetic Tree of Life image with one remaining leaf reminded me of a similar image from the television evening news. After the 1995 Oklahoma City bombing, a tree across the street from the Alfred P. Murrah Federal Building was burned and stripped, except for a few naked limbs. Left to its own devices and not chain-sawed down, it had regenerated into full foliage within one year, evidence that life persists and heals in spite of everything.

The death and destruction approach for handling Earth's affairs is winding down. That was the message Sheryl's channeled Masters wanted us to hear, when I met with her in 2005. "It is an outdated way for people to learn, and is no longer necessary," they said. When Sheryl looked into the future as a clairvoyant, she didn't see death and destruction. It was always a possibility in her far-reaching visions, but not the probable outcome. I was heartened to hear her say that. Anything positive that Sheryl perceived about the future brightened my day.

Together, Sheryl and I enumerated the many good and positive things that people were doing to help the Earth shift in a gentle way. First of all, many knew they were here for a reason—to bring about change. They had spiritual tools to create a new world. They could raise the body's vibratory rate through meditation, which, in turn, affected the vibratory rate of the planet. They could stay centered and out of fear. They had learned forgiveness and the power of gratitude. They used the power of visualization to create for good. And, Sheryl added, there were countless healing arts available that people can avail themselves of. She said that we were all being given a choice to either wallow in fear and negativity or take the high road in whatever way we felt drawn.

Sheryl pointed out that while some prophets agree that the end might come in a flash, other great masters were saying God loves us more than that. This wasn't the end of it all.

This session helped me realize that the fundamental erroneous pattern was fear. As long as we feared everyone—our neighbor, the stranger who comes to the door at ten o'clock at night, the country on the other side of the world, the next influenza pandemic, illegal immigrants streaming across our borders—we were creating a climate that bred war. We would have to change fear to trust.

I asked myself how a single person could help save the world. According to Sheryl, many people were already making the necessary changes, and it was not a given that the world would end in calamity. Louise said that we must stop dwelling on negativity and take action, even if that action was just saying no to war. Tsen Tsing said that it was not up to us to save the world, that we were not alone in this chaos. God had a plan for our planet. Metatron said that *how* this world shifted was unimportant—boom or no boom. One way or the other, this planet would shift into a new form of being, and it was happening right now.

# Chapter 10

## Healing the Matriarchal Lineage

Although I could not travel on a round-trip ticket to the Other Side with Mom, I had been at her bedside witnessing what appeared to be The End, all the while knowing that she was on the first leg of a magnificent journey. A great mystery-miracle took place the night she died.

I had read various accounts of what happens at the moment of death. Many state that the soul leaves the body through the top of the head and maintains consciousness. It experiences going through a tunnel of light. It is met by familiar family members and angelic beings who shepherd the soul through dimensions of the Afterlife. There is a review of the life just lived, and so on. Many have written first person accounts of near death experiences in which they left their bodies, spent time on the Other Side, and then returned to the physical. So I was curious about my mother's death experience. I wanted to know what kind of orientation to the Other Side was she had been given. Who met her? Were there reunions with friends and family members? I posed these questions to Tsen Tsing, channeled by Heiderose, and then to Stacey and Sheryl.

"Tsen Tsing," I asked, "What happened when Louise first died? Who met her? Where did she go? What did she do?"

He replied that the death experience varies according to the consciousness of the people before they leave their bodies. Louise, he said, was ready to transition. She didn't resist moving out of the body and leaving it all behind.

The first soul she saw was Ammon Ernst, her father. According to Tsen Tsing, Ammon met her with open arms. I was surprised to hear that it was Ammon who met Louise, rather than her own mother, Margaret. But Tsen Tsing said that Ammon needed to feel a sense of completion between them by greeting Louise with love. Apparently they still had unfinished business when he died, and this was a great opportunity for him.

I could only speculate about the unfinished business, for my mother never shared anything except fond memories of her father. However I heard that her siblings, my aunts and one uncle, had suffered from his thoughtlessness when they were children. I was heartened to hear that my grandfather's soul had come forward to make amends with Louise.

Tsen Tsing continued, saying that Louise was also met by her own spiritual teachers and by Jesus. My mother had been a devoted Christian who had attended traditional church and written dozens of religious poems. Jesus would have been on the top of her greeter wish list at the Pearly Gates, so I was happy to hear that her heart's desire was met. She hadn't written or talked much about other spiritual teachers who might have been helping her. She believed in the Catholic saints and carried a St. Christopher's medal for protection. That much I knew. She didn't expect a heaven of harps and wings with God sitting on a golden throne. None of that. She assumed the mystery of transition would be safe and loving, and I knew she looked forward to it. But my mother also believed in reincarnation. She was well read in all the great religions, as well as in parapsychology and many varieties of spirituality. I believed this was why she passed with grace and without resistance.

Tsen Tsing said Louise was held in a cocoon of light for several days where she reviewed some of her life choices and was shown which issues she didn't let go of and give over to God. While this information begged for more clarification, I didn't think to stop Tsen Tsing and ask more questions. Sheryl had already brought to light some of Louise's first experiences on the Other Side with the Way-Shower and the Field of Possibilities Screen, where Louise had to face her Earthly fears.

"Did she see the best friend of her young adult years, Bonny von der Meer, who died in a car wreck?" I asked.

Tsen Tsing replied that she "was allowed to reconnect" with Bonny's soul and "have some reunion." Being an earthbound human, I couldn't fathom what such a reunion would have been like. The two of them, Bonny and Louise, had been soul sisters as young women. I was hoping for more description. I wanted to hear of a joyous reconnection; maybe an all-night party. After all, hadn't Bonny been waiting on Louise's demise for fifty Earth years? I was a little disappointed in Tsen Tsing's short answer.

I was curious about my own father and said, "Tell me about my father, her husband, Bill."

In one swift sentence, Tsen Tsing painted a picture that helped clarify what happened when my mother crossed over.

"There is a whole group of people all coming to the one who is leaving the physical form and coming into spirit."

I could see it: souls who my mother knew during her life converging upon her, greeting her, resolving old issues—in a dimension without time, in a place without bodies. Human reunions that might take hours or days to renew and resolve on Earth might be accomplished in minutes or seconds.

As for my father, Bill Weber, Tsen Tsing said, "In some ways she was pretty complete with him. So there wasn't that much work to do between them."

*Wow! A lifetime together, and only a few minutes to say hi and bye.*

While reuniting in affection with her father was easy, it was a different story with Louise's mother, my Granny Ernst. Both Tsen Tsing and Stacey concurred on that. Tsen Tsing said that Louise's mother had possessed poor parenting skills, stemming from her own upbringing. She hadn't known how to discipline her young daughter. As a result, Louise and her mother had not been very close. Up through Louise's teenage years, there had been distance between them, and that had not been easy for Louise. She hadn't had the support she'd needed. Tsen Tsing said that forgiving her mother was one of the harder things Louise had needed to work on. Clearing the air with her father, Ammon, had been easier and had been completed first. But with her mother, there had been more to heal. When they had finally resolved their differences, a great healing had taken place.

Stacey added, "Your mother is saying that she's with her mother, your Granny Ernst. They got a lot of things worked out. They're still very different energies, the two of them, but they really like each other. She learned a lot from her mom, and part of what you're going through is dysfunction within the matriarchal lineage."

When I heard Stacey say, "dysfunction within the matriarchal lineage," my ears pricked up. The concept of a mother-daughter dysfunction running back through generations had the potential to free me from a lot of guilt. I wanted to learn more about the matriarchal line.

I dimly remembered my mother saying, once and only once, that she had hated her mother. That sentiment had seemed implausible to me, for my Granny Ernst had treated me with affection. But I'd heard it and never forgotten it, especially when I was a teenager and felt a simmering anger toward my mother. Mom's poem, "The Hard Breast," described a scene with her mother. Eight-year-old Louise had laced burdock burrs through her hair to make a queen's crown. "How could you? Brat! Brat! Brat!" screamed her mother as she "alternately brushed and banged" her head. Little Louise jerked and wriggled while her mother tore the burrs from her tangled hair. Louise said it wasn't the "pain of the tugged hair" that brought tears to her eyes, but "the hurt of the hard breast— / the first ever hiss of 'Brat, Brat.'"

My two first cousins, DeDe and Susie, helped piece together what may have been the cause of our grandmother's dysfunction. Through family constellation work, DeDe learned that our Granny (Margaret Ernst) might have married our grandfather (Ammon) on the rebound after suffering a soul-wounding trauma caused by a young man's inappropriate advance. Margaret had turned to her mother (our great grandmother, Mary Ann Conrad) for help after the trauma, but had received a cold shoulder. Her emotions had shut down and, frozen in her heart, she had married Ammon against her parents' wishes. They hadn't liked Ammon because he'd been an orphan from a troubled family without financial means or social standing. Ammon and Margaret's first baby girl had died shortly after birth, and knowledge of her existence was sealed away from later siblings. The existence of this first child was discovered by surprise only after Louise's death.

My cousin, Susie, discovered a postcard, dated 1909, addressed to Granny and Grandpa Ernst (Margaret and Ammon) from friends congratulating them on the birth of their daughter. The postcard had a picture of an infant girl in a long white dress, with the message saying how wonderful the visit had been, and that the photo looked just like the little Ernst daughter. However, the oldest daughter known to us, Susie's mother Mary, was born in 1910, one year later. We believed the first child had died. We also believed that, after the baby's death, Granny had gone through the motions of living with her heart completely closed down. In the early 1900s, there had been nowhere for her to turn for emotional assistance.

Susie's mother, Mary, remembered Granny's frequent visits to take flowers and cry at a grave with a tiny headstone, but nothing had ever been said about this first child. My mother was the next of three children that Granny bore after Mary. Granny's lot in life had been to cook three meals a day for a family of six and three field hands on a working farm. In retirement, Granny and Grandpa Ernst had accrued little to show for their labors and were partly supported by their children. It had been a hard life for Granny and she died of cancer at seventy-one, when I was thirteen.

Louise had reported fond memories of her grandmother's dinner invitations, which had been issued to each child individually. She had been treated like a princess. Louise could charm adults with her gift of gab, even as a child. Besides, she was the golden-haired one with blue eyes who had nearly died of appendicitis at age nine, the favored child in her family. At a reunion, her sisters, Mary and Rachel, claimed she had been spoiled. Mary and Rachel hadn't fared well at Grandma Benedict's table. The grandparents, who lived next door, didn't like children's clutter or chatter. Mary and Rachel remembered that the dinner table had been awkward whenever they had been invited to dine with their grandparents by themselves. Kenneth, the youngest sibling, had been too young to participate and the whole family had rarely been invited together. When I asked my cousins what they knew about our Great Grandma Benedict, the consensus was that she hadn't received sufficient mothering herself to be a supportive mother.

A medical intuitive, Barbara Noonan, told me that mother-daughter dysfunction runs through four generations on the matriarchal side of my family, manifesting in digestive troubles and fear of failure. The wound is characterized by an internalized family creed, "If you fail, you will die." Wounds such as this are passed down on a soul level until someone is sufficiently strong willed to break the pattern.

While studying The Power of the Aumakua (ancestors) in a Hawaiian Shamanism workshop, I learned that family wounds such as the one originated by my great grandmother can be healed, and when one heals oneself, healing can occur for the ancestors as well. Conditions that run in families, such as addictions, diabetes, depression, poverty, bad luck in love, cancer, and divorce are among the symptoms of family wounds visited upon the children and children's children without their knowing why. These can all be healed in the family line. It was my hope that by healing my emotional self and my relationship with Louise, these healings would help to heal the soul wounds of my Granny Ernst and her mother, Mary Ann Conrad.

In a channeling through Sheryl, Louise said to me, "I want you to know how proud I am of you, and that I am aware how much it hurt you when you didn't understand me. You can forgive yourself for that now. I played my part in that too. We are all trying to do our best with what we have."

For the first time, Mom was acknowledging my passive aggression toward her as well as forgiving me and giving me permission to forgive myself. She was also admitting her participation in the mother-daughter tug of war. In the space of ten seconds, the tension that I'd held in my stomach for most of my life had just relaxed.

Through Sheryl, Louise said she appreciated that I understood her better now that I was older. She hadn't meant to squash me when I was a child. She had thought she was bringing me out more by presenting things to me and doing interesting activities with me. Because I was an only child, she had wanted me to grow up not being totally self-absorbed all the time. She said she loved me and wanted to be more than a mom. She wanted to be a friend, someone I could see as an equal. I didn't have to view her as a mother so much any more.

That was nice to hear, because I felt the same toward her. I took a deep breath as my chest loosened and warmed up. Forgiveness in this earthly plane seemed to take a lot of work. I had been chasing it for several years, and each time I thought I'd arrived, I discovered that there was more territory to travel. I hoped that the effort Louise and I were making would help our other female ancestors.

Stacey reminded me that I was the last of the four generations of women on my mother's side—Maria, Louise Ernst Weber, Margaret Benedict Ernst, and Mary Ann Conrad Benedict. We were related to each other through blood and connected in spirit. Now healing was being created even though I was the only one in the physical world. Stacey said she believed that my individual spiritual journey could heal ancestors all the way back to my great grandmother.

Tsen Tsing expanded on that thought, saying, "It does not heal just that matriarchal line, but all of the human realm. As one soul contributes to the healing of certain patterns, all of humanity is benefited. It is beyond your own bloodline that this healing affects."

I was about to pat myself on the back for my noble effort when Tsen Tsing nailed me.

"No matter how much work you and your mother do between the both of you, you are still responsible for whatever it is you are experiencing. All souls, no matter how badly they are abused, for example, are still responsible for how they choose to respond to what happened. That is the biggest part of the healing process—taking responsibility for every single detail that a soul is experiencing, without blaming. As long as there is blame, that is a way of not taking responsibility."

Ick! I would need to reexamine my motives and my blame meter. Was I clear of all blame toward my mother? Toward my father? Toward my first husband? Toward my coworkers? Toward my women friends? Toward myself? That last one was the biggie. And I was getting ready to blame the dysfunctional matriarchal lineage for my tendency to not speak up and be heard! I liked to believe I wasn't a blamer, but it just wasn't true. More to work on. No excuses.

"You will plot your own journey," said Tsen Tsing. "Along the way, you may learn to forgive others, forgive yourself, and move forward in your own spiritual evolution. Forgiveness needs to start first with self. You can't do for someone else what you don't do for yourself."

*When I'm finished forgiving myself, I'll be guilt free and basically a happy person*, I thought. I remembered the string of wrenching events with friends over the last few years that had laid me low. Forgiveness of self and others had been the hardest undertaking of my life. Had I forgiven them totally? Had I forgiven myself totally?

"The key is forgiving yourself, for whatever the cause," Tsen Tsing said. "You don't even need to know what you're forgiving yourself for. Go beyond the intellect and just say, 'From the

God-being within me, I forgive everything and anything—anything I may not even be aware of—I forgive.' Go beyond the limitations of human thinking, because maybe what you're forgiving is your 'original sin' of pretending that you are separate from God. A lot of the forgiveness goes back to that."

Tsen Tsing said that anger and depression are not bad. Even the Great Ones from the Council of Light welcome all that is in our consciousness, because all is welcome in the realm of love. They do not judge. They do not want us to judge. They do not want us to dismiss or attempt to hide our so-called negative thoughts and emotions. In fact, they honor all the energies that we carry.

On the morning of the reading with Tsen Tsing, I felt depressed because of a personal problem. I didn't want to feel gloomy. I wanted to be happy because I was looking forward to the reading with Heiderose. But in spite of my efforts to bring back the joy, I was in a funk that weighed down my heart.

At the beginning of the session, Tsen Tsing asked how I was taking responsibility for those emotions. This advanced spirit from another dimension was reading my mind and emotional state. I felt naked, exposed, and embarrassed. I knew I couldn't hide anything from him. My goose was cooked.

"I'm taking total responsibility for my emotions," I shot back. "That's hard because I'm trying not to be in a place of blame. I'm trying to look at everything as something I created and deal with it."

"Here it is, you're blaming yourself."

"Yes."

"Here is what you need to shift," he said. "Instead of having compassion for your inner response, you are choosing blame. Why can you not have compassion with the part that is creating this internal response? Why do you need to judge that?"

"I guess I feel depressed because there's some mechanism in me that brings up a negative emotion, and I would like to change it to joy," I said.

"In order for the pattern to heal, you need to let the emotion run its course, or you will not find the origin of it."

"So it's okay to feel the sadness and grief?"

"You want to let yourself have the response. If you have the willingness to experience the emotion in its completeness, without suppressing it, without analyzing it, without trying to understand where it comes from, then at some point you'll realize where it's originating," he said. "It'll all come together."

Tsen Tsing told me I was separating. I was trying to separate myself from the negative emotion. And as long as I did that, I was creating separation in myself. He said the only way anything could integrate was if I did not separate any part of myself. If I wanted to integrate and heal, I would need to be kind to myself, as a mother is kind to a child. Instead of blaming myself—I am a bad person—I should mother that inner child, and say, "It's okay to feel that way." Anger *is*; sadness *is*. These emotions are not bad.

"My mother taught me not to express anger," I told him. "Not once but many times."

"Now you must mother yourself and tell your inner child, 'It's okay to feel angry. My mother wasn't right.' You need to take responsibility for mothering that child that you were way back then. Talk to it in loving ways and say, 'It's all right. You're not a bad person.'"

It was true that I had sometimes found myself still feeling anger brewing or guilt stewing in a relationship, even after believing I'd forgiven the other party. Tsen Tsing seemed to be suggesting that, at these times, I needed to mother myself. Although my mother had tried to be the best mother she could, one of her beliefs had been that anger should never be expressed.

She had punished me for expressing anger. It wasn't her fault. She had been raised in a repressive home by a mother who had also been raised in a repressive home.

I knew that many women had been raised the same way. As a result, many of us thought that expressing anger or feeling guilty, sad, or depressed was bad. We attempted to eliminate those emotions one way or another: practicing affirmations; using essential oils to feel happy; exercising to work out our emotions; using mind shifting, self-help CDs; taking workshops; going into analysis, or; seeing a counselor. All in pursuit of peace. Instead, what we often needed was to mother ourselves in the positive, self-affirming way that we had not been mothered as children.

Tsen Tsing was making some excellent points about healing negative patterns. He was suggesting that emotional responses are part of being human. We need to make it okay to feel guilt if we want to heal a pattern. Anything that we're making wrong, we can't heal. It's okay to feel guilt. It's okay to feel anger. It's okay to feel sadness. As we learn to accept the emotions, the patterns and the parts of ourselves that need to be healed can heal. That's how we take responsibility and we're the only ones who can do it.

We might say, "I am human. I love myself. I have compassion. I may not understand why I'm responding like this, but I'm willing to love myself no matter what!" Doing so would be choosing love for ourselves. Choosing love for ourselves was an idea I had heard repeatedly and had tried to accomplish with limited success. Now I was beginning to understand how to do that.

Tsen Tsing said that every healing of a relationship ripples through the whole human race. It followed that we were serving not only ourselves, but the world, when we forgave. If we wanted to do our part to create world peace, one great way to do that was to forgive Mom and forgive self.

I began to understand that we could heal relationships while both parties were alive, but we could also heal them if one had crossed over. If it could be done face-to-face, all the better. But in many cases, that was not possible. Apparently, none of us escapes reviewing our life and making amends. Louise had to resolve old issues with her father and mother on the Other Side. There was no avoiding it.

Through the intuitive readings of Sheryl, Stacey and Heiderose, I formed a new context for my mother's life. I no longer thought of her as the earthly mother I had shared fairy stories with as a ten-year-old or rebelled against as a teenager. She was also not the mother who had gone into a nursing home and died at eighty-five. Those pictures were in the photo album. What replaced those images in my mind was a youthful woman of light who inhabited a new and mysterious place she was eager to share glimpses of. I had been keen to hear from her, but I knew I could not cling to her. I did not want to hold her back from where she needed to go next and decided it was time for me to release her, for both of our sakes.

Tsen Tsing said, "Do you feel complete? Here's one thing you can always ask yourself: 'Am I feeling complete with receiving this guidance from my mother, or is there more?'"

"I could go on and on with the questions," I said. "But I'd like to get to the place where I can receive my own answers from my own guidance system and not have to rely on her."

"Well, you don't need your mother," he replied bluntly.

⁓

March 19, 2005. I was hunched over the bed in our guest room in my Colorado mountain home, paging through old photo albums—the kind with black and white snapshots glued to black paper pages with triangle corner stickers. I was looking for a particular photo of Louise at her easel. In the photo, she appeared to be thinking about the next brushstroke, and the wooden tip of her paintbrush touched her lower lip. An oil painting in process was on the easel. The painting was of a ballerina who had just tossed a stone into a pond. She stood on point shoes with ankles crossed, bent at the waist, and her arm curved over her head. Her eyes watched a column of water rising from the pond like a fountain. In front of this oil painting, Louise sat with her shoulder to the camera. Her hair, chestnut and wavy, curled around her neck, her pensive face, in profile. She was wearing a black flowered print dress with short puffed sleeves.

My father had shot that photo around 1953 in the cabin on the back of our property in Tennessee that we called The Shack. We had used that one-room cabin with a stone fireplace as people today use a family room. It was where my father had escaped to read, where we had retreated to on winter evenings for a steak fry, and where I had held slumber parties as a teenager.

My earliest memories included Pop documenting every-thing we did as a family with a camera. He had developed that picture of Louise in the kitchen sink, blown it up to an eight by ten, and framed it. It had hung in the sewing room. I wanted that picture for the book because it captured Louise engrossed in her art. But I wasn't going to find it in this album, for it never existed as a small print.

I turned over the last page in the album and discovered an envelope in Louise's handwriting addressed to my paternal grandmother, Lillie Pitman Weber, dated October 26, 1944—

only five days after my birth. Pop was on a minesweeper somewhere in the Mediterranean at the time. My hands shook as I
removed the letter on onionskin paper and began to read.

*Thursday, October 26, 1944*
*Dear Mother,*

*I am still flat in bed so I hope you can read this. Today
I feel able to write a few letters and I know you and my
family are anxious for some word from me. I have written
to my dear Bill three times and I hope the letters made
sense. We have received both your letters, the one of Saturday just came this morning. I am sending all the nice
letters about our baby to Bill. I also sent him a piece of her
hair tied with a ribbon. I cut it from the back of her neck.*

*I think I am the most fortunate person in the world,
for no one knows better than I all the things that could
happen. Being 32 and my first baby I expected the worst,
but I never was afraid . . . .*

*We went to the hospital at 3 p.m. I was admitted to the
labor room. Then by the time I was undressed I had hard
pains one minute apart and no relaxation between. They
gave me a hypo, pills, etc. and prep but no enema. The
doctor did a rectal and said take her to the delivery room.
I was only about three fingers dilated but he said I needed
gas to keep the baby from coming too fast. Since Maria
was born at 4:22, you know it didn't take long. I just had
enough pain to know that without gas it would be pretty
bad. I would probably be yelling my head off but as it was
I didn't make any fuss. I feel so much better today. Any
past trouble doesn't seem worth mentioning. I have had a
lot of pain in the sutures but they give me medicine when
I ask for it and something to sleep . . .*

*I was on the ward until Tuesday afternoon. Some woman next to me did a lot of talking about the war and poor mothers without their husbands, and it got me down and I cried once, but I am all right now. Dr. Nobes told me today that everyone cries one time after they have a baby . . .*

*. . . My baby cannot hold my nipples—they are too small and she is nursing with a shield. We don't know yet if I can nurse her or not. I hope so. She is gaining . . .*

*You may be glad to know I no longer think little Maria is homely. Now I think she is beautiful. I can't describe her. She is a lot like Bill's baby pictures and mine too. Dark hair, straight and dark blue eyes. She seems to be a perfect baby. I love her so and I wouldn't change her for a boy for anything. I am so happy I can't talk about it without being silly. She is so cute. I know I will spoil her rotten. If only Bill could see her, his dear little Maria. Flowers just came from my sister.*

*I think it was nice for the girls to sing to you. I hope you are feeling well and come home soon.*

*Love, Louise*

Reading this letter was like striking gold. It was Louise's heart exposed, her experience of my birth and her bonding with me still fresh and quivering. I took a deep breath and remembered how much of her writing I had discarded after my father died. Thank God this letter survived my purge. I was thrilled, elated, and wildly in love with her as I sat on the floor, hugged the letter, and cried, "I miss my mama."

# Chapter 11

## *Revelation*

For fifty years I preserved the fairy letters from Queen Thimble Bee in a Coty talcum powder box. I would pull them out of my bottom dresser drawer and read them, especially when I felt blue. The letters were the reason I talked to rocks and accepted that some people could kindle a fire by willing the sticks to ignite. Because of the letters, I believed in the unbelievable, but I never stopped wondering whether a real fairy had written them or my mother had. And if my mother had written them, why?

Those questions, along with nineteen others, were on my mind as I prepared to go under hypnosis in Melanie Smithson's office for a "Life Between Lives" session on September 28, 2006. I had never heard of Life Between Lives (LBL) sessions until I read Dr. Michael Newton's book, *Journey of Souls*. By asking the owner of my favorite Denver metaphysical bookstore whether books on the topic of life after death sold well, I discovered Dr. Newton's work.

"These are best sellers," she said, and pointed to Newton's two books.

I bought them both and couldn't put down *Journey of Souls* once I started it.

*Journey of Souls* described the case histories of clients Dr. Newton placed into hypnotic trance and regressed to the time before their births. People came to Dr. Newton for a variety of reasons, the most popular being to find their life's purpose.

They connected with their super-conscious minds—the part of our consciousness that receives messages from the divine—and experienced themselves as eternal souls on the Other Side.

Dr. Newton's clients also learned why certain souls chose to be together in this lifetime, which was what I wanted to find out. Specifically, I wanted to learn as much as possible about the agreements or contracts Louise and I had made before coming into this Earth plane, including the question of Fairy Queen Thimble Bee. Had Louise and I decided, before I was born, that she would introduce me to the world of fairies? I even hoped I might have an experience of meeting up with her soul while under hypnosis.

One week after finishing *Journey of Souls,* I attended a metaphysical fair in Denver and noticed copies of Dr. Newton's books at Melanie Smithson's vendor booth. Ms. Smithson, a psychotherapist, told me that she was trained and certified by Dr. Newton to conduct LBL spiritual regressions. Figuring this was the reason I had been guided to attend the fair, I scheduled a session for the end of the month at the Smithson Clinic in Denver, where she and her husband practiced their therapies.

Ms. Smithson gave me homework before coming to her office. I was to create a list of questions I wanted answered during my session and email this to her. My entries included: What did I decide to work on in this lifetime? Why did my mother and I choose to be together? Was the fairy letter episode planned before my birth? She also needed my cast of characters—significant people in my current life. That list included my parents, several close relatives, my first and second husbands, and several friends. I limited the list to twelve people, alphabetized it, and wrote a one sentence sketch of each person's significance in my life.

Ms. Smithson set up a recorder so I could go home with a set of CDs from the three-hour session. She hypnotized me slowly and deliberately through a lengthy guided meditation. I used a blindfold so I could "see" whatever visions or impressions might arise. In a melodious voice, she reminded me that I'd been in trance before; that, in fact, I went into trance every night as I drifted off to sleep. She asked me to trust that my body knew what to do and how to let go and said that any thoughts, worries, preconceived ideas, or expectations about the session would drift off on a cloud. There was nothing to fear and I wouldn't be affected by any gruesome scenes or frightening events.

She told me that she would first take me to a scene from a significant past life. In fact, it would be the last day of my last past life. I wasn't going to be frightened by this. She was correct. I was fully conscious, intensely aware, but never disturbed. Since I'd read *Journey of Souls*, I was expecting a continuous stream of images to move in front of my eyes and voluminous downloads of information from a higher level of intelligence to enter my mind.

At first it was a start-stop-start-stop affair, punctuated with long pauses. Finally, I was able to see a battlefield and a Roman soldier who lay dying on the beach. I felt totally removed from this man, as though I were watching a movie.

Ms. Smithson asked me to back up and view some scenes from this soldier's life. I saw him in a public building with marble columns and wide stairs, living it up with wine, women and song. He obviously thought very well of himself. He was making a speech to the revelers seated around and below him. I had seen characters like him in movies. I thought I was making this up, but I just allowed the mental pictures to come. Ms. Smithson guided me back to the battlefield and asked me how he had died. I knew that he was a leader of his group, a fairly high ranking general. He and his men had lost the battle and there were bodies lying everywhere. Detached, I didn't sense any of the misery.

Then Ms. Smithson guided me into the afterlife. I felt some confusion because I just couldn't believe that a life in Rome, 2000 years ago, would have been my last life before this one. I asked her about that, while still under hypnosis. She replied that it might not have been my last life, but it was a significant life, perhaps the life that had some karmic influence on my current life.

She asked me to tell her what I experienced right after the Roman soldier's death. I couldn't perceive anything. She asked who met me. I couldn't perceive anything. She then asked if I could see the place where I went as a soul after death. This I could see, and it was very odd. I saw a huge flesh colored ball sitting out in black space, perhaps the size of the moon. It was honeycombed on the surface. This was the "planet" I was moving toward. She asked me to go into the place where I would stay. I saw a little condo-like compartment with two or three rooms. The rooms were organic looking with low, curved ceilings and floors that curved up to meet adobe colored walls. Seating was built in, as if benches had grown out of the walls. I saw a potted red geranium in the sitting room and while I could not detect a lighting source, the area was bright and cheery. The place felt womb-like and comforting, but something wasn't right. I was alone and sad that no one had met me. I was just sitting in my compartment, wondering what to do.

Ms. Smithson said that my soul group was with me now, and asked who I saw. In *Journey of Souls*, Dr. Newton said that, after death, our souls congregate into cluster groups of intimate old friends who serve as a support group for one another. I waited and then saw, as if in the distance, a most unexpected thing: a knight of the Round Table. The identity of this person came to me in a flash and I burst into tears. It was Zoe, the friend with whom I'd split up and then reconnected after healing the relationship. Although the figure didn't resemble her—in fact this being was clothed from head to toe in armor—I knew who it was.

The knight remained there as I absorbed the full meaning of his presence. I thought of him as an archetype, a psychological pattern derived from a historical role. Zoe, who appeared as the knight, had played aspects of that archetype in my current life, representing honor, courage, steadfastness, loyalty and friendship. This information came to me in a matter of seconds, and it overwhelmed my emotions. I was grateful for the box of tissues by my side. I also instantly knew that we had been together for other lifetimes and that we were role-playing for one another. That is, I needed her to act a certain way in my present life in order for me to learn what I came here to learn. Our earthly relationship had been prearranged before we came in.

Under hypnosis, and in touch with my super-conscious, layers of meaning were packed into a few seconds that took me a minute or more to verbalize. The information downloads felt clear and true, unlike my daily muddled thoughts. The insights arrived in instantaneous bundles with layers of meaning accompanied by waves of love. That is why I needed the tissues. Seeing and sensing truth without the filters and emotional walls was overwhelming.

According to Dr. Newton, members of a soul group are united for all of eternity. They are composed of like-minded souls with common objectives, which they continually work out with each other. Usually they choose lives together as relatives and close friends during their incarnations on Earth.

The other three members of my soul group appeared hazy at first, but each finally showed his or her face. Tears flowed as

I recognized each one and what he or she meant to me. A man, over six feet tall, stood outside my chamber door and peeked around the corner. When I figured out his identity, I wept again, because I revered him so highly in my current life. I would never have expected him to be part of my soul group. Ms. Smithson asked if he might be my spiritual guide, and that felt right—at least he would play that role for me in this session, dressed in brown robes, as a monk.

I would have expected some relatives in my soul group—at least my cousins. But in this session, my group consisted only of friends and co-workers, united by a love of outdoor adventure, nature and spirituality. While the members of my soul group were friends from my current life, I understood that their purpose was to instill or strengthen particular values that I needed to learn, such as honor, integrity, compassion, sensitivity, service, perseverance, and so on. Reflecting on the Roman soldier who had died on the battlefield, I realized that he had lacked some of those qualities. While he possessed plenty of courage, self-importance, perseverance and power, I sensed that he had been a cruel and heartless man and a womanizer.

Incoming information was usually presented in chunks of knowledge rather than language. I translated each chunk into words for Ms. Smithson. When it arrived in that compressed form, my conscious mind sometimes fumbled to translate insights into coherent sentences. At other times, the words tumbled right out and I felt very bright and "on."

After meeting my soul group, Ms. Smithson asked if I wanted to see my Council of Elders. Dr. Newton defined this group as the most advanced entities his clients see in the spirit world. In the spiritual realms, according to Dr. Newton, every individual goes before this Council shortly after an incarnation is finished. He says that during this meeting, the major choices we made in the life just lived are reviewed with us.

When Ms. Smithson asked me to count the members in my Council, I heard the word "twelve." When I tried to see them as individuals, I made out eleven, and for the most part, they were hazy to the point of translucency. Two of my Council members presented themselves clearly as archetypes: the first, as a Wizard with a crystal ball; the second, as a Viking who looked like a mascot for the Minnesota Vikings football team. The other nine or ten were never clear: a figure wearing red; a Chinese male I thought might have been Tsen Tsing; a woman dressed in blue; two ancient Egyptians, one male and one female, and; three ancient Greek women dressed alike in white robes. Learning the identities of my Council of Elders was not on my list of burning questions, so it was fine that I couldn't see them clearly. This group had a sense of humor. I felt their love and heard their laughter. I knew they cared about me. I gathered they weren't there to judge me, but to assist with my spiritual advancement. That was all I needed to know. They continued to play a role throughout the session.

I first met the Council on the pinnacle of a very pointy mountain. This place was craggy, steep, and cold. I didn't like it, and besides, there wasn't room to assemble everyone. Ms. Smithson advised me to move the meeting elsewhere, so I mentally shifted us to a warm flagstone patio on a Greek isle. Everyone reclined in an overstuffed chair, arranged in a semi-circle around a big round marble table. It must have been a magical table, for objects grew out of its center on several occasions. Even though I could see the table clearly, the setting appeared vague and my Council members remained fuzzy—all except the Wizard.

When I first met the Wizard, his eyes bored into mine. He was dressed in a purple robe and wore a typical wizard's hat. Long black hair fell below his shoulders. With a quizzical smile and a raised eyebrow, he extended the crystal ball to me. I dared not touch it then, sensing that its magic was too powerful. Later, I observed the ball resting on the middle of the marble table where my Council members were seated.

The Wizard said, "Time will tell," which I translated to mean that, on a grand scale, the future is not fixed, but can change form, just as the moon waxes and wanes. Because of that, no one can see the distant future. What we can do is create the future through our powers of manifestation.

Even so, I was allowed to see into some part of my future using the Wizard's ball. During my regression, the crystal ball served several purposes. At one point, it was a device for looking into my own future. At another time, it symbolized the Sacred Circle of life. Later, it expanded into our universe, filled with incredible stars. And still later, it changed into our own blue planet as viewed from the moon.

When I saw Earth from space, it was the most incredible sight imaginable. It was as real to me as the astronauts have described it—a living jewel. Seeing it was exhilarating and also it made me very sad, knowing how we are destroying it. More tissues. The images were exponentially more vivid than they would be on an IMAX screen. Under regression, the visions were multidimensional. They looked ultra-realistic and came supercharged with joy, grief or gratitude. I never felt fear or horror. And that was a good thing. Crying for joy or sadness was all the emotion I could handle. No current film technology could touch this experience. Ms. Smithson said I was seeing and sensing with my super-conscious mind—my God-mind.

I experienced the beauty of creation, accompanied by over-powering, tangible Love. I could only dissolve into tears, time and time again.

"Let yourself be in awe," Ms. Smithson would say, as she passed me another tissue.

After I viewed Earth from space, I understood how connected I am—and my mother was—to our planet and how Louise and I were connected to one another. In my hypnotic vision, I first felt (not saw, but felt) Siamese twins connected at the belly, which was an approximation of how I was connected to Earth. And then that sensation changed like the twist of a kaleidoscope to an image of a fetus with a cord connected to the Earth. I knew that my mother had been the Earth and I was the baby attached by an umbilical cord to her, the Earth. That's who my mother was to me in this lifetime—the Earth Mother.

That the Earth was Louise, and that I had inherited the Earth from her had never occurred to me before. I had been nourished by Earth's body, synonymous with Louise's body. In my vision, she was siphoning the beauty of the Earth to me through that umbilical cord. A lifetime of interaction with my mother was reinterpreted for me in spiritual terms. I felt her significance in my heart and belly with profound awe. I understood in symbol and imagery what my mother had meant to me, spiritually. More tissues.

I also grasped that there was a positive side to my matriarchal lineage issues. My great grandmother, Mary Ann Conrad, had given the Earth to my grandmother, Margaret. In turn, Margaret had given it to my mother, Louise, and Louise had given it to me. The women in my line had all passed the love of nature's beauty down through our bloodline. For generations, we had handed the Earth to each other and had all honored the Earth in some way. Louise had done so through poetry.

While I was immersed in this thought, I saw an image of the crescent moon followed by an image of Our Lady of Guadalupe with the crescent moon at her feet, followed by the Egyptian goddess Isis with the crescent on her head, followed by a memory of seeing the bright crescent moon attached to the Earth-lit dark moon out my front door. I had no idea what the crescent moon meant for me, though I knew it had symbolized many things throughout history: femininity, Mary the mother of Jesus, the Egyptian goddess Isis, our shadow side, a return from the underworld. The crescent moon was the most pervasive single symbol in the session.

A fairy popped into my mind's eye. I said aloud, "This fairy image just came to me, and it's important that I learn if my mother had planned to write the letters before she entered the Earth plane. I am addressing my question to the Council of Elders and my mother—whomever wishes to give me answers."

I was peering into the crystal ball on the marble Council Table, hoping to see an answer. Was Louise under the influence of a fairy when she wrote the letters? Was she in a trance? Did the spirit of Fairy Queen Thimble Bee write automatically through Louise's pen? I hoped to discover if the fairy episode of my youth had been more than a fluke. I wanted to know if my mother had received supernatural help.

In my mind, I heard, "Of course she had help! Of course she had help!" But I didn't receive further explanation. My question still hung in the air. I wanted to know whether her writing the letters and my receiving and believing in the fairies had been "just a simple silly thing," or "a big important thing" in our lives. Then I heard, "There are no simple silly things. You set up your own system of symbols and they became unique for you, and they played out and manifested into whatever images you wanted to create with them."

Perhaps I needed to use the fairy as a symbol as a part of my life plan. This symbol had entered my consciousness as a ten-year-old child, representing the unseen spiritual world, especially the unseen natural world. As a result of that original symbol, I viewed the planet, universe, and all supposedly inanimate objects as sentient, conscious, and aware. And yet I still wanted to know if the fairy was also in my mother's life plan, especially whether she'd had supernatural assistance in writing the letters. The answer to that question was still unresolved.

Ms. Smithson said it was now time to travel to the place of Life Selection. In *Journey of Souls*, Dr. Newton said that before coming to the Earth plane, all souls go to the place of Life Selection and choose the one life they want to tackle from among a number of possibilities. Each has its challenges. Some may choose a difficult life in order to grow faster spiritually, while others may choose an easy life because they want to progress at a slower pace. Life choice has a lot to do with the soul's level of development. He also said that life choice is done with a lot of help from spiritual counselors. It is not done lightly. In viewing the possible lives, souls are not shown events too far into the future, because the farther they get away from the present, the higher the incidence of possible alternative realities.

Ms. Smithson asked if I saw a Life Selection room. I didn't yet, but with the help of my guide, the monk, we fetched the Wizard's crystal ball. We brought the ball to a place in the mountains. I knew that I could expand the ball to any size I wanted, so I envisioned it to be thirty feet in diameter. I stepped inside and knew that I would be able to view holographic scenes of a future life. Ms. Smithson asked me whether I could see a number of choices. Within the giant ball, I saw a big number 3. "That's about average," Ms. Smithson said. She wanted me to check out each of the options.

"How do I begin?" I asked.

She told me that before I had chosen the body of Maria, I had been shown two other possible bodies. She wanted me to describe one of those bodies.

I saw a child of about three or four years old in a jester costume. The child was doing back flips. I doubted that this was correct, but Ms. Smithson assured me that I was doing fine. She asked whether the child was male or female.

"Definitely female," I told her. "A happy, active, athletic girl."

Then I saw a young woman on a tightrope using a balancing pole. Next I saw her in a trapeze act. In this life, I lived and worked in a traveling circus with lions and elephants, the whole gypsy life.

Ms. Smithson asked if that life was attractive to me. I said it was. She asked why I chose otherwise. My first thought was that I might have died too young. I imagined a "big splat," a fall. However, I would have been using my physical skills to learn balance—literally. Trying to stay in balance was a big part of my current life, only in a different way. I had to juggle and balance all the time. So this circus life would have given me plenty of opportunity to learn physical balancing skills.

"So why did you ultimately reject it?"

"I would have enjoyed the athletics and association with circus animals. But that life would have had a dark side, for circus animals do not lead a happy existence, and I could not have stood their despair," I told her.

Ms. Smithson guided me to look at the second life possibility. A picture of that life came to me quickly. In the second life, I was a man, a climber, a mountaineer in his youth. Again it was very physical. He went to the School of Mines in Colorado, and became a geological engineer. The early part of his life would have been great. In the middle part of this life, he was into the engineering, requiring much mental involvement. I saw electronic gear and scientific instruments. But then, something was lost. I witnessed an overabundance of the masculine, of the rational, and a loss of the spiritual. I could have been very successful doing the male thing again, with books and computers. It seemed like that could have been the 20th century success story, but it wouldn't have been spiritually fulfilling. His later years were dimmed with regret and longing for his youth as a free spirit.

And now for the third life choice, the one I ultimately chose and was presently living. In this vision, I was only shown the early part of my life, the part that defined Louise's significance as my mother. I saw two images, like calendar pictures. One was a mother bending over a small child, an ethereal glow lighting up the background. The second was a teenage girl bending over a circle of fairies. Again the scene was filled with light. (I later identified the second image as the painting "Midsummer Eve" by Edward Robert Hughes). I believed I was seeing the Mother and the Magical Child archetypes. I perceived that it was my mother's intention to raise me as her magical child, not a literal magical child, but an archetypal one—a child who sees sacred beauty in all things and believes that everything is possible.

Louise's heritage had been German and she'd been brought up on old German folk tales, including the legacy of fairy tales handed down through the generations. In ancient times, people had been able to see the little people, and these experiences had been passed down to become folk tales and myths. My mother had believed that earth spirits were real and she had handed this belief to me as her gift. Once more I was moved to tears, as I felt my mother's love and acknowledged the gift she gave me. Early on, Louise had planted the seeds of mystical belief in me, and even though we later went through a swirl of teenage dramas, the seeds had sprouted and grown.

The answer to my ultimate question (Did my mother receive supernatural help in writing the fairy letters?) was partially answered. Yes, she received help from her soul. Writing the letters was in her soul's plan. But I still had not received a definitive answer to another question: Was a real fairy somehow involved in this drama?

Ms. Smithson took me back to the Council of Elders, where I could ask more questions. I wanted to know whether there was anything my Council or Louise needed me to know that should be included in the book I was writing, *I'll Be There to Write the Story.*

The answer grew out of the center of the Council Table: a tree! As I watched, it grew taller and taller, and branched outward with countless leaves. It thrived. Louise's poem "Eden's Tree," was about how war had burned and destroyed the Tree of Life in the Garden of Eden, all except for one leaf. The message in her poem was that as long as there is one leaf left on the tree, life will go on. You can't kill it. The tree growing out of the Council table was vitally green and fully leafed out. A single, beautiful, golden apple hung from one of its branches. It was Eden's Tree—The Tree of Life. Louise's biblical symbolism was coming through. I got the message: Life *will* go on and will bear fruit—a message of hope. Did it mean that humankind would be given a second chance? I believed so.

Later, I went home and asked my helpers to draw what I had seen on the Council table. The picture did not mirror what I had seen under hypnosis. In my vision, thick leaves had covered the branches. My hand drew what it wanted—a scrawny tree with buds . . . and the apple.

*Tree of Life that grew out of the Council Table.*

After four hours in Ms. Smithson's office, under hypnosis for at least three of those hours, I was so spacey that I couldn't have driven a car safely, much less recalled the details of the session. Jim was waiting for me downstairs in the car. I drank a quart of water and tried to ground myself. We drove to dinner and then spent the night in Denver. Weeks later, when I had time to listen to and transcribe the CDs, I heard the answers I was seeking. The CDs brought everything back to me. While the answers weren't exhaustive, the session was still amazing and satisfying—an experience of a lifetime.

I thought the book was finished. I had written the final chapter about my LBL session and I was ready to send out review copies when my cousin, DeDe, called to say she had heard from my mother, and Louise had a message for me.

DeDe had attended a workshop given by a group leader who could see and hear those on the Other Side. She offered to bring messages to each participant. DeDe asked about my book, which was nearing completion. Louise told her, through the workshop leader, that the book was coming along well. However, Maria needed to find an agent right away. Waiting until later might be too late. My heart sank and my head ached with this news, for I had decided to self-publish the book. I wasn't looking for an agent.

In hopes of learning what Louise really thought I should do, I set up an appointment with Stacey, one of the women who had channeled Louise for two of the book's chapters. I wanted to know if Louise had insider information from the Other Side that I needed to hear. Was self-publishing the wrong course? Did the book's success hang on my finding an agent to represent it?

Armed with my tape recorder, I met Stacey on September 23, 2008. I asked her, "If my mother told me to find an agent, then shouldn't I do that? Doesn't she know more than I about such things?"

Through Stacey, Louise said that her message had been misinterpreted by the workshop leader. Louise was still very interested in the progress of the book, and from her perspective, I was doing fine with the writing. The book was now ready for the next step—preparing it for publication. Louise thought that I needed to find someone to help me to do that. She didn't mean I needed a book agent, but someone to help me with the publishing process.

I said, "Mom, when I publish this book, no matter which avenue I choose to take, there will be people to help me."

The word "agent" was the only word Louise knew to transmit to the person speaking to my cousin. Once we had straightened out that miscommunication, the knot in my stomach relaxed. Stacey said that Louise hadn't intended to derail me, and that all she was trying to tell me was that I needed to find assistance to keep the book moving forward. My head cleared, and I knew what to do next.

I turned off the tape recorder, thinking the session with Stacey was over. But she wasn't finished. She invited me to pull one or more cards from her deck of Doreen Virtue's *Healing with the Angels Oracle Cards*. I felt guided to select three cards. When I turned them over, they were Power, New Beginnings and Divine Timing—cards that caused both of us to burst out laughing. They seemed to confirm that I was on the right track. Once again, I thought the session was over, and I reached for my checkbook to pay her.

Stacey picked up another card deck, *The Faeries' Oracle*, written and illustrated by Brian Froud, who is famous for his fairy paintings. He could see and communicate directly with fairies and very few appear as cutsey Tinker-Bell types in his pictures. Many are quirky, weird, gnome-like characters and he depicts some as clusters of light. *The Faeries' Oracle* was Stacey's favorite deck of fairy cards. She said that Froud painted his fairies the way she, herself, saw them.

The end card caught my attention, the one on the far left of the deck that she had fanned out in front of me. I drew it slowly and turned it over. It was blank. Stacey's eyes widened and she said, "That is a great card. It's from your own fairy—your own magic. It is yours to decide what it means."

I knew this card stood for Fairy Queen Thimble Bee.

"Stacey," I said, "I can't believe this is happening. I've never told you anything about the fairy letters. This is another whole piece to my book that you know nothing about."

In ten minutes, I told her the story, including the fact that I still possessed the box of letters from Queen Thimble Bee. As I spoke, Stacey began receiving images of the woods fairy and my childhood in those Tennessee woods. She said that my mother had indeed channeled a real fairy.

"We will have to schedule another session about the fairies," I said, and packed up my bags. I left, knowing there would be one more channeling with her.

One week later, I was back in Stacey's living room. This time I had brought not only my tape recorder, but my box containing all the fairy letters from the 1950s. I handed her a letter. Stacey held it and said she could feel my mother's energy all over the paper. I read letter after letter aloud to Stacey and then gave each one to her. The letters still contained Louise's energy and held the real story of the fairy episode. As the letters stacked up in her hands, Stacey relayed the story she saw unfolding.

It had all begun when I was ten and had become aware of the existence of fairies through books, movies and my neighborhood friend.

"That was Phyllis from up the street," I said. "We talked a lot about fairies and visualized ourselves shrinking down to six inches high. I shared with my mother what we were up to."

Stacey said, "Your mother was in touch with nature spirits when she was a little girl and she felt a strong urge to connect with you in that way, so she was inspired to write the first letter."

"On aluminum foil," I added. "That was Christmas of 1954. I wrote back to the fairy that night and left the letter on my windowsill. The fairy answered my letters for three years."

Stacey said that Louise had gone into an altered state when she had written those letters, just as she had done when she had written a lot of her poetry.

Mom had, indeed, claimed that her muse would visit her when she wrote poetry. In fact, she would become annoyed if her muse awoke her at 3:00 a.m. to write a poem. Some of her best poetry had come in the middle of the night.

"When the spirit moved her, she wrote them around midnight on your dining room table," Stacey said. "It is true that she was under the spell of the fairy kingdom when she wrote."

Stacey could sense my mother's little girl energy still present in the letters, which meant that my mother had allowed her inner child to come out and play when she wrote, augmenting her creativity and opening her to the fairy realm. Love still radiated from the letters, as did tremendous gift energy, Stacey said. Louise's intention, especially as time went on, was to gift me with the belief and knowledge of the unseen kingdoms. She had believed in the unseen kingdoms but had been unable to express her knowledge in any other way.

"Your mother had no one to talk to about her beliefs," Stacey said. "Nor did she feel as though she could let loose this side of herself, the little girl side. As your mother, she behaved like all mothers of her generation. She thought she had to instruct you and be the authoritarian mother. She couldn't play with you. So she reached you on the child level through the fairy letters. It was a two-way street, though, because she loved to participate in this little drama as much as you did."

As a child and teenager, I told Stacey, I believed wholeheartedly that the letters were from a fairy named Queen Thimble Bee. In my twenties, I admitted that some of the handwriting looked like my mother's, but I explained that as coincidence. When I reached my thirties, I allowed doubt to slip in but still wanted to believe.

When I reached my forties, I conceded that my mother had written the letters but wanted to believe that a fairy had helped her write them.

"Your mother thought she was channeling just one fairy but in truth, I see several woods fairies, tiny and almost transparent, glowing with different colors—blues, greens, and purples. Their substance was woven of light and movement. They didn't wear clothes and they were more female looking than male, although they were very balanced. While they were tiny little beings, they held the rhythms of the universe. Those fairies knew how everything in nature worked."

When I asked for more details about the real fairies who were behind the letters, Stacey said there were five or six, but one might have been the spokesperson. They told my mother where they lived in the woods and how they traveled. One letter I read to Stacey said fairies were creatures of light—sunlight, starlight, flower light, moonlight—every color of light. Another talked about the fairy seasons: awakening (spring), flowering (summer), bearing (autumn), and sleeping (winter).

When I read this letter to Stacey, she said, "As soon as you started saying that, I was told it's real. Your mother wasn't making that up."

Thanks to my session with Stacey, I discovered that both my mother and I had existed on two levels during my childhood. On one, we played our roles as mother and daughter. On the other, we became magical children. Louise expressed her creative, little girl side through the letters. She lit up with glee when I showed her each letter. Her reaction was genuine. She wasn't play-acting. She was right there with me.

Stacey said it helped that my mother's bloodline was German. Much of what she had channeled from the fairies was ancient, handed down in myth and fairy tales from her ancestors. It was myth, but also real. The two had become blurred over the centuries, but my mother had known, deep within her, that the fairies were real. In one of the letters, Thimble Bee told me that my great, great, great grandfather had come from Germany, where people often saw nature spirits.

Stacey said that a subtle underlying frustration emanated from the letters—a frustration about not being able to express her little girl self in the world. She had no other place in her life to share it, no woman friend with whom she could connect on that level. That was another reason why Louise wanted me to write the book—so she could at last show this side of herself.

I was surprised to hear this, but acknowledged that my mother's only public outlet for her inner child had been in the context of her poetry. She had written a few fanciful poems, and those were my favorites. In particular, "The Tale of the House that Faded Away," had won a contest, but was never published. The letters, shining with my mother's very heart and soul, weren't full of logic, weren't cerebral. They were completely free-flowing soul. That's what Louise had wanted to give to me—something she could not express to the outside world. While holding them, Stacey perceived the tremendous gift energy still flowing through them.

For almost forty years, I had turned to the fairy letters, reading and rereading them for comfort. At last I knew why. They contained the strong love energy flowing from my mother. As her daughter, I felt that her love was cloaked with rules and lessons. I refused to connect with her on that level. When she wrote as Fairy Queen Thimble Bee, her love was pure and amplified with fairy energy. Besides, each letter was filled with loving words from the fairy. I needed to know that I was loved back then, because love just wasn't expressed. The love energy from my mother and the fairies permeated those letters, and I drew on that love for decades.

I didn't want to let the magic go, even up to the day of my mother's death. Stacey said she was being told that the magic was real when I was a child, and it still was. In our contemporary culture, however, most belief in fairies and nature spirits had been lost and forgotten. At one time, the ancient knowledge was every-where—the Native Americans had it, the Mayans, the Incans and Aborigines. Some people were now working to rekindle that magic. Apparently, the fairies that Stacey was communicating with thought I was one of those helping to keep the magic alive.

The fairies' last words to me, through Stacey, were these: "Congratulations on holding a piece of this wisdom safe and not letting it get lost."

I packed up my tape recorder and gave Stacey a hug. I asked her if she could draw me a picture of one of my woods fairies as she had seen it during our session. She said she would do that for me.

*Stacey Joslin's drawing of Maria's Tennessee woods fairy.*

For more than fifty years, I had sought the true source of those magical fairy letters that had captivated me in my childhood. I received twenty-six letters and a handful of fairy gifts when I was ten, eleven, and twelve. The mystery was finally solved. While my mother had held the pen, not just one, but half a dozen woods fairies had served as her muses deep in the night and had inspired her to write those letters to me. My session with Stacey unveiled this scene with living vibrancy and also revealed that Louise had needed this experience as much as me. Her inner child awoke and danced with the fairies and let abundant love flow to me, showing that the eternal gift of life and love flowed—and continues to flow—in both directions.

# Afterword

It never occurred to me when I began writing chapters over ten years ago that this book adventure would become a joint project to be completed across the veil, with me writing at my computer in three-dimensional reality and Louise working in another dimension to assist me. I never thought it possible that this book would actually come to life. But here it is, thanks to all my friends and helpers, seen and unseen.

In honor of Louise, my co-author, who has stuck with me through the whole process and still comes close when I need her to answer a quick question, I'll leave you with her poem that inspired the title of this book.

# A Writer's Last Words

Bury me with a pencil in my hand,
For I would wake up—writing.
When Gabriel's trumpet blows and his brass bands
Begin trumpeting, I'll be there
In a front-row stand to write the story.

After the long sleep, my tired brain rested,
Think how many stored up words
I would have waiting, untried, untested;
No time for scanning or rhyme:
Pour, ecstatic flood, matching the glory!

In a channeling with Heiderose, I asked Tsen Tsing, the ancient Chinese master, whether Louise was still writing any poetry on the Other Side.

"Yes," he said. "She's doing some of that. It's a creation and is done very quickly."

# Notes and References

What follows is an annotated list of resources I used to write this story. These notes refer to quotes, websites, and print sources of my research or inspiration. I refer to them by chapter and page where they appear in the book. Additional sources may be found in the Other Sources section.

## Chapter 2: The Dream, the Vision and the Bird Call

Page 33: *I have been alone all day . . .*

Personal essay by Louise Weber, entitled "The Vision, the Bird Call and the Dream," written for Maria Weber. Undated. Contained in Louise's notebook among Maria Weber's personal effects.

## Chapter 3: Bringing Down the House

Page 41: *I wondered if she suffered from the writing disease, hypergraphia . . .*

Alice W. Flaherty, *The Midnight Disease: The Drive to Write, Writer's Block and the Creative Brain,* (Houghton Mifflin, 2004). Hypergraphia is the medical term for an overpowering desire to write. Flaherty, a leading neurologist at a major research hospital, writes from personal experience as well as the front lines of brain research. She has studied the neurology of writers, poets and other creative types and defines the lines between creativity and psychosis. She identifies the part of the brain she believes is "the God Module," a module that gives life meaning, whether religious or artistic. According to Flaherty, it is the seat of mystical and religious experience.

Page 42: *December 7, 1941 . . .*

Journal of William E. Weber and Louise E. Weber, September 29, 1938–February 23, 1952. It remains among Maria Weber's personal effects.

Page 51: *How does one summarize a life . . .*

Louise Weber's letter to her nursing class of 1934, written in 1984, and placed in a booklet with other nurses' letters. It remains among Maria Weber's personal papers.

Page 58: *It was snowing quite hard . . .*
    Mary Gallagher, personal letter to Maria Weber, October 19, 1999.

Page 62: *Carol had performed several sessions of Therapeutic Touch . . .*
    Therapeutic Touch is a form of hands-on therapy that was drawn from ancient healing practices. A Therapeutic Touch practitioner balances and promotes the flow of energy in another person. Research as shown that Therapeutic Touch reduces pain, improves wound healing, aids relaxation, and eases the dying process. It is taught in colleges around the world and has become a widely accepted alternative therapy in hospitals and other health agencies. Website: www.therapeutictouch.org.

Page 64: *Later, Sue wrote me a card that said, "As I meditated on Monday night . . .*
    Sue Elliott, personal letter to Maria Weber, April 17, 1997.

Page 69: *Left alone in the worst agony, wanting to turn to someone, I find that you are . . .*
    Letters from Bonny von der Meer in Holland to Louise Weber during 1939 and 1941. Among Maria Weber's personal papers.

## Chapter 4: The Healing Legacy

Page 86: *In her introduction, editor Lyn Lifshin writes that many women grapple . . .*
    Lyn Lifshin, editor, *Tangled Vines*, (Harcourt Brace & Company, 1992), pp. xii–xiii.

## Chapter 5: The Art of Communication

Page 96: Jane Roberts, writer of *The Seth Material* and *Seth Speaks*, typed a manuscript . . .
    Arthur Hastings, *With the Tongues of Men and Angels*, (Holt, Rinehart and Winston, Inc., 1991), p. 74.

Page 97: *Her first experience with automatic typing happened . . .*
    Susy Smith, *The Afterlife Codes: Searching for Evidence of the Survival of the Soul*, (Hampton Roads Publishing Co., Inc., 2000), p. 111.

Page 99: *The Medicine Cards said that the totem animal Raven gives us the courage . . .*

Jamie Sams, and David Carson, *Medicine Cards: The Discovery of Power Through the Ways of Animals,* (Bear & Company, 1988), p. 101.

Page 100: *For six months, I read books by Jung—just enough to be dangerous.*

Two excellent books on Jung for the beginner: C.G. Jung, ed., and authored by C.G. Jung, M.L von Franz, Joseph Henderson, Jolanda Jacobi, and Aniela Jaffé, *Man and His Symbols,* (Doubleday, 1972).

Vivianne Crowley, *Jung: A Journey of Transformation,* (Quest Books: Theosophical Publishing House, 1999).

Page 101: *I tracked down the essay, read it, and concluded that her readings in Jung had inspired . . .*

Josef Goldbrunner, *Individuation: A Study of the Depth Psychology of Carl Gustav Jung,* (University of Notre Dame Press, 1964).

Page 105: *"Well of course they're coming from your subconscious," she said . . .*

Reading with Sheryl Watson, June 6, 2004.

Page 106: *"Nothing can come near me or influence me that does not come from God in love . . ."*

Susy Smith, *The Afterlife Codes,* (Hampton Roads Publishing Company, 2000), p. 164.

Page 106: *Sheryl said, "You can call in the protection of Archangel Michael . . ."*

Reading with Sheryl Watson, June 5, 2004.

Page 107: *Virtue characterizes Archangel Michael as a leader among archangels . . .*

Doreen Virtue, *Archangels & Ascended Masters: A Guide to Working and Healing with Divinities and Deities,* (Hay House, Inc., 2003), p. 33.

Page 107: *He believed that the unconscious could create "autonomous complexes" . . .*

Arthur Hastings, *With the Tongues of Men and Angels: A Study of Channeling,* (Holt, Rinehart and Winston, Inc., 1991), pp. 174–175.

Page 107: *For example, a wise figure named Philemon showed up in Jung's mind . . .*

Vivianne Crowley, *Jung: A Journey of Transformation: Exploring his life and experiencing his ideas,* (Quest Books: Theosophical Publishing House, 1999), p. 117.

Page 107: *Napoleon Hill, who wrote* Think and Grow Rich, *created his own council of advisors . . .*

Arthur Hastings, *With the Tongues of Men and Angels: A Study of Channeling,* (Holt, Rinehart and Winston, Inc., 1991), pp. 115–116.

**Chapter 6: Uncharted Country**

Page 110: *In her first book,* Behaving As If the God in All Life Mattered, *she describes . . .*

Machaelle Small Wright, *Behaving As If the God in All Life Mattered,* (Perelandra, Ltd, 1997).

Page 121: *Brazilian medium, Luiz Gasparetto, for example, drew rapidly, creating some . . .*

Arthur Hastings, *With the Tongues of Men and Angels: A Study of Channeling,* (Holt, Rinehart and Winston, Inc., 1991), p. 20.

Page 121: *I shouted "Eureka!" when I found an article in* Artnews *magazine, about the "American Action Painters," . . .*

Barbara A. MacAdam, "Not a Picture but an Event," *Artnews,* (November, 2007), p. 176.

Page 122: *Then I read Pollack's own words, in which he said . . .*

A. Jaffe, "Symbolism in the Visual Arts," in C.G. Jung and others, *Man and His Symbols,* (Doubleday, 1964), p. 464.

Page 122: *In his artist statement, he said that to initiate a painting, he climbed a mountain peak . . .*

Freydoon Rassouli's website: www.rassouli.com.

Page 127: *Dr. Jane Greer was a psychotherapist practicing in New York City.*

Dr. Jane Greer, *The Afterlife Connection: A Therapist Reveals How to Communicate with Departed Loved Ones,* (St. Martin's Press, 2003).

Page 128: *When Edgar Mitchell became an astronaut and went to the moon* . . .

The Institute of Noetic Science website: www.noetic.org. See this website for information about why Edgar Mitchell founded IONS.

Page 128: *During his research, Rolfs even discovered* . . .

Arthur Hastings, *With the Tongues of Men and Angels*, (Holt, Rinehart and Winston, Inc., 1991), p. ix.

## Chapter 7: The Blast

Page 140: *According to Zecharia Sitchin, author of* The Wars of Gods and Men,. . .

Zecharia Sitchin, *The Wars of Gods and Men*, (Avon Books, 1985), pp. 314–315.

Eminent scholar of ancient Sumerian and Biblical history, Zecharia Sitchin, wrote about Abraham as he looked across the plains toward Sodom and Gomorrah in the year 2024 BC, and saw smoke rising from the earth. Sitchin claimed that Abraham was witnessing "the destruction of a fertile and populated plain by atomic weapons."

## Chapter 8: Side Trips to Non-ordinary Reality

Page 145: *With a mixture of anticipation and trepidation, I set out on a May morning* . . .

For those who might be interested in exploring shamanism, a beginning weekend workshop through the Foundation for Shamanic Studies is recommended. Workshops are offered all over the world. See website: www.shamanism.org.

Page 147: *Common to most shamanic traditions was the real estate: the Lower World, the Middle World, and the Upper World, which were collectively known as non-ordinary reality.*

Chapter Two, "The Three Worlds," Sandra Ingerman, *Shamanic Journeying: A Beginner's Guide*, (Sounds True, Inc., 2004), p. 13-17."

Page 148: *In the 1800s, this canyon was used by the Penitentes—a Catholic brotherhood known for their self-flagellation rituals.*

Christopher O'Brien, *Enter the Valley: UFOs, Religious Miracles,*

*Cattle Mutilations, and Other Unexplained Phenomena in the San Luis Valley,* (St. Martin's Paperbacks, 1999), pp. 244–249.

Page 156: *According to Animal-Speak, the mountain lion totem meant coming into your own power.*

Ted Andrews, *Animal-Speak: The Spiritual & Magical Powers of Creatures Great & Small,* (Llewellyn Publications, 1998), p. 259.

## Chapter 9: Eden's Tree

Page 161: *I want to emphasize that I trusted the three women I picked to channel for me.*

Maria believes it's important to use your discretion when finding a person to communicate with beings in the nonphysical planes on your behalf. Learn the person's credentials, obtain recommendations, and use your own gut feeling. A reputable channel needs to be acting in integrity and for the highest and best purpose.

Page 162: *Sheryl has been a professional medium and a clairvoyant channel for many years.*

Sheryl Watson has studied, practiced and taught palmistry, psychic development, numerology, Tarot, past life regression, and ascension techniques. She is a certified facilitator of the Melchizedek Method. Sheryl also works with Master Lanto, Lord of the Second Ray of Wisdom and Illumination. In Maria's taped interview with Sheryl Watson, June 6, 2004, Watson explained that Lanto was of ancient Chinese origin. Some people believe he was Confucious's teacher. Watson says that when he comes to her, she sees him in the beautiful golden robes of an emperor, but that he speaks with humility. She says a quiet power of humility is indicative of a great master, stemming from eons of love.

Page 162: *Metatron lived on earth as a human . . .*

Doreen Virtue, *Archangels and Ascended Masters,* (Hay House, Inc., 2004), p. 30.

Some scholars believe that Metatron was once human before being transformed into an archangel of the highest order. This myth holds that he was the prophet and scribe Enoch of the Old Testament, who "walked with God." In Virtue's book, Metatron is characterized as the archangel who works tirelessly to help Earth's inhabitants. He can sympathize with humanity more than any of the other angels because he lived one human life. Curiously, he is the archangel one can call upon for issues about writing, because in his earthly life, he served as a scribe.

Page 162: *I met Stacey at a metaphysical fair in a nearby town . . .*

Stacey Joslin is certified in Multi-dimensional Therapy from the Multi-dimensional Living Institute in Loveland, Colorado. She is a certified Angel Practitioner through Charles Virtue, the son of angel author Doreen Virtue. Since 2002, she has worked with a Navajo medicine man and medicine woman in the Navajo Nation, Arizona and New Mexico.

Page 163: *She described herself as a messenger of hope and prophecy who channels the angelic realm and the ascended masters.*

Doreen Virtue, in her book *Archangels & Ascended Masters: A Guide to Working and Healing with Divinities and Deities,* (Hay House, 2004), p. xv, defines an ascended master as a spiritually enlightened being, once mortal, now existing in a nonphysical dimension, who attends to the spiritual needs and development of humans. Various spiritual leaders such as Jesus, Moses, Buddha, the Prophet Mohammed, the Virgin Mary, Kuan Yin, and Kuthumi, from all races, cultures and civilizations, take their place among those considered to be ascended masters.

Heiderose Spang-Martindell can be reached through www.DivinePotentialMinistry.com.

Page 165: *In his emphatic masculine voice, he told me that Earth is now in a period of time called The Quickening.*

In metaphysical circles, The Quickening is called the "ascension process." This is about raising consciousness more quickly than normal, not being lifted off the planet by a space ship or ascending into heaven on a cloud. Many people find the process uncomfortable physically, mentally, and emotionally. Symptoms can include inertia, bitchiness, forgetfulness, water retention, fatigue, spaciness, achiness, and so on. On the other hand, there can be sensations of mental clarity, peacefulness and knowing that all is well. It's a time when there is chaos in the world, such as war, financial meltdown, unusual weather patterns, and earth changes. Some say the period will last for a couple of decades and that it began around the year 2000. Karen Bishop, author of *The Ascension Primer* (an e-book, available from Booklocker.com, 2006), believes that the ascension process will result in the creation of a much more highly evolved planet and much more highly evolved humans. Also see Karen Bishop's website, www.emergingearthangels.com, for bi-weekly updates about what is happening on the planet energetically.

Page 167: *Those movies are projected on the Field-of-Possibilities Screen.*
    The Field-of-Possibilities Screen sounds similar to the Life Books Library or Akashic Record noted in Dr. Michael Newton's book, *Destiny of Souls: New Case Studies of Life Between Lives*, (Llewellyn Publications, 2006). According to Dr. Newton, when souls first arrive on the Other Side, they often go to the research library in order to study their past lives. "Possibilities of future events can also be seen with the help of scribes. The word 'Akasha' essentially means the essence of all universal memory that is recording every energy vibration of existence, rather like an audio/visual magnetic tape" (Newton, p. 152).

Page 171: *Libby and I sat at the dining room table on New Year's morning, drank coffee, and silently pulled our angel cards with healing messages.*
    Doreen Virtue, *Healing with the Angels Oracle Cards*, (Hay House, 2006), book and 44-card deck. By asking and focusing on a question, and then pulling a card, the Law of Attraction causes the seeker to pull a card that perfectly applies to the current situation. Doreen Virtue, a psychotherapist, has worked with the angelic realm for many years.

Page 171: *Next we moved to the runes.*
    Runes are an ancient Viking divination tool. Each rune is a letter of an ancient alphabet. The runes are to be used as an oracle—mirroring the inner teacher or God within—rather than to tell the future or tell the seeker what to do. A seeker can pull a single rune or lay out spreads for different purposes.

Page 171: *Its name was Raido and it meant, "Journey."*
    Ralph Blum, *The Book of Runes: A Handbook for the Use of an Ancient Oracle: The Viking Runes*, (St. Martin's Press, 1987), p. 123.

Page 173: *I read Janet Catherine Berlo's* Quilting Lessons—*the story of how the author overcame her own writer's block through quilting like a maniac.*

Janet Catherine Berlo, *Quilting Lessons: Notes from the Scrap Bag of a Writer and Quilter,* (University of Nebraska Press, 2001).

## Chapter 10: Healing the Matriarchal Lineage

Page 182: *Tsen Tsing said Louise was held in a cocoon of light for several days . . .*

Time has no meaning in the spirit world, according to Dr. Michael Newton, author of *Destiny of Souls,* (Llewellyn Publications, 2000). All time on the Other Side is in the present. Linear time does not exist. When Tsen Tsing says that Louise was held in a cocoon of light for several days, he was referencing a span of Earth time.

Page 184: *. . . Through family constellation work, DeDe learned that our Granny (Margaret Ernst) might have married our grandfather (Ammon) on the rebound . . .*

Family constellation work is a kind of therapy that heals unconscious, yet influential, family discord. Conflicts that happened to dead relatives can entangle a person in a fate that belongs to an ancestor two, three, or even more generations back. In one-day workshops, group members stand in as representatives in each other's families. The commonality of the human experience allows participants to expand in the presence of each person's individual work. Website: www.systemicfamilysolutions.com.

Page 186: *For the first time, Mom was acknowledging . . .*

After several scientific studies, Dr. Frederic Luskin detailed the effects of forgiveness in his book, *Forgive for Good.* The studies bore out the fact that forgiving the hurts and grudges of our lives allows us to feel more hopeful, spiritually connected, and less depressed. These changes improve our health and give us more energy. *Forgive for Good: A Proven Prescription for Health and Happiness,* (HarperCollins, 2002), p. 88.

## Chapter 11: Revelation

Page 196: *I had never heard of Life Between Lives (LBL) sessions until I read Dr. Michael Newton's book,* Journey of Souls.

Dr. Michael Newton, *Journey of Souls: Case Studies of Life Between Lives* (Llewellyn Publications, 1994). Dr. Michael Newton is the founder of The Newton Institute for Life Between Lives Hypnotherapy. He holds a doctorate in Counseling Psychology, is a certified Master Hypnotherapist, and is a member of the American Counseling Association. He has been on the faculty of higher education institutions as a teacher and counselor, while also in active private practice in Los Angeles. He is now retired from active clinical practice and devotes his time to lecturing and training. He has written two bestselling books about his years of soul memory research: *Journey of Souls* and *Destiny of Souls*. These books have been translated into fifteen languages.

In *Journey of Souls*, Newton describes how he started doing spiritual regressions. In the early years, he was practicing traditional psychotherapy and was using age regression techniques to root out the origins of childhood traumas. He wasn't interested in metaphysics or reincarnation in particular. In fact, he was skeptical about such things. With encouragement from his clients, he regressed them farther back than this lifetime, and found that many health and psychological issues would resolve, given knowledge of past life events. One day a client regressed into a time between her past life and her current life. She called this place her permanent home. Newton knew he had stumbled on a way to access the spirit world. This incident began a journey of over thirty years and thousands of spiritual regressions. Newton now trains other advanced hypnotherapists in these techniques through The Newton Institute. A person does not have to believe in reincarnation to receive soul-level information. Regardless of a person's belief system or religious persuasion, the unconscious memories will probably reveal a spirit world consistent with the experiences from everyone who has gone through past life regression.

Page 199: *In* Journey of Souls, *Dr. Newton said that, after death, our souls congregate into cluster groups.*

Dr. Michael Newton, *Journey of Souls: Case Studies of Life Between Lives.* (Llewellyn Publications, 1994), p. 87.

Page 200: *According to Dr. Newton, members of a soul group are united for all of eternity.*

Dr. Michael Newton, *Journey of Souls: Case Studies of Life Between Lives,* (Llewellyn Publications, 1994), p. 88.

Page 201: *After meeting my soul group, Ms. Smithson asked if I wanted to see my Council of Elders.*

Dr. Michael Newton, *Destiny of Souls: New Case Studies of Life Between Lives*, (Llewellyn Publications, 2000), p. 201.

Page 206: *In* Journey of Souls, *Dr. Newton said that before coming to the Earth plane, all souls go to the place of Life Selection and choose the one they want to tackle from among a number of possibilities.*

Dr. Michael Newton, *Journey of Souls: Case Studies of Life Between Lives*, (Llewellyn Publications, 1994), pp. 201–220.

Page 208: *I perceived that it was my mother's intention to raise me as her magical child, not a literal magical child, but an archetypal one—a child who sees sacred beauty in all things and believes that everything is possible.*

Dr. Carolyn Myss, medical intuitive and author of bestselling books including, *Anatomy of the Spirit* and *Sacred Contracts*, has identified over eighty archetypes (psychological patterns that are common to all of humanity, such as Mother, Child, and so on). She says that we all carry the Child archetype within us and that there are a number of different types of Child: Divine, Eternal, Magical, Nature, Orphan and Wounded. Each has its own characteristics of light and dark attributes. To learn about Myss's take on archetypes, refer to her book, *Sacred Contracts: Awakening your Divine Potential*, Random House, 2001, or visit her website: www.myss.com.

Page 212: *Stacey picked up another card deck,* The Faeries' Oracle, *written and illustrated by Brian Froud.*

Brian Froud, *The Faeries' Oracle*, (Simon and Schuster, 2000). For books and additional information see www.worldoffroud.com.

# WORKBOOK

## Exercises, Tips, and Resources

# Workbook Contents

# ~ Section 1 ~
## Loose Ends

Come and walk with me, side by side, chapter by chapter. Although the story within these pages belongs to me, yours is just as important. If you'd like to do more than read the story—if you'd like to start a journey of your own—here is where you can begin. Maybe you have a friend or two who would like to join you—all the better. But if you are alone, that's fine too.

In my everyday life, I'm part of a writing group that meets every Monday. Sometimes all of us are present, and other times only three of us can show up because of schedule conflicts or the weather. We have learned that writing, and then reading aloud, is a healing force. We write not to compete, but to clear the fuzz out of our brains. When we're finished writing on a topic, each of us reads aloud what we've written. We don't comment or critique. We write about our inner feelings, and we write silly things that make us laugh. Sometimes we need a box of tissues on the table, because reading aloud can evoke emotions we didn't realize were there. While the act of writing what's inside of us can be very freeing, saying aloud what we've written to a silent witness is healing.

If others join you, all must be 100% trustworthy. Cardinal Rule: confidentiality. If you share your writing with another person and that person shares hers with you, you never, never take that information beyond the two of you, or beyond the circle.

The writing exercises were inspired by my experience leading our writing group. (Each member in our group takes turns leading). Every time I lead, I invent a slate of topics—and I've done that for you, using topics that reflect the themes in this book. If you and I were writing together at this moment, I would set a timer for ten minutes, read the topic aloud, and we would both begin to write. We wouldn't stop to reword a sentence that sounded awkward. We wouldn't stop and ponder what the next sentence should be. We would write, write, write. If our minds went blank, we would copy the previous phrase over and over until the juice started flowing again. That's the kind of writing I want you to do. There are no right or wrong answers to these questions. There is no judgment. As you age, your memory may become like Swiss cheese, and you must fill in the holes the best you can.

You will need a lined notebook and a pen for the writing exercises. I own a timer that allows me to clock my writings. You may want to purchase one for yourself, but all you really need is a watch. Later there will be other kinds of exercises requiring different materials. The reasons for writing these exercises are: (1) to see your words on the page, (2) to express yourself in writing and verbally, (3) to vent, (4) to recall events from the distant past, (5) to allow your subconscious to speak to you—if you let go and don't think too much, (6) to learn more about yourself, and (7) to have fun. If you find you are dredging up material that is too painful, you should seek the assistance of a professional therapist.

## EXERCISES

So let us begin. In the following exercises, I want you to write about Wonder and Regret—the theme of "Loose Ends," the first chapter in this book. Pick one exercise from this section, and then if you have time, a second one.

**Exercise 1:** When I was young, my mother told me a story about her mother, who sliced an apple across the middle and showed her the star formed by the bisected apple seeds. That small incident awakened my mother to the wonders of nature. As an adult, she wrote a poem called "Star Flower in the Fruit." Similarly, my mother cracked open pieces of slate and showed me fossil ferns, and I've been a nut for fossils ever since. Can you remember ✓ something your mother did to awaken your sense of wonder? Take out your notebook and pen. Write for at least five minutes. Try to write longer and see where it takes you. It's okay if your writing turns away from the topic and goes in a different direction. Read aloud what you wrote, even if you are alone.

**Exercise 2:** Do you believe in fairies? Have you ever seen a fairy or something that other people don't see? Write for ten minutes about your experience.

**Exercise 3:** In Chapter 1, my story begins when my mother is dying, and I cannot tell her I love her. Not only can I not utter the words, but there's unfinished business between us. I've never come clean about the anger I harbored toward her. As a result, I'm not clear about my love for her either. If your mother is gone, do you have any unresolved issues or regrets? If you do, make a list. Pick out one item that has some energy in it and write for at least ten minutes. If you have no regrets, write for ten minutes about why you have none. Now read aloud what you wrote.

**Exercise 4:** Scars. Most of us carry scars from early childhood— physical or psychological. I have one obvious one. The end of my right index finger is missing from playing "Zombie" in sixth grade. I ran through the cafeteria doors as another kid was running toward me and my finger was caught in the hinge of the door. Psychologically, I carry the scar from my parents who told me repeatedly, "Don't speak unless spoken to." Women my age remember that one. Do you? Take your notebook and pen. Think about either a physical scar or a psychological scar and write for at least fifteen minutes. Tell how the scar happened and how it has affected you throughout your life. If you still want to write more, address the scar you didn't write about first, and now write about it. Read aloud what you wrote. If you're with a friend, it is okay to talk about your experiences, but don't say, "Oh, your writing is so good." This isn't about writing well. In fact, I encourage you to write what you might consider "junk." If you start thinking you must write well, that will stifle the flow!

## TIPS

**1. Take off your adult hat and park it at the door when you write.** Put on your imaginary Mickey Mouse ears or your Harry Potter wizard's hat. Now you can write without the inner critic chattering away in your ear.

**2. Walk outdoors for ten or twenty minutes before you sit down to write.** Breathe deeply. This will shake the wrinkles out of your brain. Blankness is good, for it allows your subconscious thoughts to come forward.

**3. Don't mark out sentences that sound stupid and awkward.** It's important to keep your pen moving.

**4. Don't stop to think.** If you can't think what to write next, repeat the last few words over and over until something new pops into your mind.

## RESOURCES

"Loose Ends" is about my awakening to the unseen world. It is about wonder, trust, and faith. It's also about the birth of conflict. Writing can help us recall early memories. In this resources section, I bring you a classic book on writing and my favorite books on fairies.

1. *Writing Down the Bones,* Natalie Goldberg, (Shambhala Publications, Inc., 1986). This is Goldberg's first writing book, a slim volume that every writer needs in her library. It defines the kind of writing that we do in this workbook of exercises as "writing practice." Natalie Goldberg lives in Taos, NM, and gives writing workshops. For a complete listing of her books, tapes and workshops, see her website: www.nataliegoldberg.com.

2. *Healing with the Fairies,* Doreen Virtue, (Hay House Inc., 2001). Doreen Virtue is best known for her book, *Healing with the Angels* and her angel cards. She is a spiritual doctor of psychology who teaches about angels and fairies in her workshops and audiotapes. This book is the true story of her introduction to the fairy realm at a critical stage in her life, when she broke up with her first husband and met her new husband, who was a true soul mate. She credits the fairies for guiding the two of them together. Virtue also has developed a set of forty-four fairy oracle cards. Her books and materials can be obtained through many bookstores and her own website: www.angeltherapy.com.

3. *The Real World of Fairies,* Dora Van Gelder, (Quest Books: The Theosophical Publishing House, 1977). This little gem is a true first-person account by a young woman who later, as Dora Kunz, cofounded Therapeutic Touch. This is the most enchanting book I have ever read about many kinds of nature spirits: earth fairies, garden fairies, tree spirits, mountain fairies, water fairies, fire fairies and air fairies. As a young woman, Van Gelder could see and talk with these fairies. Her descriptions are unforgettable.

# ~ Section 2 ~
# The Dream, the Vision, and the Bird Call

In Chapter 2, my mother Louise becomes real through the story she tells about my next door neighbor who died at age thirteen. The way Mom talked and thought are as clear as if I had captured her voice on tape. Her tale jarred my memory as well. It brought my own fourteenth year back to me.

## EXERCISES

Do you remember being thirteen years old? Select one or more of the following exercises and write, write, write. Within each exercise are multiple questions. This isn't a test. You don't have to answer each and every one. Just latch onto an idea and go with it. If your ten minutes aren't up and you have run out of something to say, move on to the next question.

**Exercise 1:** Being thirteen. Describe yourself at thirteen. Seventh grade. What music did you listen to, and how did your mom react to your music? How did you fix your hair? Did you wear dresses to school or jeans? Were you dating? Were you a tomboy, a princess or a frog? What were your favorite things to do? Did you like or hate that age? Write for ten minutes, and then read aloud. Dogs and cats are great listeners—they don't criticize.

**Exercise 2:** You and your mother. Can you remember one specific event shared with your mother, and with no one else, when you were thirteen—positive or negative? If not with your mom alone, then write about any vivid memory from your fourteenth year that involved your mother. Write for ten minutes, and then read aloud.

**Exercise 3:** Synchronicities. Do you believe synchronicities are just dumb luck or that they have significance? In this chapter, the bird call might have been a sign that I was attending the funeral in spirit as my mother suggests, or that Linda was letting her family know she was still alive, or it might have been "just a coincidence." Do you pay attention to synchronicities in your life? What do they mean to you? Did you ever discuss these with your mother? Write for ten minutes about a synchronicity you have experienced. Did it change your life in any way?

**Exercise 4:** Dreams. Louise often had vivid dreams that might have been considered "second sight" or psychic experiences. Her story of seeing Linda's spirit dancing around her grieving mother was a case in point. Have you ever had a dream that you thought was extraordinary, such as seeing into another dimension, predicting the future, explaining a spiritual truth, or connecting you with powerful love? Were you able to share these with your mom, or did she share a special dream with you? Write for ten minutes about a vivid dream that you believe was inspired by an expanded state of consciousness. This can be your dream or one your mother told you. Write with as much detail as you can remember. What impact did the dream have on the dreamer? If it is difficult to remember details, then write about your dreams in general. Read your writing to yourself or another. Have you tried reading aloud to your parked car in the garage?

**Exercise 5:** Token-object Reading. Since I brought up the gifts of synchronicity and intuitive dreams, here is another one: token-object reading or psychometry—feeling the essence of a person by holding an object owned by the person. Find an object that belonged to your mother when you were young—a piece of jewelry or collectible, for example. It should be small enough to fit in the palm of your hand. Hold it in your left hand for three minutes with your eyes closed. (Your left hand receives energy, while your right hand transmits energy, which is why I'm asking you to hold the object in your left hand.) This may bring into awareness the essence of the woman. Write for ten minutes about the object as you hold it in your nondominant hand. Do not discount what you feel or what comes into your mind. Just write it down and bless it.

## TIPS

**1. Listen to the still small voice.** This is the voice of your inner being, your intuition. You may not know why you are nudged to attend a certain workshop or have lunch with a new person in your life. It could be your internal guidance system at work, setting up the next step in your spiritual progress.

**2. Keep a daybook.** My favorite is *A Woman's Diary* by Pomegranate Communications, Inc., with visionary paintings by Susan Seddon Boulet, but there are many to choose from. Each night, before you go to bed, record intuitive flashes, special dreams from the previous night, insights, synchronicities, strong desires, and cravings that came to you that day. The act of recording, forces you to pay attention to Spirit working in your life.

## RESOURCES

Here are two books that shed light on growing pains. In the first, the child is tough and resilient. She grows up fast in spite of having absolutely no parental support. In the second book, the child is severely shy. As an adult she learns why, and spends her life helping others like herself.

1.  *Behaving as if the God in All Life Mattered*, Machaelle Small Wright, (Perelandra, Ltd., 1997). This is Wright's first of many books. It describes in lively detail her early family life, which was abusive at best. Women with dysfunctional mother-daughter relationships will enjoy this true story of thriving in spite of everything parental. On her own at age twelve, Wright survived her way to adulthood by the "do or die" method, with lots of help from "luck" and synchronicities. Today, Wright owns and manages a co-creative research garden with nature where she produces flower essences, gives workshops, and writes educational materials. In *Behaving as if the God in All Life Mattered*, Wright tells how she transformed her life as a troubled teen to working with nature and became an authority on co-creative processes. It's a must-read for people whose interest lies in communicating with the plant, animal, and mineral kingdoms. This book was first published in 1981 and revised and republished in 1997. Website: www.perelandra-ltd.com.

2.  *The Highly Sensitive Person: How to Thrive When the World Overwhelms You*, Elaine N. Aron, Ph.D., (Broadway Books, 1997). Did you know that 15%–20% of the population has nervous systems that are wired differently from the majority? The roots of some mother-daughter problems stem from this fact. Highly sensitive people have identifiable characteristics that well-meaning parents and teachers often try to help them overcome—shyness, as an example. If you think you might be one of these, reading this book can help you reframe your childhood and adolescence, and even make it possible for you to more readily forgive those who didn't understand you. Website: www.hsperson.com.

## ~ Section 3 ~
## Bringing Down the House

In Chapter 3, I told about growing up with both my parents. They lived to see their fiftieth anniversary, but my father died a couple of years later, at age seventy-six. Mom came to live near me in Denver. I enjoyed her company for eight more years. But then she began failing.

When your mother dies, the shock can be almost unbearable, regardless of your relationship with her. If you loved her dearly, then you'll deal with grieving her loss. If the relationship was troubled, you may suspect that the root of your pain is gone, but that may not be the case. After her death, you may feel anger and guilt alongside the grief. In order to reach a peaceful state, you may want to start your own healing journey.

## EXERCISES

Words are like magic. They can be used for good or for ill, for healing or destruction. As such, they can be used like white magic or black magic. Words spoken thoughtlessly or in anger can leave wounds that last a lifetime, especially when directed toward a young child. Parents are usually the first humans in a child's life to nurture or negate. These exercises are for women who had issues with their mother while she was alive.

A close relative was given the first exercise by her optometrist in Chicago, a man who is able to perceive people's family relationships by examining their eyes. This exercise with its six steps is designed to help release old negative emotions about deceased parents. You will need several sheets of lined paper and some matches. Oh, and don't forget a box of tissues.

**Exercise 1:**

**Step 1:** Take a sheet of paper and fold it in half. At the top of the first half, write "Likes" and at the top of the second half write "Dislikes." Thinking of your mother, write a list of things you liked about her in the first column. In the second column, list things you didn't.

**Step 2:** Now write a letter to your mother, telling her all the things you didn't like about her. Write it with venom in your pen if that is the way you feel. Let all your emotion out. Write until you can think of nothing more to say.

**Step 3:** Read this letter aloud to yourself—or the dog. Don't read it to your writing buddy. It's for your eyes only. Read it aloud over and over until it doesn't affect you emotionally. You will know you are finished when your feelings are neutral.

**Step 4:** When you have zero reaction to anything you said in your letter, burn it.

**Step 5:** Make a list of characteristics you liked about your mother, things that you inherited from her that you are glad about and qualities of hers that you want to develop in yourself.

**Step 6:** Write a letter to your mother thanking her for the qualities you appreciate. Read it aloud as though she were sitting in front of you.

**Exercise 2:** Do you believe in an afterlife? What did your mother believe? What do you think happened to your mother after she died? Have you heard from her in any form since she departed? Write for ten minutes about any experiences you have had since she left the physical world that might be her way of contacting you.

## TIPS

**1. Harness your emotions before the passage of time dims them.** Use emotions, such as grief, anger and guilt to propel you into healing a negative relationship with your mother, either before or after her demise. Emotion is your ticket to expanding your soul. If you need therapy from a professional to resolve negative emotions, don't delay. After a couple of years, those feelings will recede into memory and will be difficult to draw out again.

**2. Pay attention to signs and symbols from your mother.** It is well documented that those who have recently crossed to the Other Side attempt to let loved ones know they are still alive through the senses of sight (symbols you would recognize), touch (such as playing with your hair), smell (such as your mother's perfume), or sound (such as your mother's favorite song on the radio—a synchronicity).

**3. Pay attention to your dreams.** Vivid dreamers often receive visitations or dream symbols that can be decoded.

## RESOURCES

There are many books that can help you process your emotions after your mother is gone. *The Afterlife Connection* is my favorite in this genre of healing relationships after death. It's packed with self-help exercises and solid experiences of contact from the Beyond. The other books listed in this section shed light on the mother-daughter relationship and on the veil that separates those of us living on earth from those living in the spirit world.

1. *The Afterlife Connection: A Therapist Reveals How to Communicate with Departed Loved Ones,* Dr. Jane Greer, (St. Martin's Press, 2003). "Promise me that when you die you'll find a way

to contact me," are the words Greer said to her mother who was dying of a brain tumor. In the years that followed, her mother found numerous ways to make her presence known. Greer, a psychotherapist, became convinced that her mother was alive and well on the Other Side. Greer documented all the incidents, making a compelling case for her mother's survival after death. Many of her clients have unfinished business with parents or others who have died, such as anger and hurt from unresolved relationships. Greer shares their stories and self-help techniques for healing painful relationships with those who have crossed over. She contends it is never too late to do that. This is a fine self-help book for those who wish to know whether life continues after death and those who want to heal painful relationships with the deceased.

2. *I Am My Mother's Daughter: Making Peace with Mom— Before It's Too Late*, Iris Krasnow, (Perseus Books Group, 2006). Krasnow's book is a good read for daughters whose mothers are still alive. She has gathered insights from adult women with varied backgrounds and experiences who made peace with their mothers before they passed on. Krasnow herself reconciled with her mother, a Holocaust survivor and former saleswoman. Krasnow contends that you can't kiss and make up with your mother at her funeral, so you had better do it while Mom is still alive. While I maintain that daughters can heal rifts with their moms after death, I recommend Krasnow's book to women who still have a chance to make amends.

3. *Mother-Daughter Wisdom: Creating a Legacy of Physical and Emotional Health*, Christiane Northrup, M.D., (Bantam

Books, 2005). This is a positively inspiring book by an enlightened teacher in our midst. Her premise is that the mother-daughter relationship is at the headwaters of every woman's mental, physical, and emotional health. She gives innumerable steps by which women can heal the legacy of mother-daughter pain where daughter blames Mom, and Mom resents daughter. As a doctor, a mother, and a daughter, she has a lifetime of experience to draw from. After scanning the Table of Contents, go straight to the Resources section. The book is doubly valuable for its extensive compendium of supplementary topics catalogued by chapter. In addition to recommended reading, you'll find organizations and websites with solid descriptions. Today's mothers can find practical advice from a true authority on how to raise healthy daughters. Daughters of elderly mothers can learn how to heal difficult relationships before their mothers cross over. The mother-daughter relationship never ends, according to Northrup. It's still there and fixable even after death.

4.  *The Wheel of Life*, Elisabeth Kubler-Ross, (Scribner, 1997). Kubler-Ross was the woman who wrote the classic psychological study, *On Death and Dying*, and transformed the way people think about dying. In her last book, *The Wheel of Life*, written when she was seventy-one and contemplating her own death, Kubler-Ross wrote this memoir that concluded death does not exist in the traditional definition. In the 1970s, she and a colleague interviewed nearly 20,000 people from many cultures who had had near death experiences. In all cases, she said, the experiences were so similar that the accounts had to be true. Up until then (the 1970s), Kubler-Ross says she had no belief in an afterlife. However this new data convinced her otherwise. In her chapter "Life

After Death," Kubler-Ross writes about the first five phases of the afterlife, beginning with leaving the body, according to what she learned in the interviews. These experiences are common to all, she says.

---

## ~ Section 4 ~
## The Healing Legacy

In Chapter 4, I told about grieving my mother after her death and healing my relationship with her through writing.

After your mother dies, you are transported to the realm of memory. Time ceases to have meaning where she is concerned. You can remember her as she was right before she died or in middle age or as your childhood mother. You can explore any avenue of your life with her through memory. You can re-create scenes to turn out differently, and you can have the last say.

I must interject here that my young life was a day at the beach compared with those of many women. I have great sympathy for women who endured physical and emotional abuse from their mothers. One of my friends is an amazing product of an abusive mother. She turned out strong and successful. But that doesn't mean she isn't wounded. Once the mother has passed to the Other Side, the relationship between mother and daughter changes, of course, but a relationship still exists, if you want to pursue it. You no longer need to fortify yourself against your mother's inappropriate behavior—if that was the case. You can grieve for yourself at last, as you grieve for your mother. You can rage at your mother too.

## EXERCISES

These exercises are not intended to heal scars, but to open doors and let in light. If the chasm between you and your mother wasn't too wide, you may achieve resolution with the help of books, various writing exercises, and persistence. My parents enforced a rule when I was a child: no back talk. I was itching to sling words at them as a teenager, but it wasn't until after they were gone that I could do it without fearing repercussions, or thoughtlessly shattering them. It felt so good to step into my teenage shoes and let loose.

**Exercise 1:** Think of a time when your mother punished you unjustly. Get out your notebook. Write for ten minutes about the incident as you remember it. Start writing with "I remember . . ." In a second ten-minute session, re-write the incident as you would have preferred it to unfold. Start writing with "I remember . . ."

**Exercise 2:** Find an old letter from your mother to you. Something in her letter irritated you. Find that. Write back to her, using some of her own words. Contradict what she said, making your own case. This will empower you. Write for ten minutes, and start with, "You said . . ." If you don't have a letter from her, make one up, writing it as you remember her writing or talking to you. Then write back to her.

**Exercise 3:** Recall a time that your mother took your power away—an angry conversation, being grounded, being slapped or being denied something you wanted. Create a dialog between the two of you that captures her side of the discussion and yours. Describe your body language—are you pacing the floor? Tell where you are—describe the room or place. Recall scents—

were the magnolias blooming? Cabbage cooking? As the scene unfolds, instead of being the victim, you stand up for yourself. This time you act responsibly and work out the situation as an adult would work it out. Write for fifteen minutes and start with "I remember the time . . ."

**Exercise 4:** What did you enjoy doing with your mother? Beach-combing? Baking cookies? Gardening? Hiking? Story time? Shopping for bargains? Playing board games as a family? Washing dishes together? Singing in the car? Reading in the living room? Make a list. Write for ten minutes about one activity on your list. Begin with "I remember . . ." Go back to your list as many times as you can and write more little scenes of enjoyment.

**Exercise 5:** Create a poem from one or more of the scenes you wrote about in Exercise 4. To create a poem, start by typing one of the scenes you like. Type each sentence on a separate line. Eliminate the sentences that don't add to the poem. Save only the sentences with strong verbs and images. Now eliminate as many prepositions and conjunctions as you can. Poetry doesn't need to rhyme. It must please the writer and convey a picture or emotion with clarity. Here's my example: What I liked doing with my mother—from Exercise 4.

**The scene:**

> I liked my mother in the dark, on a lawn chair. Summers were muggy and hot, but after sundown, after the dishes, she would stretch out on a padded aluminum chair. I would look for the glow of her cigarette and I'd join her. Fireflies twinkled in our woods like fairy candles. Crickets, cicadas, and frogs played their August symphony. The woods rang and throbbed. Honeysuckle released its perfume. We wore long sleeved shirts and long

pants at night. Dew began to fall early and mosquitoes sang their tunes around our ears. Sometimes we'd light mosquito candles, but mostly we would listen to the night sounds, our eyes fixed on the patch of sky above our heads. We lived in a cocoon of elm and oak trees. At night, sitting next to my mother in a lawn chair, the trees would breathe. I learned in school that it was called transpiration.

**The poem:**

Hot muggy summers
After sundown, after dishes,
I joined my mother in the dark
On a padded aluminum chair she stretched out
Holding a cigarette in her right hand
I followed the red glow to her
Firefly fairy candles twinkled
Mosquitoes sang around ears
Woods ringing and throbbing
With crickets, cicadas and frogs
An August symphony
Early dew dampened our long-sleeved shirts
In a cocoon of elms and oaks
Honeysuckle perfume
Sitting darkly next to my mother
The trees breathing

## TIPS

**1. Save as much written material from your mother as you can.** You will be more interested in who she was after she has been gone awhile. I learned this lesson the hard way.

**2. Join a writing group.** If you like to write prose or poetry, you will find people who share many interests with you in a writing group. The quest to understand our roots, our parents, ourselves is universal. Writers like to explore these regions.

## RESOURCES

When my mother died, I discovered writings of hers that I could respond to. Most women are not so fortunate to have the raw materials from their mother from which to begin a dialog. The first two selections will help you get back to writing—an age-old method of releasing emotions and making internal changes. The last two selections are books by writers with mothers on their minds.

1.  *The Story Circle Network* is a national not-for-profit membership organization made up of women who want to explore their lives and their souls by exploring their personal stories. Its founding member, Susan Wittig Albert, insists storytelling is healing. She says as we reveal ourselves through writing our personal stories, we become aware of the "continuing core of our lives under the fragmented surface of our experience." The Story Circle Network connects women to other women who use writing to make themselves whole. Individual membership is $35.00 per year. There are many benefits. Members receive four issues of the quarterly journal. They can submit stories to the journal, receive discounts on workshops, retreats, and conferences, plus much more. See their website: www.storycircle.org.

2.  *Writing to Heal the Soul: Transforming Grief and Loss Through Writing*, Susan Zimmerman, (Three Rivers Press, 2002). Zimmerman struggled with depression, fear, denial, guilt,

bitterness and despair after her first child developed a neurological disorder that left her unable to walk or talk. Only by writing about her experience did she begin to heal. *Writing to Heal the Soul* is her gift to anyone in crisis who is in need of hope and healing. Each chapter includes a brief essay about an event in Zimmerman's life followed by an even briefer essay that teases out the chapter's theme. For instance, in one chapter she writes of watching a glassblower who makes a mistake, destroys the vase he was blowing, and starts over. Then she writes about when we must keep on keeping on in spite of shattered dreams. At the end of each chapter she provides writing exercises that are relevant to the theme. *Writing to Heal the Soul* is a beautifully written guidebook for anyone suffering any kind of loss, be it the loss of a loved one, a relationship, loss of a job or developing of a disability.

3.  *Tangled Vines: Poems to Celebrate and Explore the Relationship Between Mothers and Daughters,* Lyn Lifshin, editor, (Harcourt Brace & Company, 1992). If you're a poetry fan, this collection of eighty poems by fifty-four acclaimed poets will certainly satisfy. Contributors include Sylvia Plath, Sonia Sanchez, Anne Sexton, Liv Ullmann, Alice Walker, Sharon Olds, Diane di Prima, Erica Jong, and Lyn Lifshin. Mothers writing about daughters, and daughters writing about mothers touch on the complexities of these two roles, from the binding closeness to intense anger.

4.  *I Am a Thousand Winds That Blow: The Healing Power of a Remarkable Death,* Gail Michael, (Bonneville Books, 2002). By healing a rocky relationship with her mother before her mother died, Gail Michael opened her heart and was forever changed. Michael writes in poetic detail about how she came

to admire the mother who appeared to have no winning attributes. In her last days on earth, Gail Michael's mother wavered back and forth between two worlds, commenting on those she saw waiting for her on the Other Side, leaving a legacy of hope for those who question whether there is life beyond this one.

---

## ~ Section 5 ~
## The Art of Communication

In Chapter 5, I told the story of how Louise used my hand to draw a picture of herself reaching out to hug me. Whether you can channel art from a deceased loved one is not important. The amazing thing is discovering that within each of us is an intelligence that wishes to express through our hands, independent of our control or conscious direction. Fine artists often harness this intelligence when they create their artwork. Governed by your subconscious mind, this intelligence can produce universal symbols. Such symbols can be interpreted by Jungian analysts or art therapists. Intuitive drawing can give you feedback on a daily basis if you wish to use it for artistic journaling. Intuitive people can connect with higher sources and channel visionary art. In fact there is a museum of visionary art in Maryland (see Resources section).

## EXERCISES

If you wish to experiment with the intelligence of automatic drawing within you, try the simple exercises below. Start with Exercise 1 and continue sequentially for best results.

**Exercise 1:** Take a *large* blank piece of paper and a pencil. The paper should be at least 11 x 14. A large drawing pad will work, as will Butcher paper. Tape a sheet of the paper to a solid surface, such as a table top, with masking tape. Relax your body and mind. Avoid any distracting noises, such as music, television, animals and children. Stand over the drawing surface rather than sit in a chair. This is important because the standing position allows your shoulders and arms more freedom of movement. Focus on the white paper, and then allow your dominant hand to draw whatever it wants without incorporating your thoughts into it. Don't expect it to be recognizable or pretty. You will create a spontaneous drawing that will reflect your present state of mind.

**Exercise 2:** Turn on your favorite music. Headphones work well with this exercise. Take a *large* blank piece of paper and a pencil. Tape the paper to a solid surface with masking tape or use a drawing pad. Stand over the drawing surface. Relax your body and mind. Focus on the white paper, and then allow your dominant hand to draw whatever it wants as you listen to the music. Allow the music to fill your mind. You will create a spontaneous drawing influenced by the music. Again, don't be frustrated if the drawing does not look like anything recognizable.

**Exercise 3:** Turn on the evening news on the radio or television. Take a blank piece of paper and a pencil. Tape the paper to a solid surface with masking tape or use a drawing pad. Relax your body and mind. Stand over the drawing surface. Focus on the white paper and allow your dominant hand to draw whatever it wants as you listen to the news in the background. Often the evening news is disturbing. You will create a spontaneous drawing that will be influenced by the news of the day.

**Exercise 4:** The exercises above work well with soft pastels or oil pastels. Allow your hand to choose the color without making a conscious decision. To do this, rest your hand over the box of colors until your hand begins to move. Your hand will move in a way similar to when you are drawing intuitively. It will stop over the color that your subconscious mind wants to use. Continue as in the previous exercises.

**Exercise 5:** Now try drawing with your nondominant hand. This hand will be less controlled, and slower, but it may draw in a totally different way from the hand you normally write with.

**Exercise 6:** If you've had success drawing in a standing position, try sitting. My favorite position is on the floor with a drawing pad to my right. I lean over the pad, allowing my right hand and arm to be as relaxed as possible.

## TIP

**Keep a visual journal.** Authors Barbara Ganim and Cathy Malchiodi (see the Resources section) have both published books that guide people in setting up and using a visual journal. The images you draw can be used for healing and for feedback on what is happening in your emotional and spiritual levels.

## RESOURCES

Art therapists utilize automatic drawing—they call it expressive art. Some of the best books on art therapy are cited below. Automatic art is sometimes found in collections of Visionary Art and in what is considered Outsider Art. In art museums, you will find automatic art in collections labeled abstract expressionism.

1. *The Soul's Palette: Drawing on Art's Transformative Powers for Health and Well-Being*, Cathy A. Malchiodi, (Shambala Publications, Inc., 2002). Malchiodi holds advanced credentials in art therapy, expressive therapies, and counseling. In the words of Jan Phillips, author of *Marry Your Muse*, Malchiodi is a modern-day medicine woman who knows the cure is within. *The Soul's Palette* includes exercises for drawing, painting, sculpting and collage. Each exercise aims to cultivate your intuition, inspiration and spontaneity.

2. *The Art Therapy Sourcebook*, Cathy Malchiodi, (McGraw-Hill, 2006). This book can be used for personal transformation and healing.

3. *Visual Journaling: Going Deeper than Words*, Barbara Ganim and Susan Fox, (Quest Books: Theosophical Publishing House, 1999). Ganim directs the Institute for the Expressive Arts and teaches in the graduate program at Salve Regina University in Newport Rhode Island. *Visual Journaling* teaches how to set up and maintain a daily journal using your own drawings instead of words to express what is happening in your emotional world.

4. American Visionary Art Museum, 800 Key Highway, Baltimore, MD 21230. AVAM is a museum "for art produced by self-taught individuals, usually without formal training whose works arise from an innate personal vision that revels in the creative act itself." Vision is defined as "the art of seeing things invisible." Visionary artworks are "entirely spontaneous and individualized." Artists "hear their own inner voice." The museum houses creations of non-artists such as street people, hermits, factory workers, housewives and psychic mediums. The museum has a collection of over 4,000 pieces. Phone: 410-244-1900; Website: www.avam.org.

5.  *Raw Vision*, an "international journal of intuitive and vision-
    ary art," is a quarterly British publication that features the
    work of the untrained, including mentally ill, artist. Out-
    sider Art is the umbrella term for all art by untrained artists
    who are also not connected with any art movements, art
    colleges or conventional art museums and galleries. It's out
    of the mainstream, yet it is becoming recognized and collected
    on both sides of the Atlantic. Outsider Art can be produced
    in a number of ways. Some are mediumistic (felt to be
    transmitted from those on the Other Side), some are psy-
    chological (felt to be downloaded from the subconscious),
    some are representations of visions, others may even be
    dictated by supernatural beings. A wide range of craftsman-
    ship is included under this umbrella—from doodles to
    elegantly executed and highly refined works of art. Website:
    www.rawvision.com.

---

## ~ Section 6 ~
## Uncharted Territory

In Chapter 6, I experimented more with automatic drawing and
also did a lot of research. I learned that traditional artists have
used spontaneous movement to create works of art that are in
museums and art books. I was losing my reticence to talk about
what I was doing.

## EXERCISES

Did you attempt the drawing exercises in the last section? Did
you have success? I hope so. Exercises 1–4 require that you
enjoyed the previous drawing exercises. If you didn't, then move
on to Exercise 5.

I found that once I had mastered the technique of automatic drawing, where my hand moved spontaneously on the page, I could combine the motion with an idea in my mind and produce a drawing of that concept. For instance, after I visited Penitente Canyon in the San Luis Valley of Colorado, I came home, sat down with my oil pastels, and automatically drew a picture of the canyon. It looked nothing like a literal canyon, but it captured the mood of the canyon. I liked it so much that I had it framed.

You might ask what this has to do with the mother-daughter relationship. For me, it had everything to do with my mother, for my mother started coming through with symbolic messages on the drawing pad. The end to which you use your own ability to draw automatically will reveal itself if you keep practicing. I'll show you a few more things you can do with automatic drawing.

**Exercise 1:** Find a poem that means something to you. A poem is a good subject because of its imagery and emotion. You should have an affinity for this piece of writing. The more strongly it affects you, the more likely your subconscious will send you strong images. If you had success drawing with colors, I suggest you use pastels or oil pastels. Assume your most comfortable position for drawing—standing up, sitting at a table, or sitting on the floor with your drawing pad beside you. This latter position is my favorite. Read the poem out loud once or twice and then begin drawing. Don't question what you're getting and don't try to control the picture. This picture may take five minutes to half an hour to create itself. Some of mine took an hour or more, but in the beginning they happened quickly.

**Exercise 2:** Do you have pets? When your cat or dog is snoozing, take your drawing pad and colors near the animal and draw it. Allow your hand to move at will. I have done this with my cats, and like the results. The picture takes form more freely than if I try to sketch my cat intentionally.

**Exercise 3:** Ask your inner being/subconscious mind/soul/God to give you a picture of your emotional state. By asking, you are alerting this part of your consciousness to take over or at least help you. The more you can let go and let this other part of you—the pure creative part—have free rein, the easier the drawing will become.

**Exercise 4:** Ask your inner being/subconscious mind/soul/God to give you a picture of joy, peace, your child or a tree. One of my favorite spontaneous drawings was of an aspen tree. I was at a weekend workshop and went hiking with a 5x7 sketch book. I took a small box of oil pastels with me in a backpack and headed up a mountainside. When I reached a good spot to sit, I connected with an aspen, a tree with black "eyes" on its white bark where

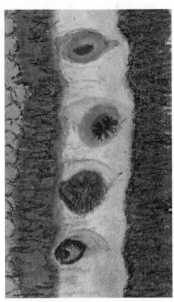

*Maria's automatic drawing of an aspen.*

it had lost branches. I started to draw this tree in the regular way, but my hand wanted to take over. It was as if the spirit of the tree came through into the drawing. As you can see, the subjects are endless.

**Exercise 5:** In this chapter, I talked about muscle testing, also called bio-kinesiology or applied kinesiology. I first learned how to get "yes" and "no" answers from Machaelle Small Wright's book, *Flower Essences: Reordering Our Understanding and Approach to Illness and Health,* (Perelandra, Ltd., 1988). Many chiropractors use muscle testing to determine whether a part of the body's electrical system is weak or strong. It can be done several ways. I use the thumb and pinkie finger method. Try this: (a) If you are right handed, place the tips of your *left* thumb and *left* little finger together. Press fairly hard. (b) Press your right thumb and pad of your right index finger together. (c) Insert the thumb and index finger of your right hand through the circle formed by the thumb and little finger of your left hand. Only the tips of your right thumb and index finger should stick up through the circle. (d) Say out loud, "Show me a 'yes.'" After saying this, try to spread the thumb and index finger of your right hand apart inside the circle. If you are doing it correctly, the circle formed by the thumb and pinkie of your left hand will hold firm. (e) Say out loud, "Show me a 'no.'" After saying this, try to spread the thumb and index finger of your right hand apart inside the circle. If you are doing it correctly, the circle formed by the thumb and pinkie of your left hand will break open. (f) Practice this over and over until you can feel the difference between "strong" and "weak." (g) Prepare your fingers for a new test, and say out loud, "My name is _____." (Use whatever your correct name is.) The fingers should hold firm. (h) Prepare your fingers for a new test, and say out loud, "My name is Marilyn Monroe." Assuming that's not your name, the fingers of your right hand should break apart. You can use this system to check information about yourself, what your body wants and doesn't want. Once you have mastered the technique, you can use muscle testing for many things. You can find a lot of information on the web about muscle testing by searching "How to Muscle Test."

## TIPS

**1. Order a set of Deborah Koff-Chapin's *Soul Cards*,** (U.S. Games Systems,1997, 2001). Koff-Chapin has produced two sets of what she calls soul cards—reproductions of some of her most evocative drawings from the thousands she has created. The decks come with no guidebook. It's up to you to interpret the card meanings. Ask a question, pull a card, and interpret. They contain wonderful images that will engage your imagination, intuition and synchronicity. Although these visionary paintings originate from Koff-Chapin's soul, they are archetypal, which means the images apply to all of us. It is uncanny how they work, but they do. Ordering information: www.touchdrawing.com.

**2. Muscle test foods in your refrigerator.** Hold a food product to your solar plexus and secure it with both wrists while you muscle test with your fingers. Ask, "Is this good for me?" I use this system to determine if leftovers are still fresh and nutritious or if I should toss them.

## RESOURCES

Deborah Koff-Chapin's book is a must-have resource if you become intrigued with automatic drawing. She calls it "touch drawing." For the nonacademic person, Vivianne Crowley's book, *Jung: A Journey of Transformation* is one of the best and easiest to read about Carl Jung and it is beautifully illustrated. Alice Flaherty's book on the brain is fascinating. I couldn't put it down.

1.  *Drawing Out Your Soul: The Touch Drawing Handbook*, Deborah Koff-Chapin, (The Center for Touch Drawing 1996). This short guide teaches people to do Touch Drawing, a form of automatic drawing. Using a sheet of glass or a similar hard surface, printer's ink, a printmaking brayer (roller), and lightweight paper such as newsprint, Koff-Chapin says that the hands become extensions of the soul, moving freely, enabling uncensored feelings to flow forth. Layers of the psyche are revealed. Koff-Chapin includes dozens of illustrations of her work and that of others. Web site: www.touchdrawing.com.

2.  A website for information about channeled art: www.crystalinks.com/art.html and automatic writing: www.crystalinks.com/automaticwriting.html. If you go to the home page and start browsing, you'll find a trove of metaphysical information.

3.  *Jung: A Journey of Transformation Exploring His Life and Experiencing His Ideas,* Vivianne Crowley, (Quest Books: Theosophical Publishing House, 2000). Jung's work is monumental in its volume and its inspiration for therapists, doctors, mystics, writers, artists, social scientists and people in all walks of life, says author Crowley. In this extravagantly illustrated four-color book, Crowley has made it possible to understand Jung's life, times, beliefs, and teachings quickly and almost effortlessly. Crowley features two contemporary artists, Robert Natkin and Freydoon Rassouli, whose work has been influenced by the ideas of Jung. Rassouli's work, in particular, appears to be guided by his subconscious—an example of "automatic art." Crowley also includes several fascinating exercises that readers can explore on their own, putting Jung's concepts into practice.

4. *The Midnight Disease: The Drive to Write, Writer's Block and the Creative Brain*, Alice W. Flaherty, (Houghton Mifflin, 2004). Flaherty, a leading neurologist at a major research hospital, writes from the front lines of brain research. She has studied the neurology of writers, poets, and other creative types and defines the lines between creativity and psychosis. Triggered by her own journey into mental illness, (hypergraphia—the medical term for an overpowering desire to write), Flaherty identifies the part of the brain she believes is "the God Module." This module is preeminent in activities intended to give life meaning, whether religious or artistic, and is the seat of mystical and religious experience. This book is especially interesting because Flaherty, a highly trained scientist, had to come to grips with her own uninvited foray into paranormal experience.

---

## ~ Section 7 ~
## The Blast

Chapter 7 is about my most difficult year writing the book. It felt as though the story was out of my control and I didn't know where to turn for clarity. I had hit a wall. I had to stop and regroup. It took a long time to dig myself out of that hole.

Think of a time when you've hit the wall—a time when the issue was how to interpret life's events, how to survive. What you thought to be true was suddenly not true. You needed a new perspective. In order to reach that state you had to take time out and return later with fresh eyes. You may have sought expert advice.

In the life of this book with Louise, I hit the wall when she drew me a picture of nuclear war. I was stunned, stopped, and stymied. My engines were down and in the repair shop for a year. I finally consulted professional mediums to help me interpret the message, since I couldn't ask Louise. My head was filled with fear and assumptions. Did this mean the end of world was coming soon? The writing came to a halt. I needed to reassess where I was going with it. This wasn't my darkest hour, but it was a showstopper. I've also been stopped by divorce, major surgery, friendship breakups, and the death of a beloved pet. On some level, my behavior and beliefs surrounding all these events were connected to my relationship with Louise and my childhood.

## EXERCISES

People write entire books about overcoming their darkest moments. I'm asking you to write for at least forty-five minutes. And since a mother-daughter thread runs through these pages, think about your mother. Was she the catalyst? Did she help or hinder? Perhaps she was already gone when you met your challenge, but your upbringing may have affected your reaction to the event. Try to hang in there and write on all three exercises, at least fifteen minutes on each.

**Exercise 1:** What was the event? Write for at least fifteen minutes about the event itself. Be as specific in your writing as you can. Give details of place, action, people involved. Don't stop and think. Don't write about what you learned from the experience. Keep writing about the drama itself. It's best not to analyze what happened. Just write.

**Exercise 2:** Did you find peace, make peace? How long did it take and what steps did you take? Again, write for fifteen minutes.

**Exercise 3:** You are now the guru. What did you learn? If a friend or your child came to you and asked your advice, what would you advise? Write for fifteen minutes.

## TIPS

**1. Rescue Remedy.** When you receive bad news or are shocked by a sudden unpleasant realization, the homeopathic solution called Rescue Remedy will calm you almost instantly. You may need to take several drops repeatedly until serenity takes hold. Look for the Bach flower Rescue Remedy in health food stores.

**2. My all-time favorite tip.** This saying was forwarded to me in an email: "One of the most delightful discoveries we can make in life is realizing that everything that happens to us can be used for our advancement. Every experience, no matter how traumatic and daunting it might appear, has just as much potential to be a stepping stone as it does to be a stumbling block. Always remember it is not what happens to us that matters. It is our reaction to what happens that makes the difference, and we always get to choose what that reaction will be."

## RESOURCES

A myriad of courses, workshops, and self-help books exist to help us regain our footing and march forward. I'm sure you have your favorites. Here are mine. When I've been in a quandary, these are the ones I've turned to.

1.  *The Four Agreements: A Practical Guide to Personal Freedom,* Miguel Angel Ruiz, MD, (Amber Allen Publishing, 1997). If

I had to choose one book for transformation, this would be it. The four agreements are: Be impeccable with your word; Don't take anything personally; Don't make assumptions, and; Always do your best. A medical doctor and Toltec shaman, Ruiz has distilled the greatest principles for enlightenment and freedom into this small volume, which benefits from reading and rereading.

2.  *MAP: The Co-Creative White Brotherhood Medical Assistance Program*, Third Edition, Machaelle Small Wright, (Perelandra, Ltd, 2006). At the core of this healing modality is the "MAP session," a forty-minute consultation and healing session with a group of physicians from an ancient nonphysical brotherhood, consisting of highly evolved souls of both genders and all races, that is available to anyone at any time. The program was created by the White Brotherhood to help people with their physical, emotional, mental, and spiritual aspects, giving only the help a person is aware he or she needs. ("White" signifies all rays of the light spectrum. "Brotherhood" signifies not only the family of all people, but also the family of all life.) MAP is ridiculously simple to do and is learned through this book. It does not require a teacher. Website: www.perelandra-ltd.com

3.  Abraham-Hicks Publications. Abraham, a group of evolved nonphysical teachers, speaks their broader perspectives through Esther Hicks. In 1986, Esther and Jerry Hicks began receiving the information that they have turned into more than 500 books, cassettes and videos. The starter set of five CDs is the edited edition of Abraham's most popular original teachings. In this CD, Abraham explains three universal laws: the law of attraction, the law of deliberate creation,

and the law of allowing. I have listened to these starter CDs over and over again and never tire of them. The information complements any spiritual path, as it clarifies where our true power lies. Website: www.abraham-hicks.com

4.  *Sounds True* catalog. Of all the catalogs that come to the house, this is the one that I read and occasionally order CDs and tapes from. With categories such as Abundance & Manifestation, Creativity Boosters, Meditation & Prayer, Metaphysics, Mind & Body Healing, Relationships & Intimacy, Self Improvement, The Spiritual Journey and The Language of Archetypes, there should be something here for you. If you are not familiar with their offerings, go to www.soundstrue.com or call 800-333-9185. You can order a free catalog from the website.

5.  *A Course in Light: A Spiritual Path for Enlightenment,* (Az Reality Publishers, LLC, 2005), channeled by Antoinette Moltzan. When I started *A Course in Light* over twenty years ago, it had to be taught by a teacher who had been trained by Toni Moltzan. Today individuals can buy the books and CDs, which are the tools to assist them to clear negative factors that contribute to their unhappiness and dis-ease. Enlightenment is only as assured as the effort people put into the lessons. This is certainly one valid path. The ascended teachers that Ms. Moltzan channels vary from lesson to lesson. Their personalities come through in the writing and audio. The lessons themselves are timeless and timely on a personal as well as on a planetary level. Ms. Moltzan also offers personal channeled readings from the masters. Website: www.courseinlight.net

## ~ Section 8 ~
## Side Trips to Non-ordinary Reality

You're on the path. It's your path, your mission, your career, or spiritual quest. The path is straight or gently meandering through the meadows and woods. You've taken enough classes, read enough books. You possess the answers. You look good on paper, and people trust you. But one day you're biking or hiking and a wasp stings you on your Achilles tendon. You don't think much about it even when it swells up and hurts like fire. Maybe a day or two later, you see an animal that's just been hit by a car and is half alive. It turns your stomach, and you ache inside for that animal. You tell your friends about it. And perhaps on the following Saturday you're heading to the grocery store. You look up at the bank's time and temperature digital display. The time reads 9:11. Are you beginning to wonder what's going on? Or are you oblivious?

I spent most of my life paying little attention to the signs and signals. I suffered the wasp sting and observed a dying deer beside the road but didn't perceive the significance of the warnings until much later. 9/11 had just happened, and my world was about to fall apart. The Universe was trying to warn me.

Chapter 8 talks about my dark night of the soul after a significant friendship broke up. There were three other less significant friendship breakups in the same general time frame that I didn't mention in the book. All together, four friendships had ended within a five-year period, three of those within two years! Luckily, my husband Jim and I were on solid ground. Eventually, three of the friendships healed.

I followed my inner urges to attend shamanism workshops, hoping for insight and healing. What I learned was that I was overcommitted and needed time for myself. I also needed to trust myself more, and I needed to pay attention to signs.

## EXERCISES

Since I'm heterosexual, I have written these exercises from my point of view. I assume that lesbian women might experience relationship breakups similar to the way I felt about my divorce from my first husband. Please adjust these exercises to express whatever works for you in defining the pain of female-female relationship breakups.

**Exercise 1:** Have you ever experienced a breakup with a close girlfriend? If so, write about the breakup. Tell about your feelings. How was this different from a breakup with a husband or romantic partner? How long did it take you to get over the girlfriend breakup? How did you heal the relationship? Write for at least ten minutes. If this exercise calls to you, write until there is nothing left to say.

**Exercise 2:** One thing I did to heal my friendship was to take colored pencils and draw the way I envisioned our reunion. I drew stick figures—my friend and me. I drew the two of us outside her house. She was greeting me at the door. Next I drew the two of us inside her house. And I drew the two of us hugging as I left. These images made an impact on my emotions and psyche. As I drew, I could feel my heart center softening. Later, this did actually happen very much as I had pictured and drawn it. This exercise is for you to do if there is an unresolved relationship hanging in your life. Take colored pencils, felt-tip pens, or crayons and draw the scenes of potential reconciliation as in a comic strip. You don't need to be an artist at all. Stick figures are fine. My pictures looked like those of a first grader.

I think the first-grader approach is appropriate, because we need to be in that innocent child-mind to reconcile after a traumatic separation.

**Exercise 3:** When I wrote about my Native American guide in this chapter, I want to emphasize that I felt gratitude for being introduced to him, and that I am not special because of this guide-human connection. We all have guides and angels who attend us, go everywhere with us, love and protect us. What is your experience with angels and guides? Write for ten minutes about an experience you've had.

**Exercise 4:** Since forever, I've sought my true home base, a religion or practice that grounds me. Some of my side trips have been Confirmation as a member of the Episcopal church, Transcendental Meditation, Science of Mind, A Course in Miracles, The Light Work, The Medical Assistance Program (MAP—from Perelandra materials), past life regressions, and studies in shamanism. What side trips have you taken along your life's journey? Make a list and describe each one in a short paragraph. What is the common thread that weaves through all of them? Where are you now, and what do you wish to learn on your path?

**Exercise 5:** How do you know when you're receiving guidance? Do you listen to your mind, your gut, or your heart? I recently had an opportunity to take a week-long workshop, a Native American Vision Quest. While it sounded wonderful, my heart didn't sing. I couldn't get excited. I felt there was something else I needed to do instead. I asked to receive clear information about the next step, accompanied by an unmistakable sign that this was it. Within two days, the answer arrived with the sign I needed. I "happened" to be in line at the annual health fair in front of a woman I hadn't seen in over a year. (This synchronicity was my sign). She is Native American. We were in line together for an hour. She told me about an Inca Shamanism workshop she was taking. I felt my emotions tingle—the excitement rising—and knew that was the next step for me. Write for ten minutes about a time when you received a clear sign about something you had asked for.

## TIPS

**1. Keep a log of synchronicities.** Synchronicities are evidence of the Universe guiding you. The more you pay attention to synchronicities, the more synchronicities you'll notice. The more you notice, the more you'll be amazed at how cared for and guided you are by angelic presences. If you keep a daybook, it is easy to write your synchronicities on the opposite page from your daily entries.

**2. Take a spiritual workshop or class every year.** Treat yourself to at least one spiritual workshop each year as a side trip of your choice.

**3. Ask for what you want.** You can do this by speaking aloud or silently (not demanding), or by writing. Writing a letter to God is one way to do this. Also, you can include your desire in a journal as long as you specifically ask for something and not just express a wishy-washy wish. Be sure to say thank you when you receive your answers and guidance.

## RESOURCES

This chapter talks about shamanism, friendship breakups and synchronicity. Here are some excellent resources to assist you in these areas.

1. *Shamanic Journeying: A Beginner's Guide, Sandra Ingerman,* (Sounds True, Inc., 2004). Through shamanic journeying, people can learn to contact departed souls to help them heal as well as to gain information. To accomplish those ends, one must be an advanced shamanic practitioner. Sandra Ingerman explains the path of shamanic journeying as a spiritual practice, answers common questions about journeying, and prepares the reader for the experience. *Shamanic Journeying* comes with a drumming CD that the beginner can use to do fifteen-, twenty-, and thirty-minute journeying sessions. There are many books about shamanic journeying. This one came highly recommended as a way to get started. It's best to learn to journey with a teacher, but short of that, you can begin with the Ingerman book. After finishing a class, Ingerman's book is a great way to review and keep the fire stoked.

2. Foundation for Shamanic Studies, www.shamanism.org. The Foundation for Shamanic Studies, founded by Michael Harner, who wrote the groundbreaking book *The Way of the Shaman,* offers workshops all over the world. Workshops and teachings through this organization are about "core" shamanism—practices that are common to most indigenous peoples and not bound by any specific cultural group.

3. *I Can See Clearly Now: How Synchronicity Illuminates Our Lives,* Mary Soliel, (iUniverse, 2008). This book is an amazing look at synchronicity. If you read this, you'll never again question whether your angels and guides are with you. They are giving you signs of their presence all the time. Once they capture your attention, and you recognize them, you can request guidance and know when you're receiving it. You'll learn to trust yourself and them as never before.

From reading this book I learned that seeing triple numbers, such as 444, means your angels are giving you messages. Synchronicities started happening for me as if by magic.

4. *The Friend Who Got Away,* by Jenny Offill and Elissa Schappell, (Doubleday, 2005). A book about friendship breakups.

5. *Art and Healing: Using Expressive Art to Heal Your Body, Mind, and Spirit,* Barbara Ganim, (Three Rivers Press, 1999). In Chapters 2 and 3 of this book, I found the inspiration to draw the friendship the way I wanted to see it. An excellent book for people who like to work with images and symbolism.

---

## ~ Section 9 ~
## Eden's Tree

In Chapter 9, I heard from my mother. She spoke through intuitive women who channeled her and a nonphysical being who knew her. She had a message to convey about what people must do to restore ourselves and our beloved planet.

Everyone agrees that our world is changing. What can we do? How can we stabilize ourselves when our footing feels shaky? There are many things we can do, such as recycle, turn off the lights, conserve water, be kind to strangers, pray for the Earth, support our local food banks, and so on. I'm sure you are already doing what you can to help the Earth Mother.

## EXERCISES

This section provides three activities that you can do for yourself and the planet, and they are fun. I've made many collages, thanks to my friend Marcy Adams. We like to do them together around the first of the year. She calls them "Treasure Maps," because when you make them, you are claiming the treasures for yourself that you include in your collage. Often, if not always, the ideas and pictured objects you put in your collage come to you.

**Exercise 1:** Create a "Soul Vision Collage." This will take you about three to four hours, and is especially fun to do with one, two or more women friends. The finished product will be a collage of visual images from magazines that represent what you and your subconscious mind wish for you to focus on and accomplish. You'll need stacks of old magazines with lots of color photos, scissors, a glue stick, and a manila file folder. Set your intention that you wish to create a picture of your life the way you want it to be. This new life can include your health, abundance, education, spiritual goals, home, friends, special creative products, job, and so forth. For at least one hour, sort quickly through the magazines pulling any pictures that appeal to you. Also cut out words and phrases from advertisements that strike you. Don't think too much about it. Let your subconscious be your guide. When you have a good stack of pictures, sort through those and select the ones that you really like. Now comes the fun. You are the artist-creator of the final product: the collage. Your file folder has four sides. Each side can represent a different aspect of your life. Or if you wish, the entire file folder can focus on one thing that you want. Or you may want only to cover the inside with pictures. Cut the pictures out to make pleasing arrangements. Then paste them down. The energy you put into this effort helps to bring about the things you want— the law of attraction. If you have room in your home where you can display your finished folder, keep it in front of you where you can see it every day. Don't forget to date the folder.

**Exercise 2:** Create a "Planet Vision Collage." Read the instructions for the Soul Vision Collage. Instead of clipping pictures that you want in your personal life, think about the planet, and select pictures to represent the way you want our world to be. By spending time focused on our planet, you are adding positive energy to our Mother, the Earth.

**Exercise 3:** The daily newspaper is filled mostly with negative stories. However, there is usually at least one story each day that is inspiring. Scan the paper for those and clip them: stories about people who are helping others, stories about animals saving people or people saving animals. You'll be drawn to the ones you need to see. Keep a clipping file or a notebook with these. Some people have stopped reading the paper or watching television altogether. By not filling your mind with negativity, and by focusing on the positive, you will help yourself and the planet.

## TIPS

**1. Join a women's circle to help the planet evolve.** There are many kinds of circles. But the best kinds—the kinds that can help elevate the state of our planet—are those that are thoughtful, rather than frivolous. Church circles, study groups, and spiritual groups qualify, as do some writing groups. According to Jean Shinoda Bolen, author of *The Millionth Circle*, groups should be heart-centered, ongoing, and supportive of the women involved.

**2. Take stock of your year.** On January 1st of each year, or close to that date, set aside some time to assess where you have been and where you are going. You can do this with New Year's resolutions. You can also do it using runes or divination cards, such as the ones noted in the Resources section below. Ask the runes or the cards to give you direction for the New Year. Write the answer in your daybook.

## RESOURCES

We face two overwhelming obstacles on this planet: rapid deterioration of our natural environment and war. Protest, advocated by my mother, has been a necessary and effective tool for change. Often, though, it pits side against side, and each side digs in its heels even deeper. The old patriarchal systems for dealing with global problems haven't worked. I am heartened to read authors who promote spiritual approaches. The resources in this section showcase spiritual methods for helping the planet and ourselves.

1. www.soulcollage.com. SoulCollage® was developed by Seena Frost. It is a process where women contact their intuition and make their own decks of cards that will have deep personal meaning and will help them answer life's questions. They create the images from pictures they cut from magazines, greeting cards, postcards, catalogues, calendars, personal photographs and other sources. See the website for a personal card reading and complete information.

2. *Urgent Message from Mother: Gather the Women, Save the World*, Jean Shinoda Bolen, M.D., (Conari Press, 2005). This small volume for our times explains why women are needed now to shift planetary energy from war to peace. Our planet is on the brink of destruction, Bolen says, because patriarchy has run amok. Our patriarchal history has been about power, possessions, and control. Women and children always suffer, and have no say in the matters of war. Every woman needs to be an activist now because time is running out.

Bolen calls women to form and cultivate women's circles where talk focuses around social, cultural, and psycho-spiritual transformation. Women already share and support one another through many kinds of circles. This trend needs to be amped up and viewed as a powerful force for change from a destructive patriarchy to the Sacred Feminine. Bolen believes that when the feminine principle dominates world consciousness, then peace can occur and our Mother Earth can be healed.

3. *The Millionth Circle*, Jean Shinoda Bolen, M.D., (Conari Press, 1999). The Millionth Circle, only eighty-seven pages, spells out how to form and cultivate women's spiritual circles. Her inspired premise is based on The Hundredth Monkey myth, which proposes when a critical number of people change how they think and behave, the culture will also. Bolen believes that when the millionth circle forms, the scales will tip and bring our world into a new enlightened state. Bolen encourages women to register their spiritual circles on her website: www.millionthcircle.com

4. *Soul on Fire: A Transformational Journey from Priest to Shaman*, Peter Calhoun, (Hay House, Inc., 2006). Calhoun, once an Episcopal priest, has followed the path of modern shamanism for nearly four decades. Each chapter reads like spellbinding science fiction. Calhoun and his partner Astrid Ganz are cofounders of the Alliance for Spiritual Ecology, which is made up of individuals all over the world who perform monthly sacred ceremonies to help heal the planet.

5. Certified mediums. Doreen Virtue's website includes a list of Certified Mediums who have completed a Mediumship Mentorship program with facilitator Doreen Virtue. These

people have received paraprofessional training in the art of mediumship. Some mediums may be licensed health care professionals, but many are not. These people are neither endorsed by nor guaranteed by Ms. Virtue. It is up to you to interview the Certified Mediums and employ your own discretion in using their services.

Website:www.angeltherapy.com/cm.php

6. *Same Soul, Many Bodies*, Brian L. Weiss, M.D., (Free Press, 2004). Brian Weiss graduated magna cum laude from Columbia University and received his medical degree from Yale University School of Medicine. In his practice as a psychiatrist, Weiss uses the therapy of regressing patients to their past lives to find the sources of their troubles or progressing them into their future lives to discover who they are destined to become. After progressing thousands of clients, he has "seen the future" of our planet, which he describes in the last chapter of his book.

7. *The Book of Runes: A Handbook for the Use of an Ancient Oracle: The Viking Runes with Stones: 10th Anniversary Edition*, Ralph Blum, (St. Martin's Press, 1993). A friend gave me Blum's book and a set of handmade ceramic runes in 1988. Each rune is a letter of an ancient alphabet to be used as an oracle (mirroring the inner teacher or God within), rather than to tell the future or tell you what to do. I've found the readings to be helpful. The new edition includes a set of runes. I've read that there are better books by Rune Masters than this one. However, reviewers agree that this set is a good place for beginners to start. For online information about runes, see the Public Broadcasting System Website: www.pbs.org/wgbh/nova/vikings/runesright.html.

8.  Oracle cards by Doreen Virtue. Ms. Virtue is a psychotherapist and intuitive who works with the angelic realm. She has produced many different sets of oracle cards. I have found them helpful and loving. Metaphysical bookstores carry her cards. Also, you can go to her website: www.angeltherapy.com, which links you to the publisher's website: www.hayhouse.com. These cards are artfully designed. Each set is accompanied by a guidebook.

---

## ~ Section 10 ~
## Healing the Matriarchal Lineage

In Chapter 10, I told about discoveries I made on my mother's side of the family. I learned that women's family lineages may be at the root of their emotional difficulties.

Even if your mother is gone, you can still do things to repair damage left over from your upbringing. Maybe the same problems you experience today were experienced by your mother and her mother. Whatever you do to heal yourself will help heal your ancestors, according to shamanic traditions and facilitators in family constellation work.

This section provides one writing exercise, several tips and abundant resources to help heal yourself and your matriarchal lineage.

## EXERCISES

The writing exercise will put you in touch with your inner child and your inner mother. The mothering side of yourself can help your inner child through writing. Anytime you help yourself to heal, you help your ancestors and the planet.

**Exercise:** This is a right-hand, left-hand journaling exercise to get in touch with your inner child—the one who may still be hurting from childhood. You will need a journal or notebook and a pencil. Using a pencil is better than using a pen, because thoughts and emotions transfer more readily to paper through a pencil. It's best if you begin by meditating to put yourself in a quiet, receptive state of mind. After meditating in whatever manner you are familiar, use your dominant hand to begin writing. You, as your adult self, are the voice of your dominant hand. Your hurting child is the voice of your nondominant hand. Begin by telling her that you are aware that she is angry or hurting and that you are here to listen and help. Also tell her that you will never abandon her. Keep reassuring her as you dialog. Tell her that you are coming to her because you love her and wish to protect her. You are not going to criticize her. Invite her to tell you what is bothering her. Your nondominant hand becomes the child's voice. Listen to what it is she really wants. She may express her anger. Respond as a loving mother would respond. Tell her you honor her feelings. If she complains about other people, as she probably will, you can let her know they were only doing the best they could. Reassure her as many times as necessary to feel a sense of peace with that little child. (Barbara Noonan, Institute of Medical Intuition & Energy Medicine, Lakewood, CO, in a reading for Maria Weber, October, 2006.)

## TIPS

**1. Withstanding criticism.** The Bach flower essence Walnut can help you shift the energetic pattern "fear of criticism," which may be a negative energetic pattern handed down through the generations. You can use Walnut to experience criticism without ill effect. Take two drops in water, four times a day until you no longer have the urge to do so. (Barbara Noonan, Institute of Medical Intuition & Energy Medicine, Lakewood, CO, in a reading for Maria Weber, October, 2006.)

**2. For protection.** Some people are sponges for other's dramas. If they listen to other's troubles, they can become so empathetic that those troubles can even affect their health. If you are one of these, here is a way to protect yourself. Visualize the Archangel Michael. His color is blue. Ask him to install that blue color within you so that it remains with you always for protection. (Claudia Hunter, clairvoyant, Lakewood, CO, in a reading for Maria Weber, March 20, 2002.)

**3. Is it yours or theirs?** Do you ever feel depressed or anxious and wonder if it is your own business or someone else's? To make that distinction, use the color violet-blue—the "X-ray color." Imagine it around you as you think about the situation. If the negative emotion (anxiety or depression) gets stronger, the problem belongs to you. If it dissipates, the problem belongs to someone else. (Claudia Hunter, clairvoyant, Lakewood, CO, in a reading with Maria Weber, March 20, 2002.)

**4. Curing temporary anxiety or depression.** Lie down and breathe deeply for fifteen minutes. Breathe in to the count of six and hold your breath until you can't hold it any longer. Breathe out to the count of six. Repeat until the anxiety or depression releases. This can work for negative emotions that seem to arise suddenly out of nowhere.

## RESOURCES

While I cannot provide writing exercises that will assist in clearing spiritual and emotional blockages handed down to you from your ancestors, I can tell you that I and friends of mine have attended the workshops and therapy sessions listed here. They are all valid and useful.

1. Larry Kessler facilitates workshops on Family Constellations and teaches Hawaiian Shamanism around the country. He also has a private healing practice in Long Beach, CA. The Hawaiians, like many other shamanic cultures, honor and work closely with their ancestors. Intimately linked to us, the ancestors actively take part in our lives. Although the ancestors can be a source of power and wisdom, they can also be responsible for stuck conditions, negative emotions, and illnesses. When we heal the family soul, we heal the entire lineage and ourselves. For more information on Larry Kessler and his workshops, go to www.hawaiishamanism.com. I have taken two of Kessler's shaman workshops and his Family Constellation workshop. His work is indeed magical and effective. Highly recommended.

2. Systemic Family Solutions—Bert Hellinger Family Constellation Work. We are often entangled in unseen forces dating back over two, three or more generations, leftover conditions and emotions that our forefathers and mothers were unable to resolve within their lifetimes. In one-day workshops, group members stand in as representatives in each other's families. The commonality of the human experience allows participants to expand in the presence of each person's individual work. Website: www.systemicfamilysolutions.com.

3. Ulrich Bold's work combines astrological intuitive work with family constellation "Origin Healing." When the natural expression of love and acceptance among the individual members of a family or partnership is blocked, violated or suppressed, the entire system will begin to manifest diverse

forms of emotional or physical distortions that are passed down to succeeding generations. An Origin Healing Workshop helps clarify and release these entanglements. Website: www.ulrichbold.com.

4.   The Hoffman Institute offers Hoffman Quadrinity Processes all over the world. Programs are designed to help heal and reverse the negative love patterns we receive from our ancestors that diminish our power, wisdom and creativity. The book, *Negative Love Syndrome,* by founder Bob Hoffman, can be downloaded from the website. It gives all the details of the process. The Quadrinity Process is a week-long experience. Website: www.hoffmaninstitute.org.

5.   Institute of Medical Intuition & Energy Medicine, LLC, Founding Director, Barbara Noonan, RN, BS, BA, CHTP, C.Ht., Lakewood, Colorado. Email: Intuitives@mho.com. Noonan can interact with people one-on-one at the office, hospital, nursing home, or by phone. Consultations are thirty minutes or fifty-five minutes. A fifty-five-minute phone consultation includes holistic nursing and medical intuitive information, guided meditation revealing source of past life or "family tree" trauma contributing to current health condition, self-help suggestions and referral options.

6.   *Forgive for Good: A Proven Prescription for Health and Happiness,* Dr. Fred Luskin, (HarperCollins, 2001). Dr. Luskin founded and codirects the Stanford University Forgiveness Project, which has provided measurable physical, psychological and emotional benefits of forgiveness. Defining what forgiveness is *not* is almost as enlightening as what it is. For example, according to Dr. Luskin, forgiveness is *not* condoning unkindness, forgetting that something painful

happened, excusing poor behavior, denying or minimizing your hurt. It does not mean reconciling with the offender or giving up your feelings. Dr. Luskin offers a proven nine-step method that he even tested on victim's families from both sides of the civil war in Northern Ireland. He also addresses forgiving oneself and how to deal with the atrocities of September 11, 2001. For groups, the DVD version is very effective: *Forgiveness: Conversations with Fred Luskin, PhD*, The Institute of Noetic Sciences, Transformative Learning Series. Website: www.noetic.org.

---

## ~ Section 11 ~
## Revelation

In the final chapter of my memoir, I recounted my experience of a Life Between Lives session, otherwise known as an LBL. An LBL can answer many questions. If you wish to know why you and your mother needed to be together in your current life, you can get this information. If you want more clarity about your life's purpose, that's also available. An LBL is rather costly, but worth every dime. But first, you need to be comfortable with past life regression. You must have experienced at least one past life regression or hypnosis session before you do an LBL.

## EXERCISES

When I did my LBL, information came to me in symbols and pictures. The wizard and crystal ball, the Viking, the crescent moon, the fairy, the ankh, a ladder—these were among the images I saw in my mind's eye. Examining your personal symbols gives you insight into your soul's purpose. So take some time to consider your and your mother's symbology.

**Exercise 1:** What symbol would others choose for you? If your daughter or best friend could define you in terms of a single symbol, what do you think that symbol would be? For example, people give me cats. I have cat pins, cat cards, cat tree ornaments, and cat pillows that people have given me. I love the sensuousness of cats, wild and domestic. Does that mean I'm catty? What about you? Write for ten minutes about symbols that others associate with you. Is there more than one? Do you think there's a connection to your soul's purpose in this symbol?

**Exercise 2:** What symbol would you choose for yourself? Do you see yourself differently from the way others see you? What symbols are deeply embedded in you? What is it about these symbols that attract you or define who you are? What animal are you? What plant are you? What gemstone? What shape? Do these symbols have special meaning for you? Write for ten minutes about your own symbols. Do you think there's a connection to your soul's purpose in these symbols?

**Exercise 3:** What symbol would you choose for your mother? Louise collected everything—animals of every stripe, especially birds. But as for a symbol, if I were to choose a symbol for Louise, it would be a tree—the Tree of Life, with roots deep in the ground, mirroring the branches spreading above. I believe she drew strength from the earth with her deep roots (she was a voracious reader and absorbed much) and gave back poetry and love to the world through her branches. That's why she's a tree, and while I have no proof that it was her soul's purpose, I feel that this could be true. What about your mother? Write for ten minutes about what would be a fitting symbol for her?

**Exercise 4:** What symbol would your mother choose for herself? I think Louise might have chosen the spiral shape as her own symbol. She spent many summer nights stargazing and her favorite galaxy was Andromeda. She also cherished the spiral form of seashells. As an eighty-four-year-old woman in a nursing home, Louise wanted a picture of Andromeda on her wall where she could see it. The spiral symbolizes a continuous upward climb, which would also symbolize Louise. How about you? What do you think your mother would have chosen for herself? Why? Write for five minutes.

**Exercise 5:** After doing the LBL and writing about it, I thought the story about Louise and me was complete, but I was wrong. There were a few pieces that fell into place a year later, which was when my clairvoyant friend Stacey Joslin told me she could see the fairy of my childhood and feel my mother's love coming from the fairy letters. It's as though my life was a jigsaw puzzle with many pieces missing. Several pieces that remained missing for most of my life were these: Did a real fairy write the letters? Did my mother write the letters? If my mother wrote them, did she have help from the fairy kingdom? Why did my mother write the letters? These pieces fell into place when Stacey did a reading for me.

Here are some questions for you: Which puzzle pieces are still missing from the jigsaw of your life? Which of those pieces include your mother? Which pieces must you absolutely find in order to feel peaceful? What must you do to find the answers you need? Take out your pen and write.

## TIPS

**1. An easy morning meditation.** I have tried a lot of different kinds of meditation. The "standing meditation" allows me to remain aware with no chance of falling asleep. It is described in *The Four-fold Way: Walking the Paths of the Warrior, Teacher, Healer and Visionary*, by Angeles Arrien, (Harper San Francisco, 1993). Before taking my shower, I stand still for fifteen minutes with my feet shoulder-width apart and arms at my sides. I look out my bathroom window, eyes fixed softly on a distant point. I allow thoughts to come and go, but enjoy those spaces where my mind goes blank. Arrien says, with this posture, you can feel what it is like to stand up for yourself, to take a stand, to stand on your own two feet. After doing this meditation, I often receive insights and answers to questions I haven't even verbalized.

**2. Treat every day as a treasure hunt.** Ask your higher self/God/guidance to show you one insight, one "aha" moment, or one answer every day. Stay tuned, aware and receptive. Answers can arrive as symbols. They also can arrive through the mouths of other people.

## RESOURCES

An LBL session is costly, but worth the expense. If it appeals to you, the information to start the ball rolling is noted below. For a less expensive exploration into the reasons you and your mother decided to reincarnate together, consider delving into the following books and cards. The oracle card decks employ archetypal images that resonate with your inner knowing. The Mother, for example, is an ancient archetype. If you have questions about the relationship with your mother, using one of these decks may help you find answers.

1.  The Newton Institute for Life Between Lives. The Newton Institute trains people to do the LBL spiritual regressions.

The trainings take place throughout the United States and in foreign countries. The Newton Institute website describes aspects of an LBL session, particularly questions about hypnosis and trance. This site also provides a list of therapists who have been trained and certified to administer LBL sessions in the United States and foreign countries. Website: www.spiritualregression.org/michael.html.

2. *Journey of Souls: Case Studies of Life Between Lives*, Michael Newton, Ph.D., (Llewellyn Publications, Fifth Revised Edition, 2005). As a hypnotherapist in private practice, Dr. Newton reaches his clients' hidden memories of the afterlife. While in deep hypnosis, these subjects remember the details of their lives as souls between incarnations. In this book, Dr. Newton presents interviews with twenty-nine different clients. They reveal specifics about how it feels to die, what people see and feel right after death, spiritual guides, soul groups, the purpose of life, views of the Creator, how and when we decide to return to Earth, selecting the right body for a new incarnation, selecting parents and other key players in the upcoming life, what happens when the soul joins the body at birth.

3. *Destiny of Souls: New Case Studies of Life Between Lives*, Michael Newton, Ph.D., (Llewellyn Publications, 2006). This is Dr. Newton's second bestseller. He uses case studies to add to the body of knowledge in *Journey of Souls*. Of special relevance to my Chapter 11 is his description of the Life Books Library where souls go to study their past lives.

4. *Sacred Contracts: Awakening your Divine Potential*, Dr. Carolyn Myss, (Random House, 2001). Myss has written many books. In essence, she agrees with Newton that souls

plan their lives before they are born. Each person's earthly purpose, divinely planned in an existence before this one, is the sacred contract. In *Sacred Contracts*, Myss guides readers through steps to discover their purpose, assisted by the archetypes that shape their lives. Also available is a set of *Sacred Contract* CDs and *Sacred Contract* cards. To locate these products go to www.myss.com and select the button for "store" and then "books."

5.  *Archetype Cards*, Carolyn Myss, (Hay House, 2003). This deck of eighty archetype cards is designed to provide basic "light" and "shadow" attributes of each archetype. According to Myss, who follows Dr. Carl Jung's work in depth psychology, we all have universal patterns of behavior embedded within us that are part of the "collective unconscious." By knowing which archetypes are most active in our psyches, we will achieve greater insight about our lives. An instruction booklet comes with the deck, which explains how to use the cards. You can use the deck by itself or in conjunction with Myss's book *Sacred Contracts*. To order, go to www.myss.com and select the button for "store" and then "cards."

6.  *Sacred Contracts: The Journey*, Carolyn Myss, (Hay House, 2004). This is an interactive deck of cards with other materials based on Myss's bestseller, *Sacred Contracts*. We all have sacred contracts with people. According to Myss, we all have a core of four survival archetypes, plus eight other archetypes that form our inner support team. It doesn't matter if you've read *Sacred Contracts* or not, because as you use the deck of archetype cards and the Archetype Wheel, you will find the essence of Myss's book within the process. With the cards and wheel, you create a Chart of Origin—a diagram of key forces throughout your entire life. The purpose of *Sacred*

*Contracts: The Journey* is to seek guidance for a particular question or issue, and work your way through the process, compiling insights and guidance along the way. To order *Sacred Contracts: The Journey*, go to the website: www.myss.com, and select the button for "store" and then "cards."

7. *Man and His Symbols*, edited by C.J. Jung, (Doubleday, 1964). This is the only book that Jung wrote for the general reader to explain his theory of symbolism, particularly dream symbolism. Jung believed that people can only become whole if they accept the unconscious aspect of mind. Lavishly illustrated, this book is written for the lay person.

8. *The Secret Language of Symbols: A Visual Key to Symbols and their Meanings*, David Fontana, (Chronicle Books, 1994). This book features more than 300 full-color illustrations accompanied by essays and detailed captions to explore the culture, history, and psychology that lie behind almost every classical symbol and symbol system. Examples of symbol systems include occult systems, alchemy, the Kabbalah, astrology, the tarot, tantra, chakras, and the I Ching.

9. *Dictionary of Symbolism: Cultural Icons & the Meanings Behind Them*, Hans Biedermann, (Meridian, 1994). Meanings of over 2000 symbols, culled from the worlds of mythology, archeology, psychology, the Bible, literature, fairy tales, folklore, and history. A black-and-white pictorial index is included.

10. *Soul Oracle Cards*, Sonia Choquette, (Hay House, 2006). This sixty-card deck (with accompanying guidebook) is loosely based on the traditional major arcana of the tarot. These oracle cards will assist in answering life's questions:

*What is my purpose in life?* and *What am I here to learn?* And they'll also show you how you can attain your goals. Each card helps you better understand your soul lessons in every situation and guides you toward the highest expression of your soul. The cards are available through the website: www.myss.com. Select the button for "store" and then "cards."

———————

# Afterword

Congratulations! If you have turned to this page, it is likely that you read through the workbook. Perhaps you even completed some of the exercises. I hope the experience was useful and that you reconnected in a healing way with some person or idea in your life.

Much of the book and many of the exercises had to do with the unseen world. In my life, fairies first symbolized that world. As I grew older, I assimilated additional invisibles into my mind for consideration: God, angels, spirit guides, my MAP team made up of ascended masters, nature spirits, souls of loved ones who have crossed over, and even the concept that our so-called inanimate Earth might be a living, conscious being. Pondering these possibilities brought forward the question—what is reality anyway? That's too big a question for this Afterword, but it's one I like to think about.

A friend who read *I'll Be There to Write the Story* asked, "Are the fairies a representation of the childlike magic and imagination within us all, or are they real creatures living in another dimension? Does keeping the wonder alive and keeping in touch with our childlike self allow us to communicate better with our loved ones? Is it through childlike innocence that we access the language of love?"

These were excellent questions. I believe the fairies are real and are made of finer fabric than we humans. Because some people can see them and because they apparently work to assist nature's processes, I believe they exist in our three-dimensional reality. Through stories read to us by our parents and fanciful movies, many of us learned of the fairy kingdom as children.

We might have believed in the magic and wonder for a short while, but most of us lost it as we grew older and still long for it.

Believing in the unseen world can shift our consciousness from cynicism to optimism. Anything that transforms pessimism to lightheartedness is bound to open our hearts and help us connect better with our families and fellow humans. Simply hearing another's story may not convince anyone there is an unseen world at work. But if we start paying attention, asking for answers, and following the trail of synchronicities, we are inevitably led to higher knowledge. Each of us has a unique lesson plan. Each is taught in the way she can learn. Fairies might not do it for you, but something else will.

It has been my intention to share my story and capture your imagination. I wanted to open some new doors and pass along information that might be helpful. Each of us has a story. If we tell it over and over, we can become stuck in our story and never move on. To move to the next level, we must leave our story behind, tell it one last time and never look back. When the story is released, a new journey begins.

# Other Sources

Besides the sources listed under Notes and References and the Resources sections of the workbook, these additional sources have inspired my memoir.

Arcangel, Dianne. *Afterlife Encounters: Ordinary People, Extraordinary Experiences.* (Charlottesville: Hampton Roads Publishing Company, Inc., 2005).

Azara, Nancy. *Spirit Taking Form: Making a Spiritual Practice of Making Art.* (York, ME: Red Wheel/Weiser, 2002).

Biederman, Hans. *Dictionary of Symbolism: Cultural Icons & The Meanings Behind Them.* (New York: Meridian, 1994).

Browne, Sylvia. *God, Creation, and Tools for Life.* (Carlsbad, CA: Hay House, Inc., 2000).

Browning, Sinclair. *Feathers Brush My Heart: Stories of Mothers Touching Their Daughters' Lives After Death.* (New York: Warner Books, 2002).

Choucha, Nadia, *Surrealism & the Occult: Shamanism, Magic, Alchemy, and the Birth of an Artistic Movement.* (Rochester, VT: Destiny Books, 1992).

Dreller, Larry. *Beginner's Guide to Mediumship: How to Contact Loved Ones Who Have Crossed Over.* (York, ME: Red Wheel/Weiser, LLC, 1997).

Faulkner, Bettilu Stein. *A Psychic in the Heartland: The Extraordinary Experiences of a Small-Town Doctor.* (Portsmouth, NH: Moment Point Press, 2003).

Friday, Nancy. *My Mother My Self: The Daughter's Search for Identity.* (New York: Dell Publishing Co., Inc., 1977).

Fontana, David. *The Secret Language of Symbols.* (San Francisco: Chronicle Books, 1994).

Greer, Steven M. *Hidden Truth: Forbidden Knowledge.* (Ladera Ranch, CA: 123PrintFinder, Inc., 2006).

Guggenheim, Bill and Judy Guggenheim. *Hello From Heaven.* (New York: Bantam Books, 1995).

Hicks, Jerry and Esther Hicks. *A New Beginning II: A Personal Handbook to Enhance Your Life, Liberty and Pursuit of Happiness.* (San Antonio: Crown Internationale, 1994).

Johnson, Robert A. *Inner Work: Using Dreams & Active Imagination for Personal Growth.* (San Francisco: Harpercollins, 1986).

Katie, Byron and Stephen Mitchell. *Loving What Is: Four Questions That Can Change Your Life.* (New York: Harmony Books, 2002).

Kennedy, Alexandra. *The Infinite Thread: Healing Relationships beyond Loss.* (Hillsboro, Oregon: Beyond Words Publishing, Inc., 2001).

Myss, Caroline. *Sacred Contracts: Awakening Your Divine Potential.* (New York: Harmony Books, 2001).

Nelson, Mary Carroll. *Artists of the Spirit: New Prophets in Art and Mysticism.* (Sonoma, CA: Arcus Publishing Company, 1994).

Northrop, Suzane. *Second Chance: Healing Messages from the Afterlife.* (San Diego: Jodere Group, Inc., 2002).

Novello, John. *The Song That Never Ended: A Jazz Musician's Journey to a Love Beyond Life.* (Boca Raton: New Paradigm Books, 2003).

Renard, Gary R. *The Disappearance of the Universe: Straight Talk about Illusions, Past Lives, Religion, Sex, Politics, and the Miracles of Forgiveness.* (Carlsbad, CA: Hay House, Inc., 2004).

Signell, Karen A. *Wisdom Of The Heart: Working with Women's Dreams.* (New York: Bantam Books, 1990).

Small Wright, Machaelle. *Dancing in the Shadows of the Moon.* (Warrenton, VA: Perelandra, Ltd., 1995).

Small Wright, Machaelle. *Flower Essences: Reordering Our Understanding and Approach to Illness and Health.* (Warrenton, VA: Perelandra, Ltd., 1988).

Vozenilek, Helen, ed. *Loss of the Ground-Note: Women Writing About the Loss of Their Mothers.* (San Diego: Clothespin Fever Press, 1992).

Waldo-Schwartz, Paul. *Art and the Occult.* (New York: George Braziller, Inc., 1975).

## Maria E. Weber

Maria Weber is a former technical writer, who started writing short stories, creative nonfiction and poetry after moving to the mountains of Central Colorado. As a member and officer of the Chaffee County Writers Exchange, she has led writing activities and coordinated workshops. Her poetry has been published in regional publications and her short stories and creative nonfiction have placed in contests. The first chapter, "Loose Ends," was adapted from a story, "Queen of the Woods," that won first place for nonfiction in the *New Millennium Writings*, 2003-2004 14th annual writing contest. Besides writing, she also collaborates with her husband in their home-based pottery business and sells her work in several Colorado galleries (www.weberbassett.com). For the past decade she has studied shamanic practices of various indigenous cultures.

### Louise E. Weber
#### 1912 - 1997

During her life, Louise Weber published many of her poems in magazines and poetry journals including *The Hartford Courant, Science of Mind, The Archer, Arizona Highways, The Lyric, The Tennessee Churchman, The Pen Woman,* and *The Watauga Review.* Her short story, "The Crossing," was published in *The Christian Herald.* Her poetry was included in *The Yearbook of Modern Poetry* and in a history of Tennessee churches (*Gentle Voices of the Chapel,* by Martha Marshall). She was an active member of National Pen Women and gave poetry readings at their conventions. Her poem, "The Land," was hand copied in calligraphy, framed and hung in the vault of the Sullivan County Courthouse in Blountville, Tennessee. Louise Weber was also a founding member of the Kingsport Art Guild and a Registered Nurse.

# Order Form

To order additional copies of this book via U.S. Mail, please remove or copy this page and return the completed form to:

Piñon Valley Press
P.O. Box 4801
Buena Vista, CO  81211

**Send to (please print):**

_____
Name

_____
Address

_____
City

_____
State                    Zip                Country

_____
Email

*I'll Be There To Write The Story* – Per copy: $19.95

U.S. Postage & Handling – Per copy: $5.00

Book Subtotal _____
         $24.95 each (U.S.) includes $5/copy shipping and handling

CO residents + 4.9% sales tax: _____

Total enclosed with order: _____

Shipments outside U.S. please contact the author directly for pricing:
www.pinonvalleypress.com

Please pay by check or money order, payable to Piñon Valley Press.

*I'll Be There To Write The Story* is also available via
www.amazon.com and www.BarnesandNoble.com.

CPSIA information can be obtained at www.ICGtesting.com
Printed in the USA
LVOW080848301211

261695LV00002BA/58/P